Gender and the Political Economy of Conflict in Africa

T0304167

Gender and the Political Economy of Conflict in Africa explores the persistence of violence in conflict zones in Africa using a political economy framework. This framework employs an analysis of violence on both edges of the spectrum – a macro-economic analysis of violence against workers and a micro-political analysis of the violence in women's reproductive lives. These analyses come together to create a new explanation of why violence persists, a new political economy of violence against women, and a new theoretical understanding of the relation between production and reproduction. Three case studies are discussed: the Democratic Republic of Congo (violence in an era of conflict), Sierra Leone (violence post-conflict), and Tanzania (which has not seen armed conflict on the mainland).

Violence affects the economy of production and the ecology of reproduction – the production of economic goods and services and the generational reproduction of workers, the regeneration of the capacity to work and maintenance of workers on a daily basis, and the renewal of culture and society through community relations and the education of children.

This book fills a significant gap on the political economy of war and women/gender for advanced undergraduate and postgraduate students as well as researchers in African Studies, Gender Studies, and Peace and Conflict Studies.

Meredeth Turshen is Professor at the Edward J. Bloustein School of Planning and Public Policy, Rutgers, the State University of New Jersey, USA.

Routledge studies in African development

Gender and the Political Economy of Conflict in Africa

The persistence of violence

Meredeth Turshen

Routledge
Taylor & Francis Group
LONDON AND NEW YORK

First published 2016 by Routledge

2 Park Square, Milton Park, Abingdon, Oxfordshire OX14 4RN
711 Third Avenue, New York, NY 10017

Routledge is an imprint of the Taylor & Francis Group, an informa business

First issued in paperback 2017

Copyright © 2016 Meredeth Turshen

The right of Meredeth Turshen to be identified as author of this work has
been asserted by her in accordance with sections 77 and 78 of the
Copyright, Designs and Patents Act 1988.

All rights reserved. No part of this book may be reprinted or reproduced or
utilised in any form or by any electronic, mechanical, or other means, now
known or hereafter invented, including photocopying and recording, or in
any information storage or retrieval system, without permission in writing
from the publishers.

Notice:
Product or corporate names may be trademarks or registered trademarks,
and are used only for identification and explanation without intent to
infringe.

British Library Cataloguing-in-Publication Data
A catalogue record for this book is available from the British Library

Library of Congress Cataloging-in-Publication Data
Turshen, Meredeth, 1938– author.
Gender and the political economy of conflict in Africa : the persistence of
violence / Meredeth Turshen.
    pages cm
    1. Women–Violence against–Africa. 2. Women and war–Africa.
    3. Violence–Social aspects–Africa. 4. Violence–Economic aspects–
    Africa. 5. Rape as a weapon of war–Africa. I. Title.
    HV6250.4.W65T84 2016
    362.88082–dc23   2015033283

ISBN: 978-1-138-79522-8 (hbk)
ISBN: 978-0-8153-9418-1 (pbk)

Typeset in Goudy
by Wearset Ltd, Boldon, Tyne and Wear

Contents

Preface

In the spring of 2010, Carleton University extended an invitation to me to speak at a workshop on sexual violence and conflict in Africa. To prepare my intervention, I revisited the literature on wartime violence against women that had appeared since my own previous work was published (Turshen and Twagiramariya, 1998, 2001). I was surprised to find the analysis somewhat stuck in accounts of individualised violence in interpersonal contexts developed more than a decade ago. Gender was now part of the conversation, but too often women were the focus of monologues about rape rather than dialogues about the altered relations between women and men. The understanding of women's experiences did advance as accounts of women as victims of abuse in wartime were superseded by reports showing that they were also actors and perpetrators, and sometimes leaders of opposition to war (Moser and Clarke, 2001). Yet I saw that much more thought was needed to make gender an analytical category of armed violence.

At about the same time, a new body of work appeared on the 'new wars' and new war economies, which, although gender-blind, did offer a broader perspective on what women go through in wartime. New wars are those funded by sales of local assets like gold, diamonds and coltan to transnational corporations, often through international criminal networks. Neoliberal capitalism has created new economic relations that have enabled new wars to be prosecuted. When protracted, new wars exacerbate the inability of states already weakened by austerity programmes to ensure human security and protect human rights. New wars are said to manipulate identity and perpetuate ethnic divisions, to use guerrilla and terror tactics, and to target public services and civilians, exploiting individual and group vulnerability to continue civil wars.

There has been little articulation of studies of women in wartime and investigations of the new wars, although the latter body of literature offers interesting insights and raises many stimulating questions relevant to women. What are women's roles in the informal economies of war zones? Has the informalisation of economies offered new opportunities to women? How are women involved in the financing and arming of conflicts? What is the gendered impact of repeated flight and relocation, capture and coerced labour? Are women's food production and marketing co-opted or undermined by these conflicts? How have the new wars changed women's relation to the state? And how do women manage to pay or avoid the irregular taxes imposed by warring groups? Answers to these questions seem important if we are to plan for the protection of human rights and legal proceedings against war crimes.

My pursuit of these questions is largely theoretical, but the answers require what Cynthia Enloe (2013, p. xiii) calls 'diving deep into the particular' because the particular offers 'the most valuable clues about the elusive big picture'. Recognising the importance of case studies, I have chosen two, the Democratic Republic of Congo (DRC), a former Belgian colony, and Sierra Leone, previously under British rule. My interest in these countries was sparked by another invitation, this one from the University of Ottawa in June 2010 to a workshop on women and girls' equality rights and the extractive industries in Africa. In autumn 2011, I was awarded the Fulbright Chair in Human Rights and Social Justice at the Human Rights Research and Education Centre at the University of Ottawa, Faculty of Law. In Ottawa I worked closely with Partnership Africa Canada (PAC), the nongovernmental organisation that had exposed the role of the illegal diamond trade in the civil wars in Sierra Leone and Liberia and was then developing a project around conflict minerals in the DRC. These two countries became the logical choice for case studies.

The paper for the Carleton workshop, now published in an anthology (Buss *et al.*, 2014), soon suggested this book project. My first questions were about the nature of violence. I had long thought that there were several categories of violence, of which social, or interpersonal, violence – such as sexual violence against women and men – was only one: violence could also be cultural, political and institutional, or economic and systemic, prompting a rejection of the narrow framing of violence as sexual violence against women and girls. Ruth Seifert (personal communication, 4 July 2015) believes that the topic of sexual violence is insufficiently theorised, that microanalyses lack a macro-analytic context.

In the past few years the conventional account of sexual violence in armed conflict has been upended. The narrative of rape as a weapon of war has been questioned: Maria Eriksson Baaz and Maria Stern (2013, p. 5), with refreshing scepticism, examine the interconnections between gender, warfare, violence and militarisation in the context of the security agenda; they note how fragile, failed chains of command can have disastrous results, that these forces differ from armies described as disciplined war machines, and that the perpetrators' sense of what is humiliating and victimising (the 'micro-dynamics of violent score settling') is strong motivation for rape. The questions of who rapes and who is raped have also been raised. Dara Cohen (2013) found that female fighters in Sierra Leone were the perpetrators of rape, including gang rape of male and female non-combatants. Chris Dolan (2009) has much to say about wartime sexual abuse of men, making it critical to check the analysis of rape of women against men's experience. Paul Kirby (2012, p. 215) reports that men and boys were targeted for rape in eastern Congo 'through sexual abuse in custody, where rape establishes hierarchy and where some men report being raped publicly by female guards'.

In addition, general questions about the nature of violence and the relation between wartime interpersonal violence and structural violence need probing. Sexual violence is not a fixed feature of all conflicts; why was it so prominent in Sierra Leone and eastern Congo? Sexual violence has been found to continue into the post-conflict period, sometimes at very high levels (Cohen and Nordås, 2014). Why does this violence persist after wars are formally concluded and peace treaties are signed? Is it a micro-dynamic or, as Patrick Chabal (2005, p. 6) suggests, is it because the present political systems in Africa are prone to produce more rather than less strife? These issues are explored in the first chapter of this book.

The history of violence in the DRC and Sierra Leone is deeply enmeshed in the colonial project of resource removal and labour exaction. This economic agenda is a major focus of the book. The colonial history of both countries has been ably recounted (Everill, 2013; Fyle, 1981; Marchal, 1996; Nzongola-Ntalaja, 2002; van Reybrouck, 2014; Zack-Williams, 1995). It is my intention not to write a political history but more modestly to pull together in the second chapter whatever evidence I could comb from secondary sources about women as actors and producers in the slave era and the colonial period in order to present a gendered narrative of violence. My purpose is to draw the threads of violence through the fabric of regional history, framed by the global economy. (The literature on the causes of the new wars is voluminous and it is not reviewed here.) Two of the few historical studies of Congo that mention women's contributions are *Beyond the bend in the river* by David Northrup (1988) and William J. Samarin's *The black man's burden* (1989). There appears to be nothing comparable about Sierra Leone, except perhaps John Grace on domestic slavery (1975); this lack of information is surprising given the early role of Recaptive women (Recaptives were Africans on cargo ships intercepted by the British navy who were resettled in Sierra Leone) who became prominent businesswomen (Bangura, 2009, p. 584; White, 1978).

The general exploration of violence and the narratives of historical violence in Chapters 1 and 2 provide the background for the second part of this book, which explores the theoretical underpinnings of the articulation of social relations of production and reproduction (that is, the social relationships people undertake to produce and to reproduce material life and which constitute the economic structure of every society). Building on the work of Isabella Bakker (2003) and George Caffentzis (2002) and assuming the foundational feminist literature, which shows how women's reproductive work (in the broad sense of the regeneration of life) contributes to men's productive work,[1] I try to break down that dichotomy in order to establish what I see as the indivisibility and complex interactions between the productive and reproductive economies. I also think that the importance of the male/female binary in the division of labour and in production/reproduction – always ambiguous in anthropological studies that show the flexibility of role assignment (Bledsoe, 1984) – is diminishing under neoliberal capitalist regimes that are increasingly transforming physical and emotional aspects of being human into commodities.

It is interesting that feminist economists accept that the divide between production and reproduction is false, but this conviction has not penetrated other
feminist studies except some analyses of the sex trade; for example, war studies
rarely use this gendered framework. The breakdown of binaries is most evident,
however, when analysing gender in conflict and its aftermath: changes in production and social reproduction are dramatic, violent, visible, traceable and
gendered. If one searches bibliographies for 'violence in production', one is
likely to find information on sexual harassment or on workers 'going ballistic' –
in other words, about worker-on-worker violence – but little about how the
organisation of work creates a violent and dangerous environment in which
individual outbursts are symptomatic of structural violence in the workplace.
Yet violence is a factor in production, and armed conflict both unleashes and
legitimates violence, contributing in some circumstances to higher productivity
and profitability for certain participants and eventual receivers of goods and services produced in this way.

If one asks about violence in reproduction, one finds reports on intimate
partner/domestic violence or stories about abuse of women in pregnancy and
childbirth, but not much about systemic violence in the provision or management of health, education or social services, let alone analyses of the contribution of involuntary social reproduction (forced pregnancy and denial of
abortion, for example) to production. The literature on the social determinants
of health only hints at this larger context of the role of violence. Yet in reproduction, too, structural violence is an organisational factor, often driven or
determined by the logic of neoliberal production. The preferred split of production from reproduction prevails: production is a matter of economics and reproduction is policy/politics. This split frees private economic forces from
democratic accountability and public oversight (Bakker and Silvey, 2008), not
to mention the expenses associated with social reproduction, which must be
absorbed by households.

Interestingly, the bodies of literature on slavery, the slave trade and the
enslavement of women in Africa articulate social reproduction to production
(Campbell *et al.*, 2007; Robertson and Klein, 1983) because slaves were productive and they were also made to reproduce slave societies. Slavery commodified
human life and introduced capitalist relations of production into Africa and the
New World; it turned mothers and fathers into producers of children for export,
fundamentally and for ever transforming Africa and Africans.

New developments in research on domestic slavery have joined the debates
on domestic labour, which in the 1970s and 1980s tried to reconcile women's
experience in industrial capitalist societies with Karl Marx's nineteenth-century
analysis of capital (Bottomore, 1991, p. 157). More recently, studies of households and how they survive in times of conflict have made connections between
production and social reproduction in their research on livelihoods. Something
of a buzzword in development circles, livelihood studies are now well established; for example, Wageningen University in the Netherlands has a Secure
Livelihoods Research Consortium, the Institute of Development Studies at the

University of Sussex has a Households in Conflict Network, and there are liveli-hood studies centres in Bangladesh, India and South Africa, among others. But even when wartime is the setting, few livelihood studies focus on what people do to endure civil wars (Mallett and Slater, 2012; an exception is Korf, 2004); generally the emphasis is on the post-conflict phase and the resettlement of internally displaced persons and refugees (Holland *et al.*, 2002). The attention to livelihoods is welcome in that it is broader than labour studies, yet it does raise questions about the shift in emphasis away from formal organisation of the workplace and trade unionism.

Researching livelihoods in mining communities, I encountered another body of literature that analyses changing relations of production in wartime; it centres on men's lives even though women also work in and around the mines. When these studies mention women (which they rarely do), they usually characterise them as sex workers. Although we know that in industrial mining camps, men assume the domestic tasks normally assigned to women (Epprecht, 1998; Moodie, 1994), it is also known that women perform many other tasks at arti-sanal mine sites and provide a large number of services including productive work critical to mineral extraction. Conflict and the presence of armed guards constrain their choices. Studies of women in mining communities in Tanzania record quite different livelihood possibilities in the absence of such dangers (Bryceson *et al.*, 2014). Taken together, these studies on new wars and liveli-hoods suggest more questions about how civil war restructures gender as a set of social relations in productive and reproductive lives.

One other project that has done much to shape my ideas on production and social reproduction is research on African historical demography and participa-tion in the Montreal group (Université de Montréal Département de démogra-phie), which challenged classic demographic transition theory, especially its failure to consider the importance of migration. In 2008, the late Dennis Cordell asked me to contribute to a new collection on African historical demo-graphy that he was editing with colleagues as a follow-up to an earlier volume in which I had participated. I chose to examine colonial population policies in the interwar period (Turshen, 2010). The articles and books I read to prepare that chapter, particularly the writings of Nancy Rose Hunt (1999) on Congo, still haunt me. Traces of my work on the demography of empire are visible through-out this book, but especially in Chapter 4 on social relations of reproduction.

Much of my previous work focused on women's health (Turshen, 2007, 2000, 1991); inevitably, looking at the persistence of violence, I wanted to know how women's reproductive lives meshed with their work lives in violent environ-ments. I wanted to understand how working women managed their family and household responsibilities in wartime. Jok Madut Jok (1998) carried out one of the rare investigations of the impact of militarisation on reproductive health, showing how war restructures gender relations and reshapes women's productive and reproductive decisions. What is the relation of very high maternal mortality ratios in the DRC and Sierra Leone to warfare and violent economies? What are the personal and political pressures for population replacement due to the loss of children during wartime or to the desire for another generation to protect one's patrimony? What obstacles do migration, repeated displacement and family dispersal present to the regeneration of material life?

Above all, I wanted to learn how reproduction, so long framed as a private woman's issue though subject to cultural compulsions and national and international population policies, fits into the economic analysis of new wars. Mark Duffield (2002, p. 1060) describes new wars as 'struggles over the terms and conditions under which commodities and populations are being integrated within the global economy'. I understand populations to include women and children as well as men; it seems to me then that these struggles are over the terms and conditions under which production *and reproduction* are being integrated within the global economy. The second part of my book explores these ideas – the violence of production in Chapter 3, the violence of social reproduction in Chapter 4, and the articulation of production and social reproduction in armed conflict in Chapter 5.

Work on the aftermath of war (Meintjes *et al.*, 2002), participation in a workshop on gender and reparations at the International Center for Transitional Justice in 2004, and indelible impressions of the International Criminal Tribunal for Rwanda, which I attended in Arusha in 1997, gave rise to more questions, this time around women's human rights and social justice. What lessons on gender were learned from the mechanisms of conflict resolution and punishment of human rights violators in previous African civil wars? What had we learned from the South African Truth and Reconciliation Commission about the inclusion of women's voices? Was the Sierra Leone Special Court a model of social justice for women elsewhere? Can accountability be achieved for crimes like the flow of conflict minerals that finance civil wars? How can the mistakes of UN demilitarisation, demobilisation and reintegration programmes be avoided, especially in respect of women and girls caught up in armed conflict? The third part of this book, on social movements and social justice, considers some of these questions in the context of violent economies. Chapter 6, on struggles for social justice, celebrates African initiatives and questions how international assistance, humanitarian aid and nongovernmental or private voluntary organisations participate in and perpetuate violent economies, and how local NGOs and PVOs organise to oppose violations of national and international law. The book concludes with an evaluation of the mechanisms the international community uses to achieve accountability, reparations and social solidarity.

This book is based on theoretical speculation, qualitative interdisciplinary research, and my decades of work in the field; it is the culmination of years of reading and of thinking aloud with other activists including leaders of programmes to reduce violence and resolve conflict. During a trip to Uganda in December 2011, I attended the fourth summit of the International Conference on the Great Lakes Region where women from 11 countries participated in the special session on sexual and gender-based violence. Rejecting a uniform international feminist agenda, their reports detailed the problems facing women that are specific to their countries and cultures (www.icglr.org). I also participated in a workshop[2] on illegal exploitation of minerals in the Great Lakes Region with participants from Burundi, the Democratic Republic of Congo, Rwanda and Uganda. The breadth of their concerns was notable: they paid attention to environmental and occupational health issues, women and children's issues, as well as the need for transparency in all government and commercial transactions.

All these experiences channelled into my efforts to understand persistent violence in Africa. Reaching back into the history of the European and American slave trade and the intensification of African domestic slavery that accompanied its decline; reading about the European colonial conquest, the imposition of unfree (that is, forced or compulsory) labour regimes and the conservative European ideologies of womanhood foisted on African women; aware of new African governments' dismissal of women's struggles for political independence and the post-colonial extension of discriminatory law; and witnessing the neo-liberal destruction of the remnants of the commons that protected women's livelihoods – one is left acutely sensitive to the historical continuity of aggression, the punishing succession of brutal regimes, the promiscuous squandering of lives, and the relentless assault on women's bodies and personhood. Who can wonder at the ferocity of civil wars or the contribution of recent conflicts to the persistence of violence?

A preoccupation with violence does not blind me to positive developments in Africa. I am not now and never have been an 'Afro-pessimist'. The continent has a history of resistance and the current period is no different, in part because capitalism has always engendered resistance: it is a core contradiction of the system. This investigation of violence and resistance touches on many subjects across a wide array of disciplines, trying to bind place, time and subjectivity to structural determinants of conflict. It has led me to conclude that, contrary to many analyses, the history of aggression is embedded in political economy, not cultural practice. The present study claims to break new ground and present new theories, but it remains a preliminary sketch that needs an even broader canvas to investigate developments relevant to conflict and violence such as Chinese investment, climate change and environmental destruction. Further work that links production and social reproduction in an integrated way to persistent violence in Africa is required to validate or correct and extend the ideas in this book.

Notes

1 For a review of the literature on women's domestic labour see the introduction to Bakker and Silvey (2008).
2 The regional workshop on training and exchanges on the collection of mining data for the implementation of the regional initiative against the illegal exploitation of natural resources in the Great Lakes Region, Kampala, 12–14 December 2011, organised by the Centre National d'Appui au Développement et à la Participation Populaire (CENADEP) and partnership Africa Canada (PAC).

References

Baaz, Maria Eriksson and Maria Stern (2013) *Sexual violence as a weapon of war? Perceptions, prescriptions, problems in the Congo and beyond.* London and New York: Zed Books; Uppsala, Sweden: Nordic Africa Institute.

Bakker, Isabella (2003) Neo-liberal governance and the reprivatization of social reproduction: social provisioning and shifting gender orders. In *Power, production and social reproduction: human in/security in the global political economy*, edited by Isabella Bakker and Stephen Gill, pp. 66–82. London: Palgrave.

Bakker, Isabella and Rachel Silvey, eds (2008) *Beyond states and markets: the challenges of social reproduction.* London: Routledge.

Bangura, Joseph (2009) Understanding Sierra Leone in colonial West Africa: a synoptic socio-political history, *History compass* 7(3): 583–603.

Bledsoe, Caroline (1984) The political use of Sande ideology and symbolism, *American ethnologist* XI(3): 455–472.

Bottomore, Tom, ed. (1991) *A dictionary of Marxist thought.* Oxford: Blackwell.

Bryceson, Deborah Fahy, Jesper Bosse Jønsson and Hannelore Verbrugge (2014) For richer, for poorer: marriage and casualized sex in East African artisanal mining settlements, *Development and change* 45(1): 79–104.

Buss, Doris, Joanne Lebert, Blair Rutherford and Donna Sharkey, eds (2014) *Sexual violence in conflict and post-conflict societies: international agendas and African contexts.* London: Routledge.

Caffentzis, George (2002) On the notion of a crisis of social reproduction: a theoretical review, *The commoner* 5, Autumn: 1–22.

Campbell, Gwyn, Suzanne Miers and Joseph C. Miller, eds (2007) *Women and slavery.* Athens, OH: Ohio University Press.

Chabal, Patrick (2005) Violence, power and rationality: a political analysis of conflict in contemporary Africa. In *Is violence inevitable in Africa? Theories of conflict and approaches to conflict prevention*, edited by Patrick Chabal, Ulf Engel and Anna-Maria Gentilli, pp. 1–14. Leiden: Brill.

Cohen, Dara Kay (2013) Female combatants and the perpetration of violence: wartime rape in the Sierra Leone civil war, *World Politics* 65(3): 383–415.

Cohen, Dara Kay and Ragnhild Nordås (2014) Sexual violence in armed conflict: introducing the SVAC dataset, 1989–2009, *Journal of peace research* 51(3): 418–428.

Dolan, Chris (2009) *Social torture: the case of Northern Uganda, 1986–2006.* New York: Berghahn Books.

Duffield, Mark (2002) Social reconstruction and the radicalization of development: aid as a relation of global liberal governance, *Development and change* 33(5): 1049–1071.

Enloe, Cynthia (2013) *Seriously!: investigating crashes and crises as if women mattered.* Berkeley: University of California Press.

Epprecht, Marc (1998) The 'unsaying' of indigenous homosexualities in Zimbabwe: mapping a blindspot in an African masculinity, *Journal of southern African studies* 24(4): 631–651.

Everill, Bronwen (2013) *Abolition and empire in Sierra Leone and Liberia.* Houndmills, Basingstoke, Hampshire: Palgrave Macmillan.

Fyle, C. Magbaily (1981) *The history of Sierra Leone: a concise introduction.* London: Evans.

Grace, John (1975) *Domestic slavery in West Africa with particular reference to the Sierra Leone Protectorate, 1896–1927.* London: Frederick Muller.

Holland, Diane, Wendy Johnecheck, Helen Sida and Helen Young (2002) Livelihoods and chronic conflict: an annotated bibliography. Working paper 184. London: Overseas Development Institute.

Hunt, Nancy Rose (1999) *A colonial lexicon: of birth ritual, medicalization, and mobility in the Congo.* Durham, NC: Duke University Press.

Jok, Jok Madut (1998) *Militarization, gender, and reproductive health in South Sudan.* Lewiston, NY: Edwin Mellen Press.

Kirby, Paul (2012) Rethinking war/rape: feminism, critical explanation and the study of wartime sexual violence, with special reference to the eastern Democratic Republic of Congo. Unpublished thesis. London: London School of Economics and Political Science (University of London).

Korf, Benedikt (2004) War, livelihoods and vulnerability in Sri Lanka, *Development and change* 35(2): 275–295.

Mallett, Richard and Rachel Slater (2012) Growth and livelihoods in conflict-affected situations: what do we know? SLRC Briefing Paper 3 December, www.securelivelihoods.org.

Marchal, Jules (1996) *L'état libre du Congo: paradis perdu: l'histoire du Congo 1876–1900.* Borgloon: Paula Bellings.

Meintjes, Sheila, Anu Pillay and Meredeth Turshen, eds (2002) *The aftermath: women in post-conflict transformation.* London: Zed Books.

Moodie, T. Dunbar (1994) *Going for gold: men's lives on the mines.* Berkeley: University of California Press.

Moser, Caroline and Fiona Clarke, eds (2001) *Victors, perpetrators or actors: gender, armed conflict and political violence.* London: Zed Books.

Northrup, David (1988) *Beyond the bend in the river: African labor in eastern Zaire, 1865–1940.* Athens, OH: Ohio University Center for International Studies Monographs in International Studies Africa series number 52.

Nzongola-Ntalaja, Georges (2002) *The Congo from Leopold to Kabila: a people's history.* London: Zed Books.

Robertson, Claire C. and Martin A. Klein, eds (1983) *Women and slavery in Africa.* Madison, WI: University of Wisconsin Press.

Samarin, William J. (1989) *The black man's burden: African colonial labor on the Congo and Ubangi rivers, 1880–1900.* Boulder, CO: Westview Press.

Turshen, Meredeth, ed. (1991) *Women and health in Africa.* Trenton, NJ: Africa World Press.

Turshen, Meredeth, ed. (2000) *African women's health.* Trenton, NJ: Africa World Press.

Turshen, Meredeth (2007) *Women's health movements: a global force for change.* New York: Palgrave Macmillan.

Turshen, Meredeth (2010) Reproducing labor: colonial government regulation of African women's reproductive lives. In *The demographics of empire: the colonial order and the creation of knowledge,* edited by Karl Ittmann, Dennis Cordell and Greg Maddox, pp. 217–144. Athens, OH: Ohio University Press.

Turshen, Meredeth and Clotilde Twagiramariya, eds (1998) *What women do in wartime: gender and conflict in Africa.* London: Zed Books.

Turshen, Meredeth and Clotilde Twagiramariya, eds (2001) *Ce que font les femmes en temps de guerre: genre et conflit en Afrique,* edited by Meredeth Turshen and Clotilde Twagiramariya. Paris: L'Harmattan.

van Reybrouck, David (2014) *Congo: the epic history of a people.* New York: HarperCollins Fourth Estate.

White, E. F. (1978) The big market in Freetown, *Journal of the historical society of Sierra Leone* 2(2): 19–32.

Zack-Williams, Alfred (1995) *Tributors, supporters and merchant capital: mining and underdevelopment in Sierra Leone*. Aldershot: Avebury.

Acknowledgements

At each step of the way towards producing this book, at each of the meetings and conferences mentioned in the Preface above, I met remarkable people. Despite the many critics of academia who condemn competitive internal faculty dynamics, I found generosity and I applaud the cooperative spirit of scholars who share their knowledge and resources freely. The interdisciplinary research undertaken for this book perforce relied on a large number of sympathetic scholars; my debts are immense to those who answered my questions, gave me references, made introductions to other scholars and in other ways took time and went out of their way to assist me. Their words, thoughts and writings shaped my ideas and inform this work. Of course I take responsibility for all garbles, bungles, botches and muck-ups.

Help has come from many magnanimous people whom I wish to thank profusely: Asma Abdel Halim, Ibrahim Abdullah, Janet Abu-Lughod, Patricia Adong, Ousseina Alidou, Shawn Blore, Carolyn Brown, Jan Burgess, Doris Buss, the Robert A. Catlin family, George Caffentzis, Bonnie Campbell, Kirsten Campbell, Morgan Campbell, Carol Cohn, Andrew Coleman, Dennis Cordell, Sally Christine Cornwell, Chris Dolan, Nicole Eggers, Oku Ekpenyon, Hala El Karib, Reverend Didier de Failly, Silvia Federici, Sara Geneen, Tefera Gezmu, Jennifer Hinton, Allen Howard, Nancy Rose Hunt, Aisha Ibrahim, Radha Jagannathan, Dida Kalinda, Jocelyn Kelly, Martin Klein, Lucie Lamarche, Joanne Lebert, Ron Lestahaege, Socrates Litsios, Paul Lovejoy, Lindsay Mossmann, Donna Mergler, Sonya Negrin, Catharine Newbury, Helen Olsen, Magda Pavitt, Amber Peterman, Kris Peterson, Myriam Pierre-Louis, Ismail Rashid, Carly Robb-Jackson, Blair Rutherford, Joanne St. Lewis, David Shapiro, Samuel Shapiro, Donna Sharkey, Dan Thakur, Monika Thakur, Annie Thébaud-Mony, Denis Tougas, Theodore Trefon, Koen Vlassenroot, Marc Weiner, Ann Whitehead, Rachel Zaslow and Lina Zedriga.

I am in debt to a number of institutions and their staff for amiable, excellent assistance: the African archives at the Belgian Ministry of Foreign Affairs, the Bibliothèque nationale de France, the British Library, Congo Research Network, Emory University, the Fulbright Program, the Institute of Commonwealth Studies, the Tervuren Museum collection in Brussels, the University of Ottawa School of Law, Human Rights and Education Centre, Partnership Africa

Canada, and the archives at UN Refugees in Geneva. I am especially grateful to my home base, the Edward J. Bloustein School of Planning and Public Policy at Rutgers University, for sabbatical leave and financial and intellectual support. The Writers Room and the Vermont Studio Center provided precious quiet space to work. My thanks to Veronica Walentowicz for excellent editorial assistance. My editors at Routledge, Helen Bell, Margaret Farrelly and Khanam Virjee, my copy editor Rosamund Howe, and three anonymous reviewers made substantive contributions to this volume for which I am grateful.

Abbreviations

AAWORD	Association of African Women for Research and Development
ADF	Allied Democratic Forces (Uganda)
AFDL	Alliance des forces démocratiques pour la libération du Congo (Alliance of Democratic Forces for the Liberation of Congo-Zaire)
AFRC	Armed Forces Revolutionary Council (Sierra Leone)
AGOA	African Growth and Opportunity Act (US)
CMS	Church Missionary Society
CNDP	Congrès national pour la défense du peuple (National Congress for the Defence of the People (Congo))
CODESRIA	Council for the Development of Social Science Research in Africa
CSO	civil society organisation
DDR	disarmament, demobilisation and reintegration
DRC	Democratic Republic of Congo
FAR	Forces armées rwandaises (Rwandan Armed Forces)
FARDC	Forces Armées de la République Démocratique du Congo (Armed Forces of the Democratic Republic of Congo)
FDD	Forces de défense de la démocratie (Forces for the Defence of Democracy (Burundi))
FDLR	Forces démocratiques de libération du Rwanda (Democratic Forces for the Liberation of Rwanda)
FNL	Forces nationales de libération (Forces for National Liberation (Burundi))
FOCA	Forces combattantes Abacunguzi (Congo)
FRPI/FPJC	Force de résistance patriotique en Ituri (Front for Patriotic Resistance in Ituri/Popular Front for Justice in Congo, Ituri)
GATS	General Agreement on Trade in Services
ICC	International Criminal Court
ICCPR	International Convention on Civil and Political Rights
ICESCR	International Convention on Economic, Social and Cultural Rights
IDP	internally displaced person

IFI	international financial institutions
ILO	International Labour Organisation
IMF	International Monetary Fund
LRA	Lord's Resistance Army (Uganda)
LURD	Liberians United for Reconciliation and Democracy
M23	Mouvement du 23-mars (March 23 Movement)
MLC	Mouvement national de libération du Congo (Movement for the Liberation of Congo)
MONUC	Mission de l'Organisation des Nations Unies en République Démocratique du Congo (United Nations Organisation Mission in Congo)
MONUSCO	Mission de l'Organisation des Nations Unies pour la stabilisation en République Démocratique du Congo (United Nations Organisation Stabilisation Mission in the Democratic Republic of Congo)
NGO	nongovernmental organisation
OAU	Organisation of African Unity
ONUC	United Nations Operation in the Congo
PAC	Partnership Africa Canada
PVO	private voluntary organisation
RCD	Rassemblement congolais pour la démocratie–Goma (Congolese Rally for Democracy)
RDC	République Démocratique du Congo (Democratic Republic of Congo)
RPA	Rwandan Patriotic Army
RPF	Rwandan Patriotic Front
RUF	Revolutionary United Front (Sierra Leone)
UMHK	Union Minière du Haut-Katanga
UNAMSIL	United Nations Mission in Sierra Leone
UNCC	United Nations Compensation Commission
UNHCR	United Nations High Commissioner for Refugees
WHO	World Health Organisation
WTO	World Trade Organisation

Part I

The persistence of violence

1 Gender and the political economy of violence

Lors des pillages au village, c'est moi qui toquais aux portes. Quand on entendait la voix d'une fillette, on ouvrait sans hésitation et les Interahamwe en profitaient pour piller et violer. En fin de compte, je les aidais à transporter ce qu'ils avaient pillé. Je l'ai fait pendant quatre ans.[1] [Congolese child soldier, 10 years old when abducted]

(Wakubenga, 2013, p. 129)

The title of this book – *Gender and the political economy of conflict in Africa: the persistence of violence* – establishes its three themes: *gender*, used here to designate the economic, political, social and cultural relations of power between the sexes; *conflict*, traced from the slave era through colonialism to the twenty-first century; and *violence*, meaning individual behaviour or collective acts that inflict injury, death, psychological harm or deprivation, or damage the natural or built environment. Violence is an abstraction that can be reified only within a historical context; it occurs within social structures that consign women, men, children and communities to roles in a highly stratified global economy. The axiomatic expression of violence is war.[2] In Africa, in the last decades of the twentieth century, 24 civil wars were fought (including one in North Africa).[3]

This book explores the persistence of violence in conflict zones in Africa using a political economy framework to situate violence against women and men in the context of criminal, corrupt and violent economies. Violence affects the economy of production and the ecology of reproduction – the production of economic goods and services and the generational reproduction of workers, the regeneration of the capacity to work and maintenance of workers on a daily basis, and the renewal of culture and society through community relations and the education of children. The political economy approach employs an analysis of violence on both edges of the spectrum – a macro-economic analysis of violence against workers and a micro-political analysis of the violence in women's reproductive lives. These analyses come together to create a new explanation of why violence persists, a new political economy of violence against women, and a new theoretical understanding of the relation between production and reproduction. The backdrop is the extractive industries in Africa, the global trade in diamonds, gold and other minerals. The case studies are the Democratic Republic of Congo (violence in an era of conflict), Sierra Leone (violence post-conflict), and Tanzania (which has not seen armed conflict on the mainland).

Chapter 1 reflects on the multiple meanings of violence in order to seat the analysis of structural violence in relations of production and social reproduction. To explain how armed conflict affects those relations, the literature on new wars is considered and linked to an assessment of the corrupting impact of war economies on gender and generational relations. The civil wars in Congo and Sierra Leone – the book's case studies – are briefly outlined with special attention to the extractive industries, the regionalised character of those wars, and the global trade networks in which they were enmeshed. This background silhouettes the economic and social consequences of civil wars for women, men and children.

The multiple meanings of violence

Most accounts of violence in Africa focus on civil war, on visible and physical violence, and on the bodies of victims and perpetrators as the 'terrain for staging violence' (Ferme, 1998, p. 555). Yet even after the truce is signed, repeated reports of deadly clashes reveal that conflict and violence continue, sometimes at even higher levels than during the war, although those who inflict violence and those who suffer are not the same wartime combatant/civilian dyad (Ibeanu, 2002). Gender-based violence appears to be brought from war zones into the community and home life: the levels of violence seen during conflict contribute to a high tolerance of violence in the aftermath (Swaine, 2012, p. 16). In spite of the disarmament and demobilisation of troops, violence persists in the economy, in politics, in everyday life, in gender and generational relations, in memory, and in the country's international affairs.

Writings about gender and war focus mainly on interpersonal attacks on women, although violence has many explanations and multiple associations. Interpersonal violence is but one dimension of civilians' wartime experience, as H. Patricia Hynes (2004, p. 433) makes clear:

> To lose one's family, home and community in conflict; to be raped by enemy soldiers and then made suspect and shunned by one's husband and community – these are a living death marked with acute impoverishment, profound culturally imposed shame and hopelessness.

An exclusive focus on sexual attacks on women misses sexual abuse of men, women's abuse of women and men, and the ways in which war changes more than familial gender relations. A corrective is to define war in its full life cycle, including preparation for war, the prosecution of war, post-war activities and 'the public ideology of militarized defense as the guarantor of national security' (Hynes, 2004, p. 433). Even this approach does not convey the full experience of violence. As Nancy Scheper-Hughes and Philippe Bourgois (2003, p. 22) write, violence is structured to harness cultural notions of femininity, masculinity, procreation, and nurturance and to put them into the service of state wars and mass murder or to fuel peacetime forms of domination that make the subordinate participate in their own socially imposed suffering.

Violence, in its manifold institutional, systemic, political, economic, social, cultural and interpersonal forms, has multiple meanings. Many specific meanings are embedded in institutions and disciplines like the criminal justice system (the analysis of interpersonal and self-inflicted violence), psychology and sociology (the study of violent behaviour and social structure), ethics and religion (considerations of intentional and unintentional violence), political science (investigations of armed violence and political and state violence), design (planning that displays the function or workings of objects and spaces) and anthropology (documentation of communal violence). One speaks of cultures of violence, of domestic and intimate-partner violence, of violent cultures, mob violence, and sexual and gender-based violence. Dan Hoffman (2011, p. 48), writing about the wars in Sierra Leone and Liberia, explores violence as a mode of production; he is thinking of the young men who cycle through the region's mines and battlefields as labourers. The fungibility of violence, Hoffman says, results from understanding war as a mode of labour, since 'the performance of violence can be traded on the market'. Some violence is legitimated in the guise of peacekeeping as in United Nations forces in Congo (Intervention by ONUC, 1960), Zaire (MONUC, 1999), Sierra Leone (UNAMSIL, 1999) and the DRC (MONUSCO, 2010).

Violence is sometimes described by the space in which it occurs. Urban violence is a concern in cities the world over. Scheper-Hughes (1997, p. 477) speaks of a 'violence transition' from political to criminal violence, referring to an epidemic of homicides, assaults, muggings, break-ins, car-jackings, gang wars and vigilantism for which urban victims hold disaffected, unattached and depoliticised youths responsible. Feminists have worked hard to bring so-called private family violence into the public realm. Movements for carceral reform have organised against the tolerance of prison violence. And educators and child protection services have argued against violent teachers and bullies in schools. Some question whether there is cross-cultural confusion around 'public' and 'private' violence, since delineations of public and private spheres differ by culture. This public/private binary is more fundamental than expressions of violence: it goes to the heart of society and differentiates cultures, religions and more. Many of the current so-called 'culture wars' are struggles around which decisions and behaviour should be individual and private and which should be collective, public and regulated. A more sophisticated analysis sees cultural and religious arguments as deliberate attempts to conceal 'international structures of inequality, novel forms of patriarchy related to politicized religious movements, and flows of transnational capital' (Abu-Lughod, 2013, p. 244). By disorganising society, by upsetting the usual hierarchies of genders and generations, violent conflict wrenches intimate behaviour out of private spaces and forces it into the public arena.

Hoffman (2011) uses spatial imagery in another sense – to describe the need of young Sierra Leoneans searching for work to be ready to move at any moment, to displace themselves as opportunities arise. Violence was not intrinsic to the search for work, but the men were willing to exchange violence on the market; the volition to commit violent acts was fungible.

> That same capacity might as easily be called on for labor in the diamond pits, labor tapping rubber, labor felling trees, or labor standing in line at a disarmament center. As laborers in a violent economy these were all qualitatively similar opportunities for work.
>
> (Hoffman, 2011, p. 53)

Gender continues to be overlooked in studies of the genesis of war violence even though local and international bodies such as the World Bank recognise armed conflict in resource-rich countries as a major cause of human rights violations (Lebert, 2010; Vines, 2006). UN Security Council Resolution (UNSCR) 1653 acknowledges the link between the illegal exploitation of natural resources, the illicit trade in those resources, and the proliferation and trafficking of arms as key factors fuelling and exacerbating such conflicts as the one in the Great Lakes Region of Central Africa. Recognition of the particular nature of women's and girls' vulnerability in conflict is now nearly universal, heightened in such international instruments as UNSCR 1325, 1820, 1888 and 1889; but there is little talk about women as perpetrators of sexual assault on women and men. Rape among boys and men is beginning to be noticed but is still largely ignored in official circles. The full gender dimension is omitted from studies of the mechanisms and economic, social and political impacts of the extractive industries in African conflicts.

Researchers from a range of disciplines (anthropology, conflict studies, history, law, political science and sociology) have studied the increasingly popular topic of sexual violence in conflict, but there is little if any consideration of how larger regional and globalised trade relations, both legal and illicit, manipulate gender dynamics, gender relations and gender-based violence. For example, reports of the UN panel of experts on the illegal exploitation of natural resources and other forms of wealth in the Democratic Republic of Congo make little mention of gender (UNSC, 2002, 2003). State-sponsored regional studies, such as those carried out by the UK Department for International Development, examine mineral extraction and trade in the region (Sunman and Bates, 2007), but they do not consider the gender aspects of either benefits or vulnerability, nor do industry statements and ethical guidelines (EICC, 2009). Studies of gender and sexual violence in the eastern DRC have focused on international law, justice, impunity, masculinity, the motivation of perpetrators, public health, female combatants and the vulnerability of the girl child, rarely in context (Lebert, 2010).

Beyond war-related state and non-state activities lies the meta-context of the political economy: how each armed conflict fits into global commerce and international relations. How are we to understand the extortion of people's livelihoods, the dispossession of their economic activity, the disruption of long-established economic, social and political relations, the imposition of taxation by force, summary killings, detentions and executions, as well as unrelenting sexual violence against women and girls (Beneduce *et al.*, 2006)? Are these examples of interpersonal violence or the violent behaviour typical of those who abuse their power and privilege? Are they symptoms of the chaos of civil war in which state institutions like the judicial system rarely function to prevent violence or avenge victims? If these exactions point to an increase in the use of violence at all levels of society, do we investigate the violence that accompanies armed conflict as personal violence, or do we analyse the situation as structural violence? How do we take account of the shifting nature of violence over time in protracted wars, of the changing rationale of the conflict itself (for example, from idealistic overthrow of a tyrant to predation and banditry)? Finally, does neoliberalism spawn violence (Springer, 2015), or does the violence of war lead to a neoliberal regime (Klein, 2008)?

Structural violence and relations of production and social reproduction

Limiting an analysis of violence to agents and intentions fails to convey the pervasive forms of violence that are integral to structures, institutions, ideologies and histories. Through an engagement with the concept of structural violence, a term coined by Johan Galtung in his seminal 1969 article, 'Violence, peace, and peace research', it is possible to investigate the violence that models of agency and force based on liability cannot account for (Dilts, 2012). Indirect (structural) violence 'shows up as unequal power and consequently as unequal life chances' (Galtung, 1969, p. 171):

> *Resources* are unevenly distributed, as when income distributions are heavily skewed, literacy/education unevenly distributed, medical service existent in some districts and for some groups only, and so on. Above all the *power to decide over the distribution of resources* is unevenly distributed. (italics in original)

Paul Farmer (1996) writes eloquently on structural violence, which he defines as the violence of organised racism, sexism, political aggression and poverty. He calls for an analysis that is geographically broad and historically deep, one that is informed by intersectionality[4] or the overlapping of gender, race/ethnicity and class; and he warns against conflating cultural difference and structural violence. Scheper-Hughes and Bourgois (2003, p. 1) define structural violence as 'the violence of poverty, hunger, social exclusion and humiliation', claiming that its power derives from its social and cultural dimensions, the assaults on 'personhood, dignity, sense of worth or value of the victim'. Structural violence, they say, inevitably translates into intimate and domestic violence. Mariane Ferme (1998) investigates the link between structural forms of violence and the processes of enumeration and classification embedded in elections, the census, development planning and taxation, noting that numbers are also crucial in documenting such violence, which is of special importance in accountability for criminal acts.

Galtung (1969, p. 173) finds no reason to assume that suffering is less with structural than with physical violence even though the latter is visible and the former is silent. He believes that personal violence may provoke a complaint whereas structural violence silences its victims through the workings of stratified social systems. Because stratification embodies a hierarchy, inequality is built into structural violence, which becomes a mechanism of conflict control. Galtung (1969, p. 179) also thinks that repressive structures are internalised and become accepted as the norm. While agreeing with much of what Galtung has written, I recognise that racism, sexism and class bias are missing from his analysis. Here, in particular, I take issue with the notion that all structural violence is invisible: for example, racist violence, especially when institutionalised, is obvious to the racial and ethnic groups that are the targets of discrimination. Both the apartheid regime in South Africa and Jim Crow laws in the American south were silencing, but they were not silent to the blacks and whites living under them.

Internal structures hide behind the overt functioning of systems, and visible social relations should not be confused with interior structures; the laws of social practice depend on the functioning of these hidden structures (Copans and Seddon, 1978, p. 5). Scheper-Hughes and Bourgois (2003, p. 2) contrast the transparency of revolutionary violence, community-based massacres and state repression with the '*everyday* violence of infant mortality, slow starvation, disease, despair, and humiliation that destroys socially marginalized people with even greater frequency'. This quotidian violence, which I call the violence of social reproduction, is easily disguised as a concomitant of poverty and often unrecognised as structural. Its very familiarity leads some to shrug their shoulders ('the poor will always be with us') and others to blame the poor for their plight or to elaborate theories like the culture of poverty. Similarly, the violence of social relations of production is obscured by accounts of sexual harassment and attacks of one worker on another; the structural violence of the organisation of work responsible for high rates of productivity and profitability is not visible to those who receive and use the goods and services produced in this way.

Structural violence in social relations of production and reproduction is disguised in democracies, concealed behind legal edifices that promise unbiased protection. Despite assurances of equal opportunity, economic and social policies continue to erode human security. Reproductive activities, as well as divisions of labour, social relations and welfare provisions (among others), have been subject to much 'creative destruction' under neoliberalism, which is characterised by a belief in free markets and demands that the state create markets in health care, education and social security if none exist (Harvey, 2005, p. 3). Because neoliberalism values market exchange, it emphasises the cardinal role of contractual relations in the marketplace – even unto arrangements for child-bearing, as in commercial surrogacy contracts. The interference of powerful non-state actors hinders our ability to identify the impact of neoliberalism on reproductive activities; for example, religious authorities wielding significant influence in legislative, moral and ethical domains block from view the new political economy of human reproduction. The concept of reproductive govern-ance traces political shifts in the monitoring and control of reproductive behavi-ours and population practices in Latin America (Morgan and Roberts, 2012). Economic studies of women's health usually focus on the introduction of the market into all aspects of social reproduction. The commercialisation of the care economy is another aspect of neoliberal development. Isabella Bakker (2003) goes well beyond these approaches in relating neoliberal governance to the rep-rivatisation of social reproduction and social provisioning, a theme developed further in Chapter 4, 'Violence in biological and social reproduction'.

A direct relationship between everyday violence and the violence of wartime has been suggested by Franco Basaglia (1987). In the idea of 'peacetime crimes', according to Scheper-Hughes (1997, p. 474), Basaglia sees a continuity 'between extraordinary and ordinary violence, between the everyday forms of violence that are normalised, naturalised and unmarked, and the explicit, sensational and remarkable crimes and violations of war-time'. These ideas of structural violence in wartime and peacetime inform my investigation of the under-explored activ-ities of women and men in the economies of extended civil conflicts. Structural violence is inherent, not only in relations of social reproduction, but also in labour relations and work organisation in neoliberal capitalist economies. By favouring the deregulation of markets and industries, neoliberalism increases the riskiness and precariousness of employment, and civil wars exacerbate both con-ditions. The question explored in this chapter is how the social relations of pro-duction and reproduction for civil war economies affect gender relations.

Theories of structural violence help analyse the experiences of women living in conflict zones, their contributions as workers in mineral extraction that has supplied the conflicts, and their biographies as lovers, wives and mothers, as well as victims of sexual assault. Structural violence frames the analysis of the viol-ence of reproduction, both biological and social, and the violence of produc-tion. My contention is that manifestations of violence in work (production) and childbearing, child rearing and regeneration of community (reproduction) are interdependent, indeed inseparable. The binary that sets up production as a male domain and reproduction as a female arena is false, not only because what happens in the productive domain affects reproduction (and vice versa), but because women are workers too and men also contribute to procreation and the socialisation of children. Divisions of labour are not fixed gendered categories since they shift over time in different modes of production and in diverse societies.

Unfree labour

Violence is manifest in conditions of labour: an increase of unfree labour is reported in Africa as elsewhere, generating profits of US$13 billion per year in Africa and global profits of US$150.2 billion (ILO, 2014). Labour relations exist on a spectrum of unfree to free (Lerche, 2011). Unfree labour, labour that is restrictive or forced, takes many forms – chattel slavery, serfdom, indentured service, debt bondage, prisoners of war and convict labour (and, some would add, military conscription). Free labour refers to contractual labour relations, usually for wages in a job the worker can quit without punishment (Lintvedt, 2003). The ILO (2009, p. 5) prefers the term forced labour. ILO Convention 29 adopted in 1930 defines forced labour as involuntary entry and participation in work or a service that is extracted 'under menace of any penalty and for which the said person has not offered himself voluntarily' (ILO, 1930).[5] Unfree workers constitute a special kind of labour force that generates maximum flexibility for firms and employers by limiting the ability of workers to negotiate the production process; in this way it augments returns. In the context of a global labour force that is increasingly pitched towards greater insecurity, competition drives the creation and maintenance of unfree labour relations across a wide variety of economies, sectors, types of work and social settings. The key dynamic relates to the ability of powerful firms to impose weighty commercial pressures on conditions of price and supply and to vary them at any given time in order to maximise value (Phillips, 2013, p. 182).

Violence in labour relations is one aspect of violent production; another is the relation between unfree labour, exports and global production. In the recent literature on global supply chains, global value chains and global production networks and in analyses of unfree labour, one finds a far more embedded approach to international trade in comparison with neoclassical economic trade theory. Stressing the institutional structures that govern commodity transactions, these analyses draw attention to how firms set up production and maintain trade. Global supply chain theory also accounts for adaptations of labour exploitation that trace back to the slave trade. Feminist commodity chain analysis considers women's subsidies to the global production network: the exploitation of unpaid household and informal sector labour constitutes chains of hidden surplus extraction at every node; this value is externalised from prices to the benefit of capitalists and consumers alike (Clelland, 2014).

Well covered in the press and in research are the distinctive experiences of women and girls in sex trafficking. But nearly two-thirds of all forced labour today is for economic exploitation, not sex work (Barrientos, 2013). Private agents (labour contractors and other intermediaries) are the primary channels for the supply of these workers.[6] Forced labour plays an integral, not residual, role in global production and is connected both to wartime supplies of raw materials and to international commodity markets. One could say that the imperative to earn a living is the initial compulsion that pushes workers into disadvantaged working conditions, particularly work in the shadow economy, both locally and internationally. From the corporations' viewpoint, the benefits of various forms of unfree labour include short-term contracts, the ability to hire and fire at short notice, and the freedom to dispense with a permanent workforce by outsourcing work.

The incorporation of workers into the global labour force on precarious and exploitative terms is well illustrated in the employment of children. Child labour is a peculiar form of productive work that is unfree – employers, including armed forces, set the lower productivity of young children against low wages or none at all. Commercial processes that are socially embedded (traditions of family artisanal labour in the mines, for example) and associated with contemporary global production (local use of artisanal labour to extract minerals for export through transnational mining companies) facilitate child labour, which may be based at home or in a factory, depending on shifting local conditions (Phillips *et al.*, 2014, p. 429). The commercial dynamics of global supply networks act to reinforce the employment of children, directly by fostering their engagement as workers, and indirectly by favouring the use of children, especially girls, in the reproductive household economy so that adult workers are available for waged labour.

In Sierra Leone, children represented a sizeable percentage of the labour force in the diamond mines, a pattern that the civil war exacerbated and that did not end with the truce (Surtees, 2005, p. 35). During the war, RUF (Revolutionary United Front) and AFRC (Armed Forces Revolutionary Council) fighters captured and abducted many children and forced them to work in the mines; the yields financed the rebel forces. Such cases constitute trafficking and were apparently numerous. Generally, children working in the mines are young boys, although girls also work in mining, commonly as cooks, domestic labourers, traders or prostitutes.

In addition to employing children, businesses that use artisanal labour under adverse terms are rewarded by global production networks. Businesses run by militias and armies in Africa have engaged artisanal labourers under wartime conditions in mining, ivory hunting and manual palm oil production.[7] There are similarities in the way the products of forced labour and work on adverse terms enter the legitimate marketplace, though the links in the chain are not the same. For example, in the late 1990s Ugandan businessmen, not wishing to invest in developing gold mines in Congo, took the expedient of working with militias that used artisanal labour to extract the ore. Ugandan trade statistics testify to the success of the tactic: in one year gold became Uganda's second export earner, despite the country's lack of domestic gold sources (Renton *et al.*, 2007, p. 192).

A third dimension of the neoliberal system is the new political ecology in which production and reproduction are situated. This ecology is the product of economic, social and political policies, and the people who hold economic and political power have created it. This third dimension, which can be a vector of violence, includes the disease ecology, the environment and the exploitation of natural resources. Political ecology crosses the boundary between production and social reproduction when multinational corporations privatise environmental resources like water. Neoliberal transformations in the water sector – understood as acts of primitive accumulation because neoliberal states implement a new round of enclosures of the commons to open up new territories to capitalist development and to capitalist forms of market behaviour – bring commodification into households (Ahlers, 2010; Roberts, 2008).

Economies adapt to long-running conflicts. Globalisation and neoliberalism have altered the role violence plays in the new political economy just as global neoliberal capitalism has altered such basic human activities as production and reproduction. Neoliberalism prefers temporary labour contracts, which affect not only trade unionism and labour markets in wartime, but also emotional, sexual, cultural and family life. Trends like the increase in unfree labour track to a host of specific neoliberal production practices: the squeeze of labour market reforms and privatisation, resulting in lower wages, fewer jobs and more poverty; the burgeoning informal economies within countries and with transnational links; the casualisation of work with no health and safety protections and no social benefits; the changed position of Africa in the international division of labour and labour conditions in global supply chains; the rise of the BRICS[8] and the new scramble for African resources and markets; and intensified processes of primitive accumulation (Lebaron and Ayers, 2013). Many of these changes precipitate armed conflicts and profit from them.

Capitalist organisers of production prefer to separate the political from the economic, casting violence in the political sphere. This is another false dichotomy, which transnational corporations use to deflect attention from the political and policy implications of their business practices and to disguise the externalisation of social reproduction costs. Although economic violence has a long and brutal history, Galtung (1969, p. 171), writing before neoliberalism was hegemonic, eschews the use of the term 'exploitation'; he claims that it belongs to a political vocabulary and has so many political and emotional overtones that it doesn't facilitate communication. In addition, he states that the term lends itself too easily to expressions involving the verb 'to exploit', which in turn may lead attention away from the structural as opposed to the personal nature of this phenomenon, 'and even lead to often unfounded accusations about intended structural violence'. Marxists interpret exploitation in terms of power, particularly over the use of the surplus produced by others in capitalist economies. By promoting the elimination of controls on capital, neoliberal policies have changed the balance of class forces decisively in capital's favour (Kotz and McDonough, 2010). Exploitation would seem to be the correct term to use in this context.

The new wars and the new war economies

New wars[9] is the term used to describe international or civil wars that involve so many transnational connections that it is difficult to support distinctions between internal and external, aggression and repression, and local and global.

The term grew out of the perception that new forms of violence have emerged with globalisation – militias, ethnic rebels, gang conflicts, sectarian violence, criminal insurgencies – which blur the boundaries between war and peace and between political and criminal violence. New wars signal the end of the state monopoly on violence, so long held as a way to maintain and justify order, and they mark the rise of armed non-state actors – militias, mercenaries, gangs, bandits, private security companies and military contractors. Unlike state armed forces that are marked by unproductive consumption of government expenditure, non-state armies must find ways to support themselves.[10] The new wars are also disputes about who controls the values and ideologies that supported the old order, leading to violence over representation: non-state actors contest who belongs, who qualifies as a citizen and who is an alien subject to deportation or ethnic cleansing (Deb *et al.*, 2012).

The military use the term low intensity to distinguish new wars from conventional warfare in which heavy weaponry and battlefield tactics are used between two or more states in open confrontation. (Low intensity is a cruel misnomer from the perspective of civilians, as will be shown.[11]) Globalisation has changed conventional warfare into new wars in three ways, according to Mary Kaldor (1999): new wars base their claims on identity; they use guerrilla or terror tactics; and they finance their attacks by exchanging natural resources for weapons, using parallel trade and international criminal networks. These exchanges, which are current and common in conflict zones, establish new economic configurations that are creatures of neoliberalism. They are so entrenched in global markets that they constitute a new economic formation; their influence necessitates a political economy analysis that situates the violence of production and reproduction in the context of criminal, corrupt and violent economies.

Violent economies provide a fast track to profit for legitimate businesses dealing in minerals such as gold, diamonds and coltan,[12] as well as criminal organisations smuggling weapons, drugs and people (Cockayne, 2010, p. 190). Violent economies also encompass all the shadowy combinations between legitimate and criminal commerce. Violence is available to these businesses as a resource – a factor of production, supportive of distribution, a dynamic in competition, and a shortcut to regulating reproduction. Violence deforms prevailing relationships to economic assets (Jackson, 2005, p. 155). In the context of Congo and Sierra Leone, armed conflict has allowed the use of violence to turn goods and services that would not normally be available into commodities such as forced labour, sexual servitude and illegally extracted or plundered mineral wealth (Cockayne, 2010, p. 194).

Neoliberalism has facilitated the criminal activities of the new war economies by reordering global trade and financial arrangements.[13] Cockayne (2010) names three financing strategies: *predation* (the use of violence to acquire capital, a strategy also called primitive accumulation; bank robberies are an example, whether old-style stickups or modern internet forms of fraud, and resource theft – everything from bottled beer (tax avoidance) and cattle to coltan); *parasitism* (extortion, protection money, taxation and kidnapping); and *symbiosis* (investment in licit businesses – bars, phone cards, temple management – and in illicit activities – drug production and human trafficking).

Another link between neoliberalism and the new war economies is the opportunity to solve a post-Cold War dilemma: how to supply Third World militaries? After the end of the Cold War, Third World leaders could no longer plead anti-communism or anti-Americanism to attract military aid from the superpowers; and, whereas the civil wars of the Cold War era were proxy wars dependent on the US and USSR for military equipment, now insurgents and state militaries alike must find new sources of weapons and supplies. A criminalised and globalised economy enables all sides to arm their fighters through sales of local assets to transnational corporations; the intermediaries of these deals are often international criminal networks adept at navigating financial byways. The necessary resource base enclave for the purchase of weapons is found in those areas of high-value minerals and raw materials that have become centres of contention for competing international and regional networks of control (Duffield, 2002, p. 1060). The inhabitants of these areas – that is, those who are unable to flee – become the productive and reproductive workforce of the occupiers.

In the process of converting assets into weapons, war economies often entail campaigns of immiseration and violent population displacement – indeed these disruptions are essential preconditions of asset realisation (Duffield, 2000, p. 81). Thus poverty and dislocation are not unfortunate eventualities or indirect consequences of conflict; they are usually its intended outcomes. In the short term, wars involve robbery and plunder; in the medium term, forms of slave labour (Münkler, 2005, p. 14). In the long term, the new wars involve shadow economies that inextricably intertwine exchange and violence, because where the aim is to force a population to support and supply armed groups on a permanent basis, the boundaries between working life and war become blurred. War becomes a way of life.

Neoliberalism and protracted new wars have further weakened the state, making it ever more difficult for governments to ensure human security and protect human rights. The role of the state is equivocal in the complex mutual penetration of legitimate businesses and illegitimate operations. In these conflicts, the state is both guarantor of human rights and complicit partner in criminal networks. The rebels who engage in armed violence, the rulers who are supposed to disarm them, and the transnational corporations that make use of rebels and rulers to procure the minerals they trade may perceive greater political and financial payoffs from continued violence than from peace. Only the local population suffers greatly, when it resists and when it submits – the poor women, children and men who are unprotected by the state and subject to coercion, corruption and violent criminal rule (Cockayne, 2010, p. 198).

A further characteristic of the new wars is said to be the use all sides make of ethnic divisions and the ways that they perpetuate them (Kaldor, 1999). Hoffman (2011), however, shows the flexibility of ethnic and national identity in the Liberia/Sierra Leone wars where fighters changed sides as gainful opportunities opened up. New wars also use guerrilla and terror tactics, and they target civilians. The wars in Congo and Sierra Leone militarised not only the production of minerals but also the societies in which mineral wealth is produced. Militarised production is a kind of slave labour – work at gunpoint – and changes how wealth is shared with workers. Instead of free labour able to negotiate payment, female and male workers at the eastern Congo mines occupied by armed forces were allowed to keep just half of what they produced; soldiers appropriated the other half and paid no compensation (Global Witness, 2009, p. 37). A similar practice operated in Sierra Leone: the 'two pile' system – one pile for the boss and one for the diggers. 'Compensation was completely unpredictable, less dictated by the certainties of the labor market than the capriciousness of the gods' (Hoffman, 2011, pp. 44–45). In the early and mid-1990s soldiers of the Sierra Leone army were observed not only looting and engaging in illegal diamond mining, but also killing civilians, dressing up as rebels, selling arms to rebels, and coordinating movements with rebels so as to minimise clashes and maximise the exploitation of civilians (Keen, 2002, p. 4). Incredibly, the RUF leadership took credit for violence carried out by soldiers, while soldiers used the excuse of the rebellion to plead impunity for their own abuses.

The impact of militarisation on social reproduction is even more dramatic. In eastern Congo, the age of marriage and childbearing dropped, families were repeatedly separated and displaced, many were reduced to extreme poverty, poor nutrition was chronic and health care was poor or non-existent; ultra-violent rape, which is still prevalent, leaves survivors severely injured as well as psychologically traumatised, and the incidence of sexually transmitted infections continues to rise, as do rates of pregnancy termination under unsafe conditions. In Sierra Leone, the civil war's impact on health was equally striking, with high rates of death and disability from war-related injuries, as well as the breakdown of the existing health infrastructure. At war's end, Sierra Leone had the world's lowest life expectancy (34 years) and the highest level of child mortality (316 per 1,000 live births); maternal mortality peaked at 1,800 per 100,000 live births in 2000 (WHO, 2004, p. 117). A decade later, the country is still recovering from the effects of the war. The long-term consequences of what Nancy Rose Hunt (2008) has described as 'reproductive ruination' are incalculable.

Contemporary studies of new wars are, nonetheless, gender-blind, and while I agree with Mark Duffield (2002, p. 1060) that the struggles in strife-afflicted lands are fundamentally about the terms and conditions under which production is being integrated within the global economy, I would add reproduction. My argument is that the battles in Congo and Sierra Leone are about the terms and conditions under which production *and reproduction* are being integrated within the global economy. This discussion goes beyond the gendering of warfare, which is the consideration of what women do and what is done to them in wartime (Turshen, 1998). The contention is that the violence of the new wars extends into home life, reorganising everyone's productive and reproductive activities. Although some writers admit that prolonged armed conflicts remake relationships between women and men (Bayart, 1999), few consider gender as part of the vocabulary of new wars. The omission of gender is doubly unfortunate because the new analyses break with past understandings of civil war and have much to offer on how wartime experiences change productive and reproductive relations between generations as well as how women and men reorganise their intimate relations and social responsibilities (Bayart *et al.*, 1999; Duffield, 2001; Le Billon, 2001).

Integration of states weakened by conflict into the globalised economy is not proceeding smoothly or according to neoliberal plans. The new wars can be seen as a form of resistance made possible by the opportunities globalisation has created and made necessary by structural adjustment programmes that dismantled the old patronage networks based on public bureaucracies (Duffield, 2002, p. 1056). Privatisation of public assets may have provided an opportunity for foreign corporations to shop at bargain basement prices, but it also afforded an opening for many African elites to develop trans-border networks as a new basis for political power. For young women and men seeking to survive in conflict zones, the shadow economy seems to have opened an alternative to fighting in rebel militias. Ray Bush (2007, p. 117) sees miners in small-scale operations, who access mineral wealth and trade it beyond the limits of established official markets and state control, as engaging in strategies of opposition to the plunder of resources by transnational corporations or state elites. William Reno (2009) notes that illicit commerce underlies new political relationships in West Africa, but then again pre-war regimes also incorporated significant elements of criminal networks into their strategies of rule. Reno believes it is important to understand criminality as one of the few avenues open to former armed groups for active participation in post-war economies and politics. I prefer to think about the protests behind the criminality, about the protesters who are entrapped and used by the criminal networks, and about the ways in which corporations use state and private militaries to crush dissent.[14] When they cannot master crooked organisations, companies join in the prosecution of outlaws, masking their own criminal behaviour.[15]

A further reason young people seek work in the shadow economy is the effect of austerity measures, which cut back the size of the public sector and standing armies, creating widespread unemployment. As workers are pushed out of formal employment, they seek income in the informal sector, and a shadow economy of extra-legal trade expands. The economic adjustments mandated by the International Monetary Fund (IMF) and the World Bank reduced the size of government, often costing women the decent work[16] they were just becoming qualified to perform as low-level bureaucrats, teachers and health workers. Cutbacks in bureaucracies, which spelled the loss of state services or required clients to pay for their privatised substitutes, combined with layoffs to compel many women to enter the overcrowded informal economy. War, Hoffman (2011) suggests, is a mode of violent accumulation in the absence of viable economic alternatives.

Civil wars in Congo and Sierra Leone

Comparative studies of gendered wartime experiences of violence are few, and generally the literature on women and war does not take into account the political economy of the new wars. An analysis of young female fighters in Liberia, Mozambique, Sierra Leone and Uganda compares women's roles as soldiers, army wives and support staff in camps (Coulter *et al.*, 2008). Bariagaber (2006) looks at UN peacekeeping operations in Africa; without considering gender issues, he concludes that the different dynamics of conflicts in Congo and Sierra Leone far outweigh their similarities and on this basis rejects the comparison. Wong (2012) finds the roots of what he calls the African post-colonial governance imbroglio in the histories of Congo, Liberia and Sierra Leone. Missing are comparative studies of women's work in areas occupied by rebel armies, for example women's coerced labour in the illegal exploitation of natural resources.

The conflicts in Congo and Sierra Leone do bear similarities. Neither was a classic civil war between citizens of the same country as both were regional conflicts that involved many nations. They were both also new wars profiting from conflict minerals and both were infamous for their abuse of women. Sierra Leone, with a pre-war population of 4.5 million, suffered traumatically in its 11-year civil war: 75,000 deaths, 100,000 mutilated, two million people internally displaced, 500,000 made refugees, and 250,000 women and girls abducted and raped (Abdullah *et al.*, 2006, p. 2). During the conflict, which began in 1991 and ended in 2002, rebel militias looted and burned villages, destroyed schools and health clinics, pillaged the capital, Freetown, and ruined the economy. Rebels financed the war by selling diamonds extracted by forced labour in the mines under their control in exchange for guns. When Sierra Leone emerged from the war, the country ranked last (177th) on the 2004 UN Development Programme human development index (UNDP, 2006).

Two successive wars, the first from 1996 to 1997 and the second from 1998 to 2003, left Congo devastated; perhaps five million people died, some due to violence but many as a result of preventable disease and starvation. The extent and nature of the violence in Congo have been widely reported in the international press and well documented by the UN. The number of deaths is in dispute. The International Rescue Committee estimated that from 1998 to 2007, 5.4 million excess deaths occurred,[17] more than two million of them since the formal end of war in 2002, and over 90 per cent the result of disease and malnutrition, not war-related injuries. (Excess deaths are those over and above what is expected.) To put these numbers in perspective, consider that Congo's population is about 65–70 million. In 2008 the crude mortality rate in the five provinces of eastern Congo was still 2.6 deaths per 1,000 per month, a rate that is 85 per cent higher than the sub-Saharan average.[18]

Since 2000, the International Rescue Committee (IRC) has documented the humanitarian impact of war and conflict in DR Congo through a series of five mortality surveys. The first four studies, conducted between 2000 and 2004, estimated that 3.9 million people had died since 1998, arguably making DR Congo the world's deadliest crisis since World War II. Less than 10 percent of all deaths were due to violence, with most attributed to easily preventable and treatable conditions such as malaria, diarrhea, pneumonia and malnutrition.

(IRC, n.d., p. ii)

The fifth survey, covering the period January 2006 to April 2007, found the national crude mortality rate to be 2.2 deaths per 1,000 per month, which is 57 per cent higher than the average rate for sub-Saharan Africa and unchanged since the 2004 survey. Clearly the conflict in Congo continued to claim lives despite the nominal end of the war in 2003. Every day, more Congolese join the ranks of the disabled as a result of landmines, unexploded ordnance and sporadic fighting (McCormick, 2014).

Not everyone agrees that the war in Congo fits the description of new wars. Koen Vlassenroot (2003, p. 341) believes that, although war seriously destabilised the economic order of eastern Congo, his research suggests that the situation in 2002 did not differ essentially from that before 1996, except perhaps for the slippage from informal to illegal activity. Even that, he says, is due less to the war than to the nature of the Congolese state under Mobutu, who allowed warlords to rise. Globalisation, far from marginalising local plutocrats and kleptocrats, offers them new advantages. The greatest difference, he concedes, is that the economy is now based on the logic of violence.

The violence of extractive industries

The United Nations examined the details of Congo wars' financing and arming (UNSC, 2002, 2003, 2008). Whatever may have been the motives for war in the early 1990s, at their height the conflicts became a contest for the control of land and the resources that lay beneath the surface (Johnson, 2009).[19] The sales of minerals, principally diamonds, gold and coltan, paid for the war materiel of the conflicting armies and enriched their backers. To give an idea of the economic value of these operations, in 2010 Bisie, a tin mine in Walikali, North Kivu, provided local soldiers more than $100,000 per month; in addition, some commanders took control of individual pits and also received kickbacks from trading houses (Stearns, 2010).

Despite attempts to integrate militias into the regular army after each peace accord, shifting coalitions of state and non-state armed groups sponsored principally by Kinshasa, Kigali and Kampala continued to control the mineral deposits.[20] They or civilians working for them do the digging, or they tax the output of local diggers. *Comptoirs* (buying houses) typically transport the output by road and air to their headquarters, many of which are located in Goma and Bukavu, the capitals of North and South Kivu provinces respectively. They also deploy roadblocks to tax trade passing along roads under their control, and they tax markets. Groups that control border crossings tax other rebel groups who pay them for safe passage of goods.[21] Internal and regional smuggling networks supply weapons to armed groups in eastern Congo. According to the 2008 UN Security Council report, the governments of Uganda and Rwanda have explicitly denied any official cooperation between their armed forces and the CNDP military wing, but it is widely accepted that both nations financed proxy militias in Congo.

The UN Security Council also appointed expert panels to look at minerals smuggling in support of rebel activity in Sierra Leone (UNSC, 2000). They concluded that diamonds, of which the estimated annual value was anywhere between $25 million and $125 million, represented a primary source of income for RUF, sustaining its military activities. RUF commanders and Liberian couriers carried the diamonds to Foya-Kama or Voinjama and then to Monrovia. Some local diggers, in a modified form of forced labour, worked four days a week for RUF, two days for themselves and had a day off; others worked on the 'two-pile' system, but all sizeable diamonds went to RUF (UNSC, 2000, p. 16). S. Balimo Jalloh (2001) describes wanton acts of arson, mutilations and amputations committed by rebels as designed to provide cover for the extraction and smuggling of diamonds.

Regional trade networks

The regional integration of Sierra Leone predates colonialism and the formation of nation-states in West Africa, as we know them today (Howard, 2006). The Atlantic coast of Congo was similarly integrated early on (Heywood, 2009), and eastern Congo developed important exchanges with its neighbours from the mid-nineteenth century (Northrup, 1988). European and Arab contacts and the slave trade were significant in the development of regional trade networks (Manning, 1983).

Regional integration took on new significance during the civil wars of the 1990s and those ties continue to shape life and death (as the West African Ebola epidemic demonstrated). Trading networks flourished in the context of neoliberal rules of engagement, as trans-border networks became conduits for the growth of multiple forms of extra-legal trade in legitimate and illicit goods. Through trans-border networks, new wars are tied to new economic arrangements as well as new relations of production and reproduction. Inventive 'local–global shadow networks' have become the basis of reintegration with the liberal world-system (Duffield, 2002, p. 1057). New war economies function through trans-border networks, relying on external markets to turn local assets into cash as well as to furnish all kinds of essential supplies and services that are not available in the neighbourhood – everything from fuel, spare parts and munitions to clothing, food and bottled beer.

Shadow economies now constitute the major part of international trade over much of the global South (Duffield, 2002, p. 1056; Naím, 2003). The shadow (or parallel) economy is not necessarily associated with criminality or organised violence and can represent a normal way of life for many people, but in conflict zones the shadow economy is almost always brutal. Gutiérrez (2010) claims that private–public networks of militarised commerce need not be predatory or particularly aggressive because they can conduct business and coordinate rent extraction with the private provision of security, as in Colombia. Duffield (2002,

p. 1066) points out that altered trans-border arrangements have changed the perception of international security, with profound implications for international governance: metropolitan monitoring, intervention and regulation are at levels not seen since the colonial period.

Extra-legal trade often adapts and draws on resources and networks based on locality, kinship or ethnicity, and these social networks tend to inscribe their own forms of legitimacy and regulatory codes on the shadow economy (Duffield, 2001, p. 156). Social and political elites in control of trans-border trade are generally opposed to economic regionalism or integration, since profit depends on maintaining differences and discrete forms of control. The nodes within parallel networks that command real influence remain under patriarchal control (Duffield, 2001, p. 156). This patriarchal control differs from previous arrangements because neoliberal structural adjustment programmes transformed women's status, downgrading their worth and their work and altering relations between genders and generations.

Several characteristics of trans-border activity have specific implications for women. The dynamics of trans-border trade are likely to encourage and enforce informal protectionism. Circuits of extra-legal activity lend themselves to different forms of socially structured control. With few formal qualifications required for positions of power and control, what prevails are ethnic, local, kinship, religious, political or diaspora connections. These considerations are likely to spell trouble for women who marry across lines (for example, inter-ethnic or inter-religious marriages). Ethnic cleansing and forcible transfer of assets between groups may be features of conflict situations, and women with multiple affiliations or loyalties will be caught in the crossfire. The suspension of legality is often a necessary precondition of asset realisation through parallel and trans-border manoeuvres. Duffield (1999, p. 8) notes that 'the rule of law and protection of customary rights have been an important casualty of the qualification of nation-state competence'. This contradictory development means that, just as ethnicity becomes salient in new trade networks, women's customary land rights are in jeopardy.

Changes to the conditions of reproduction, analysed in detail in Chapter 4 below, are more difficult to articulate in terms of local–global networks. Seay (2013, p. 85) observes that many civil society organisations step in to provide social services in response to the withdrawal of weak states and that many of these CSOs establish partnerships with international donors and NGOs to support their work. This pattern of international partnerships is particularly characteristic of religious service providers, whether Christian or Muslim. CSO substitution for state services represents the privatisation of health care, education and social work and is consonant with the predominant neoliberal model, posing no challenge to the norms of structurally adjusted economies.

Trans-border trade: the DRC

As conflicts were layered on top of an already decrepit infrastructure, fracturing the links between the eastern provinces and the western half of Congo, trans-border trade to the east assumed greater prominence. Trans-border networks have long extended across the eastern borders of Congo into Uganda and Rwanda; from the 1990s, they became conduits for the growth of multiple forms of extra-legal trade in legitimate and illicit goods.

The sale of resources and the procurement of arms and supplies, which depend on access to global markets, rely on women and men who traverse mountainous forest trails transporting goods to waiting fleets of light planes that land on roads rather than airstrips. Entry to transcontinental smuggling or grey commercial arteries is arranged through these networks, which may be involved with the government or independent of state apparatuses, particularly police, tax and customs functions. Private security firms maintain the threat of force: over 100 firms employing 30,000 guards are registered in Congo. A spiral of violence accompanies mining companies' increased use of private security in Congo (Aoul *et al.*, 2000).

Women dominate the small-scale cross-border trade in legal agricultural goods between some countries, for example Congo and Rwanda (Kimanuka and Lange, 2010). The women described by Janet MacGaffey (1991) as heavily involved in smuggling in the 1970s and 1980s do not appear to have survived the wars of the 1990s. Women also run the illegal petty trade in processed goods like soft drinks between Congo and Uganda (Raeymaekers, 2009). New field studies of smuggling detail how women function in these illicit networks (Laudati, 2013). Timothy Raeymaekers (2009, 2010) tracked hidden smugglers with open official ties and rebel entrepreneurs seeking high political protection: their activities sustain the transformation of politics at the Semliki border crossing between Congo and Uganda. For most participants in the smuggling economy of the border town of Lubiriha, fraud is necessary because the Congolese customs service taxes imports at rates that severely reduce profits. For these smugglers, fraud just means operating covertly; for example, they shift commodities like crates of soft drinks across the border.[22] Smuggling generates many livelihoods and ensures survival. According to interviews Raeymaekers conducted in January 2008 with female smugglers, women are prominent actors in the traffic over Lubiriha's side-paths. Aside from smugglers, there is a much larger group of men and women (lower administrators) operating on the border, who often nurture close connections with the innumerable intelligence and military services that circle Lubiriha's markets, connections from which they can derive benefits.

Trans-border trade: Sierra Leone

Mark Shaw (2003, p. 23) draws a graphic portrait of the trans-border activities involved in supplying the war in Sierra Leone: he investigated the internal RUF supply organisation, Lebanese trading networks (Lebanese traders were commercial allies who exchanged food and cash for diamonds), the Liberian connection (the role of intermediaries operating with contacts in Charles Taylor's government), various bandits and businessmen involved in the trade of supplies or military expertise, as well as how the Sierra Leone state was supplied with weapons and protection.

Trans-border human trafficking of girls and boys appears to flow in all directions: proximity to borders was a key determinant in a child's destination (from Kambia to Guinea, for example, or Pujehun district to Liberia) (Surtees, 2005, p. 25). Some children are recruited for agricultural labour on plantations as far away as Côte d'Ivoire, which shares no border with Sierra Leone. Trafficking of unaccompanied minors to Europe has also been recorded (29 to Ireland between 2003 and 2005, 38 to the Netherlands between 2002 and 2005) (Surtees, 2005, p. 23). Child trafficking entails the use of false documents or the payment of bribes to border officials to allow children with no documents to pass; traffickers may use or threaten violence or abuse as a means of exerting control over the children as they travel long distances across rough terrain and covertly cross borders (Surtees, 2005, p. 68).

Trans-border trade is not limited to material goods or human trafficking, unfortunately: disease travels with people. An epidemic of Ebola, a virus carrying a high risk of death that causes fever and internal bleeding, began in 2014. Originating in Guinea, it spread through Liberia and arrived in Sierra Leone[23] following the route of the second Liberian civil war, which began in 1999 when the rebel group LURD, backed by the government of Guinea, emerged in northern Liberia. Cross-border clashes between Liberia and Sierra Leone peaked in 2001, 'coinciding with a sudden increase in violent events in Liberia' (Dowd and Raleigh, 2012, p. 14). In this case trade, disease and conflict converged.

As a social body, the borderlands have opened up new types of economic and social policy; new levels of poverty and new degrees of popular participation have appeared; corruption and criminal activity are extensive; respect for human rights, the status of women and psychological wellbeing have declined; and the roles of media and political institutions have been transformed. Trans-border economies have dramatically altered the lives of women in conflict zones.

The economic impact of civil wars on women

The economic impact of civil wars on women cannot be separated from the issue of displacement, which was the experience of 2.6 million people in Sierra Leone (more than half the population) and of 2.7 million from the eastern provinces of Congo. Displacement is the euphemism the UN uses for forced eviction, ethnic cleansing, expulsion, forced removal, house demolition, land expropriation, population transfer, relocation and resettlement, all of which are common in conflicts involving competing territorial claims. When all weapons are increasingly accurate, and destructive battles are costly and difficult to win, territory is gained by controlling or displacing the people who live there (Kaldor, 2006).

Eviction disrupts economies, destroys local markets and disconnects people from their sources of income. Every time people flee (and they may be expelled two, three, four, five or more times), they lose almost everything – their homes and material assets, their jobs and schooling for their children – and they must deal with trauma, death and physical injury. If they are separated from family and community, they may lose their social support networks as well. With each flight, a person's ability to cope is further eroded (Wissing and Pagot, 2014).

V. Spike Peterson (2008, pp. 15ff.) examines the new war literature through a feminist lens, analysing the shadow economies of war zones. She describes three (somewhat overlapping) categories, which are useful for pinpointing the effects on women. *Coping economies* facilitate individual survival and the social reproduction of families and households; they force women to deal in black-market goods, engage in sex work, go into debt bondage and even sell their body parts to the human organ trade. *Combat economies* include activities like looting, theft, kidnapping and smuggling to supply and fund fighters and insurgent activities. Stereotypically masculinised, combat economies disrupt traditional gendered identities, yet harshly discipline nonconforming women; they objectify, abuse, rape, assault and kill women; they use them as sexual decoys, abduct them for ransom and traffic them. Peterson (2008, p. 10) refers to this conduct as 'devalorisation of the feminine' and understands it as discrimination against insufficiently masculine men; masculinised identities, practices and objectives are prioritised as necessary for military success.

Overlapping both of these categories are *criminal economies*, defined by activities like smuggling, trafficking, predatory lending, aid manipulation, natural resource expropriation, fraud, tax evasion and money laundering. Criminal economies also provide opportunities for women and men to profit from activities that fall outside state regulation. Striking about all three types of economy is the criminalisation of the working class, forcing us to question assumptions about people's choices and latitude to choose, as well as about what women, men and children must do to survive in war zones. What we decide about wartime behaviour enjoins determinations about justice and reparations in the aftermath.

The economic impact of civil wars on women extends to extractive industries, which have figured so prominently in the conflicts in Congo and Sierra Leone. Women are often the first to bear the negative impact of fighting for control of mine sites, as the mining encroaches on their farms and they lose the land they work. The influx of migrant workers and cash into mining sites makes women likely targets of sexual violence; and the pollution of rivers and streams near mine sites means they often have to travel longer distances to collect clean water, which can expose them to attack.

We know that there are women miners but we do not know much about how they profit from their labour.[24] Women provide the majority of services at mine sites and adjacent mine camps; they run restaurants, markets and small kiosks. They work both voluntarily and under coercion in the sex trade, often unprotected or under intimidation (Perks, 2011, p. 180). In Congo, for example, women more often perform support service work to the industry than engage in the physical act of mining, though there are women pit bosses in Rwandan tin mines (Joanne Lebert, personal communication, 14 September 2011). According to Colette Braeckman (2004), a Belgian journalist who has written several books on Central Africa, gold diggers in Congo take the rocks to women who grind the stones for hours until they have reduced them to powder mixed with spangles of dust, which is then carefully sifted. Women get a dollar a day for this work – and another dollar if they prostitute themselves at night.

We also know that women were bartered by a new generation of local commercial actors who joined the coltan mines where they became the leaders of the coltan diggers; these leaders made payments called tributes to the owners of the mine sites and offered food, beer, manufactured products – and women – to the diggers in return for coltan, transactions that brought them lots of money (Vlassenroot and Romkema, 2002). The abduction of women and girls to work in the camps and provide housekeeping as well as sexual services is a common theme of rebel operations everywhere, but there is little detail available of rebel camp experience in Congo. One group that operated in South Kivu, known as the Rastas and composed mostly of Rwandan Hutus, boasted of their extremely violent and brutal gang-rapes of underage girls; often they confined these girls for months as sex slaves and sometimes 'gave' them to FDLR-FOCA militia (IRIN News, 26 May 2005).

Stories of women who profit from war are rarely published. Emerita Munyashwe is known because she was a close associate of Laurent Nkunda[25] and was assassinated in Goma in August 2010. She handled CNDP finances during Nkunda's reign as commander of the movement. She was also allegedly close to General Kayumba Nyamwasa,[26] which led some commentators to speculate that the men who assassinated her came across the border from Rwanda (the border is just several hundred metres from where she was shot) (http://congosiasa.blogspot.com, 30 August 2010).

An example from the Mano River wars (Liberia, Sierra Leone and Guinea) is Aicha (or Ayesha) Keita Conneh, daughter of the Guinean president Lansana Conté and wife of Sekou Conneh who successfully led LURD against Charles Taylor; she was accused of transporting heavy war-making weaponry across the border into Guinea (*Inquirer*, Monrovia, Liberia, 19 May 2004, www.theperspective.org/inquirer/aishaconneh.html, accessed 12 June 2014). In 1999 she had performed the same task in the other direction, persuading her father to arm LURD (*The Economist* 16 December 2004, www.economist.com/node/3490667, accessed 12 June 2014).

Tracking women's activities in the criminal world or seeing how women have profited from war economies has proved difficult (Malu Muswamba, 2006). Little of the literature on wartime violence against women looks at women's livelihoods in the broad context of economies transformed by neoliberal policies, a question discussed in detail in Chapter 3 below. Margaret Niger-Thomas (2001) studied women smugglers on the Cameroon-Nigeria border, but this is not a conflict zone, and she defines smuggling as evading customs to avoid paying taxes; also the commodity smuggled (fuel oil) is legitimate. She does offer important information on both the profitability of this trade and the hazards, namely sexual harassment, as customs officers have been known to demand sex from female entrepreneurs. She notes that some of these women had been sex workers before becoming entrepreneurs, and officers made such assumptions about all of them. Scattered reports suggest that like men, women are cashing in on the new asset transfers of trans-border activity, at increased risk to their personal safety. Occasional news reports surface, telling of the arrests of female arms dealers (several stories of Nigerian women running weapons-smuggling operations),[278] drug smugglers (again, mainly Nigerians but also reports of women from Kenya, Tanzania, Zambia and South Africa),[28] and human traffickers (60 per cent of prosecuted persons in trafficking cases in Nigeria are women and 50 per cent of convicted traffickers are women).[29]

The social impact of civil wars on women

Social impacts of wartime violence are fairly readily described but are much more difficult to quantify with precise numbers and even harder to convey in terms of raw lived experiences. The social impacts are displacement, rape and the loss of access to social services – unless refugees and (more rarely) internally displaced women and girls are served by the UN High Commission for Refugees or one of the many international emergency relief NGOs like Médecins sans Frontières or OXFAM. Mass displacement takes a huge social toll on populations, as the estimates of death, disability and sickness for Congo and Sierra Leone demonstrate. Abduction of girls, as the epigraph at the head of this chapter shows, subjects them to all the ambiguities of civil war: use as decoys, as porters and as sex slaves (Wakubenga, 2013, p. 129).

The epidemic scale of rape in Congo, which seemed to reach a peak in 2007–2008, has caused great misery. In one report, 32,000 rapes were registered in the eastern district of South Kivu in the period 2005–2007 (Holmes, 2007). Another estimate of rape among women aged 15 to 49 years, based on data for the year 2007, translates into 1,150 women raped every day (Peterman *et al.*, 2011). This figure does not include sexual violence against girls younger than 15 years or women older than 49 years who account for about 16 per cent of reported rapes; it also does not include sexual violence against boys and men. It is likely then that these estimates are lower than the true prevalence of sexual violence. Doctors at Panzi Hospital in Bukavu in eastern Congo reported that a high percentage of the rapes were extremely violent:

> Seventy-two percent of women reported that they were tortured during the rape itself (beaten, wounded with machetes, genitally mutilated/burned by drops of plastic melted by flame), and 12.4% had had objects inserted into their vaginas (sticks, bottles, green bananas, pestles coated in chili pepper, rifle barrels); some women, after being raped, were killed by shots fired into their vaginas.
>
> (Mukwege and Nangini, 2009, p. 2)

In 2009 President Joseph Kabila signed an amnesty law that, according to the International Center on Transitional Justice, perpetuates Congo's pattern of rewarding violence; it created a blanket amnesty for scores of crimes perpetrated by rebel groups, Congolese armed forces (FARDC), militias and police alike.

Similarly, the 1999 Lomé peace accord gave a blanket amnesty to all combatants in the Sierra Leone conflict in exchange for demobilisation and peace, a pardon that meant a complete lack of accountability for the massive human rights abuses of the war including rape and forced marriage, abduction and conscription of children and youth of both sexes. As a result, human rights activists pushed for mechanisms of transitional justice that would pay special attention to child victims and perpetrators of the conflict, as well as women and girls who suffered violence. One assessment of the Special Court for Sierra Leone evaluated four judgments and concluded that considered together they failed to make a significant progressive contribution to gender-sensitive transitional justice (Oosterveld, 2009).

Summing up

When interpolating the findings of the literature on new war economies with that on women in wartime, some changed circumstances stand out. With weakened states has come the loss of public goods and services. Feminist economists have written about the destructive impact of neoliberal economic regimes imposed upon state borrowers by the international financial institutions (Balakrishnan, 2005; Sparr, 1994). They have highlighted the effects of structural adjustment programmes on state services formerly available to women and on which they depended, perhaps more than men. Many commentators have noted the hollowing out of the state that resulted from the imposition of structural adjustment (Niemann, 2007). Wars destroyed the remaining infrastructure and services, throwing women on the charity of private care providers.

This chapter introduces gender into the political economy of armed conflict by examining the multiple meanings of violence, especially structural violence, in the war-altered relations of production and social reproduction. It considers unfree labour in the context of the new wars and the new war economies. The case studies of civil wars in Congo and Sierra Leone are comparable in the wartime violence of their extractive industries and assaults on women; they offer compelling evidence of regional trade networks and trans-border trade in both countries. The chapter concludes with a general assessment of the economic and social impacts of armed conflict on women.

The analysis of war economies is important for women and for the struggle to end sexual violence because women need to know their enemies. Proximate enemies are most often men, but sometimes they are women, just as men are sometimes victims of sexual violence. Ultimate enemies are those who pull the strings and hold the power that provokes and maintains these conflicts. We need to look beyond interpersonal violence to understand better the causes of the use of force and to see how violence is embedded in global systems of trade and grey commercial networks. We need to comprehend how deeply rooted these systems are in world markets; how destabilising it is to penetrate and disassemble war economies. We need to enumerate and name the vested interests, not just of the armed groups that directly inflict violence on women, but also of the legal transnational corporations that benefit directly from the rebels' dirty work. We may know the trajectory of the exploitation of minerals through their sale to intermediaries and ultimate users, but we know less about women's collaboration or involuntary participation in these activities. We need to know in a gendered way all the links in the chain that ties armed groups to transnational corporations, including the governments – those so-called failed states – that are complicit. We need, in effect, the gendered story of persistent violence. This knowledge will at least enable us to evaluate our strategies for bringing an end to sexual violence against women in wartime.

Notes

1

> When looting the village, I was the one who knocked on doors. When they heard the voice of a little girl, they opened without hesitation and the *Interahamwe* took the opportunity to loot and rape. In the end, I was helping to transport the looted goods. I did it for four years.

> [my translation]

2 Chenoweth and Cunningham (2013, p. 273) in a discussion of nonviolent resistance maintain that violence is neither the only nor necessarily the most potent form of conflict.
3 Civilians accounted for 90 per cent of deaths directly or indirectly related to these civil wars. One source (Scaruffi, 2009) estimates the death toll from 15 of those conflicts to be 9,267,700, including 200,000 deaths in Sierra Leone and 4.6 million in the Democratic Republic of Congo. These estimates are not disaggregated by sex: the assumption is that with the shift from a majority of combatant deaths early in the twentieth century to a greater number of civilian deaths at the millennium's end, more women are dying in recent conflicts. All war mortality statistics for Congo are in dispute: see the debates between the International Rescue Committee (www.rescue.org) and the Human Security Report Project, Simon Fraser University, Vancouver, British Columbia (www.hsrgroup.org/human-security-reports/20092010/text.aspx). Also see Spagat (2010) and Note 18 below.
4 The key assertion of intersectionality, an interdisciplinary analytic approach to social categories inflected by relations of power, is that the various systems of societal oppression do not act independently of each other. Different systems of inequality such as racism, sexism and class oppression are transformed in their intersections.
5 For a useful discussion of the various forms of unfree labour, see McGrath (2005, 2013).
6 Forced labour accounts for an estimated 21 million workers globally, and their work generates more than US$150 billion in illegal profits annually (which bypass national tax collection systems); women and girls account for 55 per cent of the total (ILO, 2014, p. 7).
7 This type of forced labour differs from labour in adverse conditions on plantations producing for global supply networks (like the production of soybeans, cotton, sugar and coffee in South America).
8 The BRICS are the emerging economies of Brazil, Russia, India, China and South Africa.

9 For a review of civil wars since the end of the Cold War, see Kalyvas (2003); for a critical view questioning whether this literature identifies new phenomena, see Mama and Okazawa-Rey (2012) and Newman (2004).

10 Neoliberalism dictates that as many military functions as possible should be privatised; non-state actors by definition are private sector entrepreneurs. Because in Congo the national army so rarely receives wages or benefits, it is often forced to support itself in much the same way as non-state actors.

11 In November 2014, a forum of 190 representatives of civil society organisations met in Addis Ababa and declared, inter alia, that the definition of conflict should be expanded to include internal disturbances, protracted and low-intensity civil strife, political strife, ethnic and communal violence, state of emergency and suppression of mass uprisings, and their impact on women's security (http://femnet.co/index.php/en/beijing-plus-20/item/326-africa-cso-position-statement, accessed 20 June 2015).

12 Coltan is an abbreviation for columbite-tantalite, the mineral ore from which the metal tantalum is extracted by artisanal miners using rudimentary tools. European and Asian companies process tantalum into tantalum powder; it is an essential component for making capacitors that store energy in nuclear reactors, mobile phones, pagers, PlayStations, laptops and other electronic devices.

13 Congo is not ranked because data on national accounts, balance of payments and bilateral trade data are missing for the period 1980–2009; Sierra Leone, despite some missing data during the civil war years, ranks among the top 20 countries in illicit financial flows as a percentage of GDP (Kar and LeBlanc, 2013, pp. 26–27). By deregulating money transactions and allowing banks to operate in secrecy, for example, an estimated US$5.9 trillion in illicit funds flowed out of the developing world in the period 2002–2011 (Kar and LeBlanc, 2013). By not imposing restrictions on capital flight, profits from trade misinvoicing amount to US$424 billion each year (Baker *et al.*, 2014).

14 Chinua Achebe (1972, p. 114), writing about the Biafran War in a short story, speculates about

> heartless attack-traders who traffic in foreign currencies and make their hundreds of thousands by sending young men to hazard their lives bartering looted goods for cigarettes behind enemy lines, or one of those contractors who receive piles of money daily for food they never deliver to the army.

15 See the Anvil case (www.ccij.ca/cases/anvil-mining/, accessed 30 September 2011). It is alleged that the company, Anvil Mining Limited, provided logistical assistance to the massacre by Congolese military of more than 70 people in the Congo in 2004.

16 Standing (2014) restricts the term decent work to unionised jobs in the primary employment sector; here the term is used more colloquially with reference to steady employment protected by a contract that binds employers' duties to workers' rights.

17 The Human Security Report Project (2010) finds this figure far too high and estimates the dead at only half that number. Even so, 2.7 million excess deaths in a decade is an astounding number.

18 The five provinces are Maniema, North Kivu, Orientale, South Kivu and the northern part of Katanga. The estimated population of North and South Kivu is 6.3 million, that of the much larger Orientale and much smaller Maniema provinces is 6.6 million, giving a total of 12.9 million. Katanga is very large and only portions of the north are in conflict; the population of the area is unknown. These figures are very rough guesses: the last census was carried out in 1984.

19 According to Johnson (2009), the economic dimension of conflict in eastern Congo began with disputes about rights of access to land and control of trade routes, not control of minerals. The history of conflict in the Kivus shows that the existence of a trade in minerals is not a factor favouring either conflict or its absence. Conflict is linked to nationality and ethnicity and to political and administrative power. The

economic issues revolve around competition to control trade routes and trade revenues between elites as well as competition to control access to land and water between rural populations. It is precisely because conflict revolves around issues other than minerals that the mineral trade can serve as a substitute source of revenue for parties who have lost their other, really important livelihoods. Johnson maintains that in the past, fighting never occurred over control of the cassiterite mines of Walikale, the gold mines of Lubero, the coltan mines of Masisi or the pyrochlore mine of Lueshe in Rutshuru. In South Kivu, large-scale artisanal gold mining began as a means for displaced populations in remote areas to survive.

20 For example, in 2008 the FDLR-FOCA operated as part of an informal network of armed groups (UNSC, 2008).

21 The CNDP taxes border crossings, and receives payment from the FDLR for the safe passage of goods.

22 For example, Nordstrom (2004, p. 73) gives another scalar dimension to the trade in beer and soft drinks in her interviews at a truck stop: 'This beer that costs 60 cents here, I can sell this for ten US dollars a bottle in the eastern province.' Each truck carries 30–50 tons of drinks, and trucks travel in convoys of 100–150 vehicles.

23 The Ministry of Health of Guinea first reported an outbreak of Ebola haemorrhagic fever on 25 March 2014; suspected cases in the neighbouring countries of Liberia and Sierra Leone were reported at that time (www.cdc.gov/vhf/ebola/outbreaks/guinea/recent_updates.html; www.afro.who.int/en/clusters-a-programmes/dpc/epidemic-a-pandemic-alert-and-response/outbreak-news/4069-ebola-haemorrhagic-fever-guinea-27-march-2014.html, accessed 21 August 2014).

24 Women are – or are only minimally – involved in the mineral sector in developed countries in technical occupations, skilled trades and senior leadership roles.

25 Laurent Nkunda was formerly a general in the Congo armed forces and a warlord operating in the province of Nord-Kivu; he was sympathetic to Congolese Tutsis and Paul Kagame's government in Rwanda.

26 Faustin Kayumba Nyamwasa is a Rwandan former lieutenant general who was chief of staff of the Rwandan army. He also headed Rwandan intelligence and served as Rwanda's ambassador to India. Nyamwasa fled to South Africa in February 2010.

27 A Nigerian mother and her three daughters belonging to a syndicate that specialises in supplying weapons to criminals for armed robbery were sought (Mac-Leva, 2009).

28 Four women including a nursing mother and a young girl were arrested in Enugu for allegedly supplying cocaine (Achife, 2008). Two African women (Tanzanian and Kenyan) drug smugglers carrying 110 and 93 heroin-filled capsules in their stomachs were arrested by anti-narcotics force personnel at Peshawar airport when they were about to leave for Dubai; they told the court that they were working for an international gang of drug smugglers in their respective countries (Ahmad, 2003). This is part of a growing trend: Zambia's drug enforcement commission said it had arrested 15 Zambian women for drug-related offences around the world and at Zambia's various entry and exit points in 2010 (Kabange, 2011). For South African women's arrests, see www.sabc.co.za/news/a/e6afe900430fb82c85e79d45a23ba143/SA-woman-arrested-for-drug-smuggling-in-Kenya-denied-bail-20140225, accessed 21 January 2014.

29 According to the 2008 report of the UN Office on Drugs and Crime on women traffickers, 53 per cent of recruiters are men and 42 per cent are women; 21 per cent of victims are recruited by women and a further 27 per cent are exploited by women. Despite these statistics, which suggest that sex trafficking is a crime with a relatively high rate of female involvement, the numbers for Africa are low (about 20 per cent of traffickers are women), and many Nigerian traffickers are thought to be victims who later become members of the criminal group exploiting other victims and may have another member of the same group still exploiting them (UNODC, 2012, pp. 29–30).

References

Abdullah, Hussainatu J., Aisha F. Ibrahim and Jamesina King (2006) Women's voices, work and bodily integrity in pre-conflict, conflict and post conflict reconstruction processes in Sierra Leone, http://r4d.dfid.gov.uk/PDF/Outputs/WomenEmp/Abdullah_SierraLeoneCountryPaper.pdf, accessed 20 January 2014.

Abu-Lughod, Lila (2013) *Do Muslim women need saving?* Cambridge, MA: Harvard University Press.

Achebe, Chinua (1972) *Girls at war*. London: Heinemann.

Achife, Chukwudi (2008) Nigeria: police nab 22 robbers, 4 female cocaine dealers, 14 October, *allafrica.com/stories/200810140975.html*, accessed 25 August 2014.

Ahlers, Rhodante (2010) Fixing and nixing: the politics of water privatization, *Review of radical political economics* 42(2): 213–231.

Ahmad, Shafiq (2003) Drug traffickers enticing youth, *DAWN* (Peshawar), 17 March, www.dawn.com/news/88272/drug-traffickers-enticing-youth, accessed 25 August 2014.

Aoul, Samia Kazi, Émilie Revil, Bruno Sarrasin and Bonnie Campbell with the collaboration of Denis Tougas (2000) Towards a spiral of violence? The dangers of privatising risk management of investments in Africa. Mining activities and the use of private security companies. Montreal: Working Group on Human Rights in Congo/Kinshasa, and Development and Peace, MiningWatch Canada.

Baker, Raymond, Christine Clough, Dev Kar, Brian LeBlanc and Joshua Simmons (2014) Hiding in plain sight: trade misinvoicing and the impact of revenue loss in Ghana, Kenya, Mozambique, Tanzania, and Uganda: 2002–2011. Washington, DC: Global Financial Integrity.

Bakker, Isabella (2003) Neo-liberal governance to the reprivatization of social reproduction, social provisioning and shifting gender orders. In *Power, production and social reproduction: human in/security in the global political economy*, edited by Isabella Bakker and Stephen Gill, pp. 66–82. London: Palgrave.

Balakrishnan, Radhika (2005) Why MES with human rights? Integrating macro economic strategies with human rights, www.cwgl.rutgers.edu/globalcenter/gcpubs.html, accessed 22 November 2013.

Bariagaber, Assefaw (2006) United Nations peace operations in Africa: a cookie-cutter approach?, *Journal of third world studies* XXIII(2): 11–29.

Barrientos, Stephanie (2013) 'Labour chains': analyzing the role of labour contractors in global production networks, *Journal of development studies* 49(8): 1058–1071.

Basaglia, Franco (1987) *Psychiatry inside out: selected writings of Franco Basaglia*, edited by Nancy Scheper-Hughes and Anne M. Lovell. New York: Columbia University Press.

Bayart, Jean-François (1999) The 'social capital' of the felonious state. In *The criminalization of the state in Africa*, edited by Jean-François Bayart, Stephen Ellis and Béatrice Hibou, pp. 32–48. Oxford: James Currey.

Bayart, Jean-François, Stephen Ellis and Béatrice Hibou, eds (1999) *The criminalization of the state in Africa*. Oxford: James Currey.

Beneduce, Roberto, Luca Jourdan, Timothy Raeymaekers and Koen Vlassenroot (2006) Violence with a purpose: exploring the functions and meaning of violence in the Democratic Republic of Congo, *Intervention* 4(1): 32–46.

Braeckman, Colette (2004) The looting of the Congo, *New internationalist* May: 13–16.

Bush, Ray (2007) *Poverty and neoliberalism: persistence and reproduction in the global south*. London: Pluto Press.

Campbell, Howard (2008) Female drug smugglers on the U.S.–Mexico border: gender, crime, and empowerment, *Anthropological quarterly* 81(1): 233–267.

Chenoweth, Erica and Kathleen Gallagher Cunningham (2013) Understanding nonviolent resistance: an introduction, *Journal of peace research* 50(3): 271–276.

Clelland, Donald A. (2014) Unpaid labor as dark value in global commodity chains. In *Gendered commodity chains: seeing women's work and households in global production*, edited by Wilma A. Dunaway, pp. 72–87. Stanford, CA: Stanford University Press.

Cockayne, James (2010) Crime, corruption and violent economies. In *Ending wars, consolidating peace: economic perspectives*, edited by Mats Berdal and Achim Wennmann, pp. 189–218. Milton Park: Routledge for International Institute for Strategic Studies.

Copans, Jean and David Seddon (1978) Marxism and anthropology: a preliminary survey. In *Relations of production: Marxist approaches to economic anthropology*, edited by David Seddon, pp. 1–46. London: Frank Cass.

Coulter, Chris, Mariam Persson and Mats Utas (2008) *Young female fighters in African wars: conflict and its consequences.* Uppsala: Nordiska Afrikainstitutet.

Deb, Basuli, Pascale Perraudin and Annedith Schneider (2012) Introduction to special issue: transnational inquiries: representing postcolonial violence and cultures of struggle, *Postcolonial text* 7(1): 1–4.

Dilts, Andrew (2012) Revisiting Johan Galtung's concept of structural violence, *New political science* 34(2): 191–194.

Dowd, Caitriona and Clionadh Raleigh (2012) Mapping conflict across Liberia and Sierra Leone, *Accord* 23: 13–18, www.c-r.org/accord/westafrica, accessed 12 July 2013.

Duffield, Mark (1999) Globalization and war economies: promoting order or the return of history? Fletcher forum of world affairs. Boston: Tufts University.

Duffield, Mark (2000) Globalization, transborder trade, and war economies. In *Greed and grievance: economic agendas in civil wars*, edited by Mats Berdal and David M. Malone, pp. 69–89. Boulde, CO: Lynne Rienner.

Duffield, Mark (2001) *Global governance and the new wars: the merging of development and security.* London: Zed Books.

Duffield, Mark (2002) Social reconstruction and the radicalization of development: aid as a relation of global liberal governance, *Development and change* 33(5): 1049–1071.

EICC (2009) *Statement on use of minerals in electronics products.* Electronic Industry Citizenship Coalition, www.eicc.info/documents/EICCStatementonMinerals.pdf, accessed 31 March 2013.

Farmer, Paul (1996) On suffering and structural violence: a view from below, *Daedalus* 125(1): 261–283.

Ferme, Mariane C. (1998) The violence of numbers: consensus, competition, and the negotiation of disputes in Sierra Leone, *Cahiers d'études africaines* 150–152, XXXVIII(2–4): 555–580.

Galtung, Johan (1969) Violence, peace and peace research, *Journal of peace research* 6(3): 167–191.

Global Witness (2009) Faced with a gun, what can you do? War and the militarization of mining in eastern Congo. London: Global Witness.

Gutiérrez, Francisco (2010) Colombia: the restructuring of violence. In *Economic liberalization and political violence: utopia or dystopia?*, edited by Francisco Gutiérrez and Gerd Schönwälder, pp. 209–244. London: Pluto Press.

Harvey, David (2005) *A brief history of neoliberalism.* Oxford: Oxford University Press.

Heywood, Linda M. (2009) Slavery and its transformation in the kingdom of Kongo: 1491–1800, *Journal of African history* 50(1): 1–22.

Hoffman, Daniel (2011) Violence, just in time: war and work in contemporary West Africa, *Cultural anthropology* 26(1): 34–57.

Holmes, John (2007) Congo's rape war, *Los Angeles Times*, 11 October.

Howard, Allen (2006) Nineteenth century coastal slave trading and the British abolition campaign in Sierra Leone, *Slavery and abolition* 27(1): 23–49.

Human Security Report Project (2010) *Human security report 2009/2010: the causes of peace and the shrinking costs of war*. Vancouver: Simon Fraser University.

Hunt, Nancy Rose (2008) An acoustic register, tenacious images, and Congolese scenes of rape and ruination, *Cultural anthropology* 23(2): 220–253.

Hynes, H. Patricia (2004) On the battlefield of women's bodies: an overview of the harm of war to women, *Women's studies international forum* 27(5–6): 431–445.

Ibeanu, Okechukwu (2002) Healing and changing: the changing identity of women in the aftermath of the Ogoni crisis in Nigeria. In *The aftermath: women in post-conflict transformation*, edited by Sheila Meintjes, Anu Pillay and Meredeth Turshen, pp. 189–209. London and New York: Zed Books.

ILO (1930) Convention 29 concerning forced or compulsory labour, www.ilo.org/dyn/normlex/en/f?p=NORMLEXPUB:12100:0::NO::P12100_ILO_CODE:C029, accessed 20 July 2014.

ILO (2009) The cost of coercion: global report under the follow-up to the ILO declaration on fundamental principles and rights at work. Geneva: International Labour Conference 98th Session.

ILO (2014) *Profits and poverty: the economics of forced labour*. Geneva: International Labour Office.

IRC (n.d.) Mortality in the Democratic Republic of Congo: an ongoing crisis, New York: International Rescue Committee.

IRIN News (2005) DRC: Latest killings in South Kivu part of long-standing abuses, www.IRINNews.org, 26 May.

Jackson, Stephen (2005) Protecting livelihoods in violent economies. In *Profiting from peace: managing the resource dimensions of civil war*, edited by Karen Ballentine and Heiko Nitzchke, pp. 153–182. Boulder: Lynne Rienner.

Jalloh, S. Balimo (2001) Conflicts, resources and social instability in Subsahara Africa – the Sierra Leone case, *Internationales Afrika-Forum* 37(2): 166–180.

Johnson, Dominic (2009) Minerals and conflict in Eastern DRC. Pole Institute, July, www.pole-institute.org/site%20web/echos/echo114.htm, accessed 21 August 2013.

Kabange, Sanday Chongo (2011) Zambian female drug traffickers invade Asia, *News*, 31 August, http://wiredproject316.wordpress.com/2011/08/30/zambian-female-drug-traffickers-invade-asia/, accessed 25 August 2014.

Kaldor, Mary (1999) *New and old wars: organized violence in a global era*. Oxford: Polity Press.

Kaldor, Mary (2006) Evaluation of UNDP assistance to conflict-affected countries: case study of Sierra Leone. New York: United Nations Development Programme.

Kalyvas, Stathis N. (2003) Les guerres civiles après la fin de la guerre froide. In *Guerres et sociétés. États et violence après la guerre froide*, edited by Pierre Hassner and Roland Marchal, pp. 107–135. Paris: Éditions Karthala.

Kar, Dev and Brian LeBlanc (2013) Illicit financial flows and the problem of net resource transfers from Africa: 1980–2009. Washington, DC: African Development Bank and Global Financial Integrity.

Keen, David (2002) Since I am a dog, beware my fangs: beyond a 'rational violence' framework in the Sierra Leonean war crisis states programme. Development Research Centre, DESTIN, London School of Economics, London, working paper 14.

Kimanuka, Celestin and Maria Lange (2010) The crossing: small-scale trade and improving cross-border relations between Goma (DR Congo) and Gisenyi (Rwanda). London: International Alert.

Klein, Naomi (2008) *The shock doctrine: the rise of disaster capitalism*. Toronto: Vintage Canada.

Kotz, David and Terrence McDonough (2010) Global neoliberalism and the contemporary social structure of accumulation. In *Contemporary capitalism and its crises: social structure of accumulation theory for the 21st century*, edited by Terrence McDonough, Michael Reich and David M. Kotz, pp. 93–120. Cambridge: Cambridge University Press.

Laudati, Ann (2013) Beyond minerals: broadening 'economies of violence' in eastern Democratic Republic of Congo, *Review of African political economy* 40(135): 32–50.

Lebaron, Genevieve and Alison J. Ayers (2013) The rise of a 'new slavery'? Understanding African unfree labour through neoliberalism, *Third World quarterly* 34(5): 873–892.

Lebert, Joanne (2010) Women and girls' equality rights and the extractive industries in Africa: background note to the POWER project and the June 28, 2010 workshop. Ottawa: POWER Africa-Canada project, University of Ottawa.

Le Billon, Philippe (2001) The political ecology of war: natural resources and armed conflicts, *Political geography* 20: 561–584.

Lerche, Jens (2011) The unfree labour category and unfree labour estimates: a continuum within low-end labour relations. Manchester papers in political economy, working paper 10, http://eprints.soas.ac.uk/14855/1/Lerche_unfree_working_paper_2011.pdf, accessed 23 December 2014.

Lintvedt, Ane (2003) Free and unfree labor: a review essay, http://worldhistoryconnected.press.illinois.edu/1.2/br_lintvedt.html, accessed 28 August 2014.

McCormick, Ty (2014) In Congo, a disabled peace, *Foreign policy*, 31 July, www.foreignpolicy.com/articles/2014/07/31/congo_disabled_peace_aid_camps_security_refugees, accessed 13 September 2014.

MacGaffey, Janet (1991) *The real economy of Zaire: the contribution of smuggling and other unofficial activities to national wealth*. London: James Currey.

McGrath, Siobhán (2005) Unfree labor, capitalism and contemporary forms of slavery. Graduate faculty of political and social science, New School University, www.peri.umass.edu/fileadmin/pdf/UM-NS_Workshop/SiobhanMcGrath.pdf, accessed 20 May 2014.

McGrath, Siobhán (2013) Many chains to break: the multi-dimensional concept of slave labour in Brazil, *Antipode* 45(4): 1005–1028.

Mac-Leva, Fidelis (2009) Nigeria: four female arms dealers declared wanted, 10 June, http://allafrica.com/stories/200906100313.html, accessed 22 December 2013.

Malu Muswamba, Rosalie (2006) Le travail des femmes en République Démocratique du Congo: exploitation ou promesse d'autonomie? Paris: UNESCO.

Mama, Amina and Margo Okazawa-Rey (2012) Militarism, conflict and women's activism in the global era: challenges and prospects for women in three West African contexts, *Feminist review* 101: 97–123.

Manning, Patrick (1983) Contours of slavery and social change in Africa, *American historical review* 88(4): 835–857.

Morgan, Lynn M. and Elizabeth F. S. Roberts (2012) Reproductive governance in Latin America, *Anthropology and medicine* 19(2): 241–254.

Mukwege, Denis Mukengere and Cathy Nangini (2009) Rape with extreme violence: the new pathology in South Kivu, Democratic Republic of Congo, *PLoS Medicine* 6(12): 1–5.

Münkler, Herfried (2005) *The new wars*. Cambridge: Polity Press.

Naím, Moisés (2003) The five wars of globalization, *Foreign Policy*, 28 December, www.mafhoum.com/press4/131E62_fichiers/fivewars.htm, accessed 12 December 2013.

Newman, Edward (2004) The 'new wars' debate: a historical perspective is needed, *Security dialogue* 35(2): 173–189.

Niemann, Michael (2007) War making and state making in Central Africa, *Africa today* 53(3): 21–39.

Niger-Thomas, Margaret (2001) Women and the arts of smuggling, *African studies review* 44(2): 43–70.

Nordstrom, Carolyn (2004) *Shadows of war: violence, power, and international profiteering in the twenty-first century*. Berkeley: University of California Press.

Northrup, David (1988) *Bend in the river: African labor in eastern Zaire, 1865–1940*. Athens: Ohio University Press.

Oosterveld, Valerie (2009) The Special Court for Sierra Leone's consideration of gender-based violence: contributing to transitional justice?, *Human rights review* 10(1): 73–98.

Oxfam International and Harvard Humanitarian Initiative (2010) Now, the world is without me: an investigation of sexual violence in eastern Democratic Republic of Congo, www.oxfam.org/sites/www.oxfam.org/files/DRC-sexual-violence-2010-04.pdf, accessed 12 January 2015.

Perks, Rachel (2011) Towards a post-conflict transition: women and artisanal mining in the Democratic Republic of Congo. In *Gendering the field towards sustainable livelihoods for mining communities*, edited by Kuntala Lahiri-Dutt, pp. 177–196. Canberra: Australian National University epress, Asia-Pacific Environment monograph 6.

Peterman, Amber, Tia Palermo and Caryn Bredenkamp (2011) Estimates and determinants of sexual violence against women in the Democratic Republic of Congo, *American journal of public health* 101(6): 1060–1067.

Peterson, V. Spike (2008) New wars and gendered economies, *Feminist review* 88: 7–20.

Phillips, Nicola (2013) Unfree labour and adverse incorporation in the global economy: comparative perspectives on Brazil and India, *Economy and society* 42(2): 171–196.

Phillips, Nicola, Resmi Bhaskaran, Dev Nathan and C. Upendranadh (2014) The social foundations of global production networks: towards a global political economy of child labour, *Third World quarterly* 35(3): 428–446.

Raeymaekers, Timothy (2009) The silent encroachment of the frontier: a politics of trans-border trade in the Semliki Valley (Congo–Uganda), *Political geography* 28: 55–65.

Raeymaekers, Timothy (2010) Protection for sale? War and the transformation of regulation on the Congo–Ugandan border, *Development and change* 41(4): 563–587.

Reno, William (2009) Understanding criminality in West African conflicts, *International peacekeeping* 16(1): 47–61.

Renton, David, David Seddon and Leo Zeilig (2007) *The Congo: plunder and resistance*. London: Zed Books.

Roberts, Adrienne (2008) Privatizing social reproduction: the primitive accumulation of water in an era of neoliberalism, *Antipode* 40(4): 535–560.

Scaruffi, Piero (2009) Wars and casualties of the 20th and 21st centuries, www.scaruffi.com/politics/massacre.html, accessed 15 April 2015.

Scheper-Hughes, Nancy (1997) Peace-time crimes, *Social identities* 3(3): 471–498.

Scheper-Hughes, Nancy and Philippe Bourgois, eds (2003) *Violence in war and peace: an anthology*. Hoboken: Wiley-Blackwell.

Schouten, Peer (2014) Private security companies and political order in Congo: a history of extraversion. Doctoral dissertation in Peace and Development Research, School of Global Studies, University of Gothenburg.

Seay, Laura E. (2013) Effective responses: Protestants, Catholics and the provision of health care in the post-war Kivus, *Review of African political economy* 40(135): 83–97.

Shaw, Mark (2003) 'The middlemen': war supply networks in Sierra Leone and Angola. The Hague: Netherlands Institute of International Relations working paper 10.

Spagat, Michael (2010) Estimating the human costs of war: the sample survey approach. Brighton: Institute of Development Studies, University of Sussex, HiCN research design note 14.

Sparr, Pamela, ed. (1994) *Mortgaging women's lives: feminist critiques of structural adjustment*. London: Zed Books.

Springer, Simon (2015) The violence of neoliberalism. In *Handbook of neoliberalism* edited by Simon Springer, Kean Birch and Julie MacLeavy, pp. 1–21. London: Routledge.

Standing, Guy (2014) Understanding the precariat through labour and work, *Development and change* 45(5): 963–980.

Stearns, Jason (2010) Mass rape in Walikale: what happened? *Congo Siasa blog*, 24 August, http://congosiasa.blogspot.com/, accessed 6 September 2010.

Sunman, Hilary and Nick Bates (2007) *Trading for peace*. Research report for UK Department for International Development. London: DiFD, www.wilsoncenter.org/events/docs/Trading%20for%20Peace%20ENG.pdf, accessed 20 January 2014.

Surtees, Rebecca (2005) *Child trafficking in Sierra Leone*. New York: UNICEF.

Swaine, Aisling (2012) *Learning from practice: the experiences of GBV programming by Irish Joint Consortium Members in Sierra Leone*. Dublin: Irish Consortium on Gender Based Violence.

Turshen, Meredeth (1998) Women's war stories. In *What women do in wartime: gender and conflict in Africa*, edited by Meredeth Turshen and Clotilde Twagiramariya, pp. 1–26. London: Zed Books.

UNDP (2006) UNDP human development index. New York: United Nations Development Programme, www.nationsonline.org/oneworld/human_development_low.htm, accessed 20 March 2014.

UNODC (2012) *Global report on trafficking in persons 2012*. Vienna: United Nations Office on Drugs and Crime.

UNSC (2000) Report of the panel of experts appointed pursuant to Security Council resolution 1306 (2000) paragraph 19, in relation to Sierra Leone. United Nations Security Council document S/2000/1195.

UNSC (2002) Final report of the United Nations expert panel on the illegal exploitation of natural resources and other forms of wealth of the DRC. United Nations Security Council document S/2002/1146, 16 October.

UNSC (2003) Final report of the United Nations expert panel on the illegal exploitation of natural resources and other forms of wealth of the DRC. United Nations Security Council document S/2003/1027, October.

UNSC (2008) Letter dated 11 February 2008 from the Chairman of the Security Council Committee established pursuant to resolution 1533 (2004) concerning the Democratic Republic of the Congo addressed to the president of the Security Council. United Nations Security Council document S/2008/43, 13 February.

Vines, Alex (2006) Dousing the flames of resource wars, *South African journal of international affairs* 13(2): 85–100.

Vlassenroot, Koen (2003) Économies de guerre et entrepreneurs militaires: la rationalité économique dans le conflit Sud-Kivu, RDC. In *Guerres et sociétés: états et violences après la guerre froide*, edited by Pierre Hassner and Roland Marchal, pp. 338–368. Paris: Éditions Karthala.

Vlassenroot, Koen and Hans Romkema (2002) The emergence of a new order? Resources and war in eastern DR Congo, *Journal of humanitarian assistance*, available at http://jha.ac/articles/a111.htm, accessed 20 July 2015.

Wakubenga, Faida (2013) La voix des filles: la perception féminine du processus de réinsertion. In *Filles ex-soldats du Congo: la route cahoteuse de la réintégration*, edited by Gunhild Odden and Milfrid Tonheim, pp. 127–139. Paris: L'Harmattan.

WHO (2004) *World health report 2004: changing history.* Geneva: World Health Organisation.

Wissing, Melanie and Anaïs Pagot (2014) Why is aid not working? A fresh approach to displacement in the DRC, www.internal-displacement.org/blog/2014/why-is-aid-not-working-a-fresh-approach-to-displacement-in-the-drc, accessed 29 August 2014.

Wong, Pak Nung (2012) Discerning an African post-colonial governance imbroglio: colonialism, underdevelopment and violent conflicts in the Democratic Republic of Congo (DRC), Liberia and Sierra Leone, *African & Asian studies* 11(1/2): 66–94.

2 The gendered history of persistent violence

> One day when my husband went into the forest to gather rubber, the sentry
> Ikelonda came, finding me in my hut where I stayed, and asked me to give myself
> to him. I rejected his proposition. Furious, Ikelonda fired a gun shot at me, which
> gave me the wound whose trace you can still see. I fell on my back; Ikelonda
> thought I was dead, and to get hold of the brass bracelet that I wore at the base
> of my right leg, he cut off my right foot. This happened at the time when the
> white man Ekolakauba (M. Rogers) was at the post of Baringa. [Boali of Eko-
> longo, 1905]
>
> (Hunt, 2008, p. 225)

Violence has a long history in Africa: the starting points here are merchant
slavery, European conquest and colonial rule of sub-Saharan Africa. European
powers used violence to extract human and material wealth, to conquer the subcontinent, to impose and maintain dominion, to command the economy, and
to exploit the labour power of the people. Women were always part of that
history, part of the workforce, if rarely paid for their labour, and manipulated as
procreators, even when European attempts failed to raise, lower or otherwise
control the birth rate. Feminist historians have begun to chronicle women's
stories even as gender-blind accounts continue to be published. In the course of
this history, gender relations within families and between generations were
transformed irrevocably and irremediably.

This chapter establishes the contrasting colonial backgrounds, British and
Belgian, to violence in the former colonies of Sierra Leone and Congo. Though
the countries are of unequal size and population (Congo is 33 times larger than
Sierra Leone and its population today is ten times greater), the reasons for comparison are compelling. Both are resource-rich countries that lost millions of
dollars in mineral wealth to rebel militias during regionalised armed conflicts in
the 1990s. Both became notorious for the sale of minerals like diamonds and
gold to fund civil wars which were infamous for inhumane physical and sexual
abuse of civilians. Both wars were enmeshed in broad regional and transnational
dynamics that were shaped by colonial legacies and linked to the workings of
international markets and shadow economies. And in both countries, the
contribution of women in the minerals business, historically and in the war

economies, is little known. One more similarity: both countries emerged from civil war highly unequal, as shown in Gini coefficients: 44.4 DRC (2006) and 42.5 Sierra Leone (2003). The historical dissimilarities are important to note, and they force one to limit generalisations and check the geographical and historical specificity of any claims or conclusions. One striking difference between Sierra Leone and Congo was the different level of experience of the colonising powers: Britain's exercise of colonial rule dated to the seventeenth century; Belgium's to 1908 (or 1877 if one includes King Leopold's dominion, Congo Free State).[1] A commonality is the impact of abolitionist movements on slavery in both countries, which are discussed below in Chapter 6, 'Social movements and the struggle for social justice'.

African women and slavery

The story begins with the practices of slavery, chosen on three accounts – violence, women and work. 'Slavery arises from an economy of theft, in which people are stolen through acts of violence, and are then converted into commodities' (Lovejoy, 1991, p. 8). In a spiralling tragedy, the pursuit of captives in ever-larger numbers for sale overseas, peaking in the hundred years from 1750 to 1850, became the motive for increasing violence, mounting insecurity, massive migration and frequent wars (Manning, 1983).[2] Paradoxically, the end of the Atlantic trade, which coincides with the growth of legitimate export-import commerce, increased slavery within Africa, as demand rose for the cheap labour that slaves provided and as British naval vessels intercepted slave shipments.[3] The history of bondage reveals the histories of women and women's migration in Africa, the histories of women's productive and reproductive work, and the history of violence against women.[4] This story also puts sexual slavery of girls and women in contemporary African civil wars into a historical context (Lawrance and Roberts, 2012).

Roughly 11 million people were shipped out of Africa and as many died in Africa in slave raids and transhipment over the course of ten centuries; an unknown number, perhaps 8 million, were reduced to slave status within Africa (Manning, 1990).[5] By the mid-nineteenth century, the proportion of children carried on slave ships bound for the Americas reached over 46 per cent (Lovejoy, 2006, p. 200). Dennis Cordell (2013) describes this as the largest forced migration in world history; it severely disrupted and reshaped the demographic regimes and social reproduction of African societies for a millennium, robbing African households of 30 million young women, men and children. The practices of slavery – what Miller (2012, p. ix) describes as 'historical strategies rooted in times, places, cultural heritages, and momentary opportunism' – entwine relations of production and reproduction, bringing their indivisibility into sharp relief.

The production of human beings for enslavement has been examined from many angles (Whatley and Gillezeau, 2011), including the fertility of enslaved women (Klein, 1994). From the viewpoint of motherhood and fatherhood in

Africa, the death and disappearance of so many of the daughters and sons birthed by women recast family, kinship and community relations.[6] Was the response tempered by very high rates of infant and child mortality? The value of children was not everywhere the same in the slave trade. In the nineteenth-century East African trade, boys and girls were a significant portion of the traffic, and the violence and trauma of capture and rupture left indelible scars. The march from the interior to the coast was arduous, and if they failed to keep up, children were sometimes killed. On long-distance caravans, traders used children as small capital to settle debts or establish credit or as bargaining chips to negotiate deals (Morton, 2009, p. 55). Between sales – and the children changed hands several times – they were easily controlled and taught, were productive in a variety of tasks, and usually appreciated in value as they grew older. Slave children were sold on the East African coast to work as servants in urban Muslim homes on the Indian Ocean littoral, or they were exported to the Middle East and other Indian Ocean markets.

Technically, slave labour is unfree labour or work under some kind of non-economic compulsion.[7] The slave is a privately owned commodity, denied control over her or his labour or the products of that labour and over her or his reproduction. Slaves were outsiders, people who had been forcibly removed from their kin and culture – which amounted to what Patterson (1982) has called social death – their status more exploited and fixed in large, state societies, more flexible and impermanent in smaller, less centralised communities. Slave owners invested in both production and reproduction because, as slaves could be bought and sold, reproduction was an act of production. Servile, slave and slave-like relationships and methods of oppression were varied, intense, highly developed and widely spread in pre-colonial and colonial Africa. Work was the common denominator, with women preferable to men because women could perform both reproductive and productive work. Slavery could bypass the rights and obligations of kinship, depending on the setting and society (Meillassoux, 1991).

Most slaves in sub-Saharan Africa were women: the internal demand and prices paid for women were higher than for men, especially after the Atlantic slave trade was prohibited.[8] Slave women's versatility was remarkable: they could serve as 'field hands, artisans, mothers of rulers, breeders of lineage members, rewards for warriors, wives for male slaves, or simply as domestic servants', and their manual labour was often valued more highly than their ability to bear children (Miers, 1983, p. ix). Slave women and girls could be displayed as items of conspicuous consumption, used as pawns to cement alliances with neighbours, transferred to pay off debts or exchanged as bridewealth; in some cases they were valued as transmitters of coveted skills or knowledge from other cultures (Robertson and Klein, 1983, pp. 6, 8, 11). Violence was, obviously, a reality of slave life. But slave women were not only victims, some also engaged in the slave trade and owned slaves; some were commercial entrepreneurs, held political power or exploited 'their position as mediators between two different cultures' (Robertson and Klein, 1983, p. 13).

Catherine Coquery-Vidrovitch (2009) suggests that overall one of two Africans was held in slavery in the nineteenth century. Domestic slavery, which is internal slavery within Africa (sometimes also called indigenous slavery or African slavery), usually included household labour and sex work as well as farm labour and other external duties.[9] Children born into slave status had some exchange value, but those caught up in a raid were sometimes left behind when their mothers were taken, presumably because few would survive the long, gruelling treks. Patrick Manning (1990, p. 114) notes the account of Gustav Nachtigal in Baghirmi (today's Chad) who reported in 1872 that women who could not escape capture in a raid often killed their infants. The widespread African demand for slave women, especially in the eighteenth and nineteenth centuries, reflected men's desire for women who would become subordinate members of their families, performing domestic labour and producing children. Masters, particularly big men who collected women in harems, sexually exploited their slaves. Slave women's work was mostly in the fields, then in menial domestic tasks, and only a very few achieved other, more interesting and varied occupations (Manning, 1990, p. 115). In addition to farm labour, women carted firewood and water, pounded grain and yams into meal or flour, washed clothes and swept floors and yards. Slave women also participated in craft production and provided such services as porterage. In urban areas and along trade routes, female slaves were put to work as petty traders.

Domestic slavery predates the slave trade in Sierra Leone and in eastern Congo, and the two countries bear similarities as to the source and use of domestic slaves. The history of the slave trade in the two places is quite different: Europeans initiated contact with Sierra Leone (late fifteenth century) much earlier than with eastern Congo (second half of the nineteenth century), where they were preceded by Arabs; and the slavers came from different directions – in the case of Sierra Leone initially from Portugal, which started the Atlantic trade on the West African coast, and across the Indian Ocean via Zanzibar on the East African coast in the case of eastern Congo.[10] Lines crossed: the expansion of domestic slavery was an invention of the overseas trade, and the export commerce supplied the domestic market.

Slavery in Sierra Leone

Although slavery was well established and widespread in the West African coastal zone before 1800, all evidence suggests that enslavement increased greatly during the nineteenth century, boosting the volume of human trafficking. At the end of the nineteenth century, perhaps 15 per cent of the Protectorate and 20 per cent of the coastal population of the north-west region was locked in domestic slavery (Howard, 1994, p. 268). Of course the irony of slaving in Sierra Leone lies in the origins of the colony, founded by Great Britain in 1787 for emancipated slaves.[11] The initial settlers of Freetown were the Black Poor of London, Recaptives (who were Africans from cargo ships intercepted by the British navy; they were also known as Liberated Africans),

Maroons (Africans from Jamaica) and Africans from Nova Scotia. Allen Howard (2006, p. 26) notes that in Sierra Leone abolitionists faced sensitive issues at the legal and political boundary between trading captives bound for shipment overseas and holding or moving domestic slaves. The British did not formally abolish slavery in Sierra Leone until 1928.

The secondary material on women in domestic slavery in Sierra Leone is thin, in part because many historians fail to differentiate between male and female slaves. The proportion of slaves in the population of north-west Sierra Leone was high, likely in the range of 30 per cent. James Thayer (1981, p. 5), relying on a report from 1923 which gives the 1921 Sierra Leone population census as 1,446,375, says that 15.5 per cent or 219,275 were domestic slaves; there is no breakdown by sex. Howard (2006) cites evidence suggesting that once groundnut production developed in the mid-nineteenth century, the volume of people forcibly moved along the corridor was substantial, possibly rising to several thousand per year.[12]

In a blurring between free and unfree labour, Africans repatriated to Sierra Leone paid the redemption money for female slaves and then employed them as domestic servants in their households; presumably the ex-slaves were not paid for their labour. 'This ambiguous term [domestic servants] suggested that the women were freely employed when in fact they were indebted to and, whether by choice or not, dependent upon their patrons for paying their manumission costs and taking them into their households' (Shields, 2000, p. 193). Carol MacCormack (1983, pp. 273–274) says of slavery in the Sherbro society of coastal Sierra Leone that it was 'not simply an institution facilitating men's greater control of the productive and reproductive capacities of women, but was used by [aristocratic] women for economic and political enhancement'.

Bruce Mouser (2007, p. 35), writing about Sierra Leone, recounts a report from 1778, qualifying domestics as slaves born on the coast who were guaranteed certain privileges and protections. They fell into two groups: those ministering to the daily demands of their masters, and the labouring class who lived in the owners' rice- and cotton-growing and salt-production villages and were esteemed to be no better than beasts of burden. Because this account is not gendered, we do not know whether it was women who ministered to the daily demands of masters and men who constituted the labouring class.

As to how slaves were acquired in Sierra Leone, Howard (2006, p. 31) says the majority were victims of raiding and warfare. Armed groups known as the Ceddos pillaged villages to enslave civilians who were sold to European slave traders (Gberie, 2007, p. 214). Raiders kidnapped children, and adults sold children to raise funds, typically at times of ecological crisis. Betrayal, deception and trickery were common: Thayer (1981, p. 7) quotes one of his informants

> who related that a Susu slave trader made a habit of travelling down the Sherbro or Gallinas Coast and arranging to marry one or two women. Upon arriving upcountry in Susuland, he introduced his wives as 'slaves' he had bought on the coast. Being far from home and relatives, the women had no

one to protect them and their protestations and denials were regarded by one and all as egregious and self-serving.

Thayer (1981, p. 7) claims that it is difficult to gauge the economic importance of slaves in rural Susu life, but one informant (born about 1910) told him that 'when he was a youth his father never worked. His "work" consisted of traveling to his slave-villages to supervise their work.'

Slavery in Congo

Slavery is known to have existed in Congo from the earliest period of the Portuguese trade, notably in the lower Congo region of West-Central Africa where it continued after abolition (Vos, 2012). Slaves were acquired mainly through capture in warfare and sold into the transatlantic traffic. Writing of the old kingdom of Kongo, Wyatt MacGaffey (2008, p. 75) notes that slaves were the basic convertible currency, articulating domestic and Atlantic circulation: a slave could be both a unit of social reproduction and a commodity to be bought and sold for gain. In eastern Congo, however, examples of economically motivated slavery were rare before the mid-nineteenth century Afro-Arab intrusion (Cordell, 2013; Northrup, 2007, p. 112). Domestic slavery was not uncommon in eastern Congo where men took prisoners in local wars; those not ransomed became slaves for life, but slave status was not hereditary.

The constitution of a productive unit began with marriage, by which a man acquired a wife; other wives and perhaps slaves could be added later. The marriage money was calculated and distributed conventionally (by offering domestic livestock and slaves), not commercially (MacGaffey, 2008, p. 65). The constant and inescapable play of power in the competitive transfer of persons from one group to another by marriage, purchase, debt payment, judicial processes and various kinds of ritual entrapment was much the same everywhere in Central Africa (MacGaffey, 2008, p. 72). Most slaves were women, obtained to build lineages and to produce food. The purchase or capture of women as wives was widespread; to attract followers, rulers distributed food and slave wives.

From the 1840s Arabs from Zanzibar began to penetrate the interior of East Africa, and in the 1870s Zanzibari traders established a commercial empire in eastern Congo, with access to world markets (Northrup, 2007, p. 111). The initial purpose was to collect ivory; to find and transport it the Zanzibaris needed thousands of porters, which markedly increased enslavement for labour purposes. From 1881 the conquests of Tippu Tip, the most famous late nineteenth-century Arab trader in Central and Eastern Africa, led to a great increase in captives, who were incorporated into Zanzibari armies, caravans and settlements. King Leopold II of Belgium absorbed the region by legal annexation in 1887 and made Tippu Tip its first governor. The Berlin Conference (1884–1885) confirmed Congo Free State as the private property of the Congo Society, and the King formalised his control in 1892–1894 through military conquest. Because the regimes of Zanzibari traders and King Leopold

II overlap, they are treated together in this synopsis of the history of women and slavery.

All slaves were used as porters and units of exchange for other products; female slaves were regarded as currency, better than cowries for long-distance transactions. The armies that conquered East Africa and Congo for European powers were forces of African soldiers commanded by European officers.[13] Expatriate soldiers (non-Congolese, usually African) acquired wives locally. In the Belgians' 1895 expedition to explore Katanga, each of the 300 soldiers was allowed to take at least one woman and a boy; the number of women was even higher if some of the 200 porters brought along a wife or female relative (Samarin, 1989, p. 214). The number of women among the soldiers was not trivial. In 1892 at Equator Station there were 150 men and 72 women, though possibly not all were wives. Some may have been relatives or even slaves forced into this kind of domestic service.

> The presence of women on military expeditions was regulated in an official manner. It was argued that they served many useful purposes. People would be less fearful for the safety of their own women in seeing women amongst the soldiers. They could also forage in 'abandoned fields' for food. Hired at very little cost, they could prepare food for the unmarried soldiers, now relieved from this domestic chore for more useful training. In this way they contributed to the health of the soldiers. Moreover, on expeditions they animated the long marches with their laughter and conversation. Coming in contact with the people through whose territory they travelled, they established friendly relations and picked up useful information.
>
> (Samarin, 1989, p. 215)

Johannes Fabian (1986, p. 27) confirms these observations, quoting a nineteenth-century traveller, Jerome Becker (1887). Women served as scouts and cooks, and as they gathered information they were widely recognised as contributing to military intelligence.

The Belgians included women in expeditions by design, even when space on boats and ships was limited and expensive. Women were more than camp followers in expeditions, being deliberately included as auxiliary workers and sent for military training along with male recruits. At government posts women's housing was separate from the rows of workmen's huts. In the late 1880s the Belgians were buying female slaves from convoys and villages on the Ubangi River for the men, probably deducting the cost from their wages. They also took female hostages and held them in stockades whenever they forced chiefs to perform certain services or until they received restitution for a perceived crime like theft. The chiefs might redeem the women, but not before soldiers had raped some of them; or the whites might not recognise the offer for restitution, desiring to keep the women for themselves or for their men (Samarin, 1989, p. 215).

The Belgians regarded women as cheap labour for the construction and maintenance of stations, where they cut grass, carted wood and water, cooked and carried. The guide to military affairs, *L'art militaire au Congo* (https://archive.org/details/lartmilitaireau00unkngoog), stipulates that women could be used as porters, carrying 15–20 kg for the same distance each day as men. For work in station gardens the chiefs, not the women, were paid two brass rods per day per woman. The Belgians moved women about like the men to wherever their work was needed. Women clearly made the whites' projects easier (Samarin, 1989, p. 217).

Work levies and forced labour, along with displacement from birthplace to workplace, affected gender and inter-generational relations. The massive involvement of women in unfree labour altered living patterns for thousands upon thousands of women and girls. Women worked at every centre established by whites; some of the women came from far away and were strangers who, like slaves without the protection of their kin, were exposed to the will and caprices of local men. Some were hostages transformed into unwilling workers; some were liberated slaves; some were local village women forced by their chief at the command of the whites to perform chores. Government posts, trading centres, towns and eventually cities all had more men, but women's presence was perhaps more significant than their numbers suggested. William Samarin (1989, p. 221) concludes that, in the name of civilisation, the Belgians mobilised women, 'an act of violence greater, if that is possible, than ... that of men'.

Marcia Wright (1993, pp. 160ff.) has published the most detailed intimate account of slave women at the time of Congo Free State, in Katanga, an area to the south of the Kivu provinces of eastern Congo. She describes much exchanging of slaves without official concern, except when peace was disturbed by quarrels over the price of a slave woman; it would be unlikely, she notes, for the judiciary to notice a woman without a male advocate or economic resources. Wright illustrates the point with the story of Bwanikwa, which is astounding for the number of displacements and resales recounted – ten enslavements in different locales in the space of six years (1892–1898). As a Christian convert, Bwanikwa's last move was to a missionary station in north-east Rhodesia, where she dug clay, and moulded and baked cooking pots and water jars which she bartered or sold. She cultivated and sold produce, kept chickens and sold eggs, bought breeding goats and traded the kids. With the money accumulated she bought her freedom, but stayed with her (last) husband (Wright, 1993, p. 167).

Congo Free State administered by Belgians working under King Leopold II no longer officially recognised slavery but continued the Zanzibaris' cruel regime. The sentries and auxiliaries who served the Force Publique (police force) in the outlying villages were untrained and poorly supervised, had no loyalties and abused their power, but the Belgians ignored their excesses so long as the quotas in rubber, ivory and copal (resin) were met (Northrup, 2007, p. 116). The Force Publique regularly employed violence to secure porters: armed attacks, village raids, capture of the able-bodied who were tied together and led off to transport ivory and rubber. Labour *corvées* built and maintained roads and, later, telegraph routes. When ivory supplies dwindled, rubber tax exactions increased, provoking rebellions (Northrup, 2007, p. 118).

The atrocities committed in Congo Free State of King Leopold II from 1876 to 1908, a reign of terror that hid under the hypocritical cover of liberating slaves, are well documented (Hochschild, 1998; Marchal, 1996; Northrup, 2007; Roes, 2010). In the scramble for ivory, rubber, copal, wax and gold, and in the rush to create plantations of coffee, cocoa and oil palm trees, Leopold's agents used every form of violence: massacre of indigenous peoples, shooting the unarmed with rifles, cutting the throats of recalcitrants, amputation of hands (in exchange for bullets), application of the *chicotte* (a whip made of rhinoceros hide), chain gangs, tracking men to force them to produce even more of the desired products, burning of villages, eviction of farmers, requisitioning of food reserves and building materials, taking of hostages, long forced marches bringing death to thousands, capture of thousands of children in raids, and the rape of women. The Belgians surpassed the Zanzibaris' brutality in scope and duration, all the while bragging that they had liberated the slaves; in fact they redeemed former slaves by buying them from Zanzibaris, while Belgian military campaigns against Zanzibaris produced large numbers of new captives who were pressed into state service – into the Force Publique or into food production for military and administrative posts (Northrup, 2007, p. 115).

Slavery and violence against women: a summation

Slavery and the slave trades – across the Sahara, over the Atlantic Ocean and beyond the Indian Ocean – changed everyone in Africa: they affected women, children and men, kinship and community across generations, social relations of gender and work, sex and status, procreation and demography, hierarchy and stratification. Domestic slavery, the enslavement of women, may have been widespread throughout pre-colonial Africa but the historical record makes clear that it intensified after abolition and with the rise of export trading. Slaves were the most significant capital asset of most owners, male and female. Slavery reinforced patriarchy[14] by increasing concubinage and slave women's dependence on men, as well as by redefining the concept to mean the power to enslave rather than the ability of senior men to lead their communities (Manning, 1990, p. 3).

The abolition of slavery was a decades-long process across the continent, and emancipation, which came late in law, took hold even more slowly in reality. Research is limited on the long-term effects of slavery on conditions of family labour, marriage patterns, family and household composition, violence against women, rates of maternal and child mortality, and on the status of women and esteem for their productive and reproductive work. The surmise is that the transformations were persistent, lasting long after abolition and emancipation. Slavery blurred the lines between free and unfree labour, between pawn and slave, between production and reproduction. It changed the status of women from esteemed wife and mother to chattel, a commoditised property. Slave labour devalued the work of free women, and at the end of the slave era all women were likened to slaves and seemed to be treated as such. In a reinforced patriarchy that strengthened the power of men over women, slavery under-pinned heterosexuality, leaving a legacy felt today: efforts to criminalise homo-sexuality in several parts of Africa are one expression of renewed patriarchy, and struggles over the privatisation of social reproduction are another. In many cases the end of slavery led to increased exploitation of family labour: wives, children and junior kin became the new captive labour of household heads (Miers and Roberts, 1988, p. 41). The fact that so many women remained enslaved after formal emancipation, that for many a change in legal status made no change in either their place of residence or the master whom they served, and that their children (whether slave or free) remained the property of their former owners, reverberated profoundly in gender relations (augmenting the power of men over women) as well as the accepted terms of marriage (productive and reproductive duties and responsibilities of each partner).

Slavery profoundly destabilised African families, fundamentally restructuring African social organisation long after abolition. As slavery faded, a renewed pat-riarchy obliterated women's individuality, flattened the diversity of women's lived experiences, and denied their 'intersectional' personhood as human beings with multiple identities and attachments. Male leaders, both European and African, imposed highly restrictive gender roles on women in the names of national security and religious or cultural morality. Extreme patriarchy reduced women to their biological functions while cloaking this negation, this essential-ism, in fiats and fatwas about femininity. In a mirror image, military and reli-gious training also normalised a tamping of male personality and a similar essentialism of manhood. Although life in a hierarchical, racialised and strati-fied society introduced contradictions to this rigidified binary, the set of attributes ascribed to women appeared necessary and natural to female identity and function.

There is speculation that free women who were slave owners had much to lose with the end of slavery since senior wives rather than male slave masters profited most from slave girls' work (Harms, 1983, p. 101). The burdens of free women's productive and reproductive work beyond childbearing would increase without the labour of slaves. Francine Shields (2000, p. 192) suggests that gender relations deteriorated in this period. Suzanne Miers and Richard Roberts (1988, p. 42) note that where slaves had performed fieldwork, now wives had to replace them. Monogamous Christianised couples would exact even higher labour demands on wives who lost the labour of junior wives and concubines with the renunciation of polygamy.

Emancipation might have become an era of new possibilities and opportun-ities for women. Religious conversion offered some escape from traditional rule, and the introduction of biomedical healing systems promised relief from new and old diseases. Instead, the imposition of colonialism and capitalist demands for labour circumscribed women's prospects. Slavery declined but not servitude or forced labour; and in the period between abolition and colonial rule internal slave trading continued, linked to the developing trade in commodities (Vos, 2012). Colonial administrators redefined African customs and traditions in new statutory and customary laws drafted to their own advantage. Colonial taxation and labour migration systems once again separated families. And the individual-isation and privatisation of property, especially land, excluded most women from farm ownership and limited their access to gardens and plots. The pattern of women remaining on farms to supply food for male labourers, already developed in the slave era, was now intensified, codified and regulated by colo-nial administrators. The new laws did not reverse those aspects of customary systems tending to favour the land claims of men over those of widows or women separated from spouses, nor did they correct the denial of female chil-dren's land rights under some systems (Huggins, 2010, p. 10).

From slavery to colonisation

Across Africa, colonial administrators dominated and controlled workers without actually owning them by using physical and psychological violence (or threat of violence), coercion and exploitation. The epigraph at the head this chapter illustrates vividly the reality of that violence for women (Hunt, 2008, p. 225). Wages were low and working conditions were hard, but workers did not have the ability to enter and withdraw from particular labour markets and labour processes (Seibert, 2011, p. 373). Despite these hardships, slave agency – rooted in the specific way that slaves took advantage of the historical juncture when the colonial political economy destabilised structures of power and control – played a role in the demise of colonial slavery (Brown, 1996).

Labour markets and unfree labour in Congo

Like other European governments, the Belgian state was not eager to pay for empire, and it made no net contribution to the financing of the Belgian Congo. The government permitted Leopold II to become king of Congo Free State on the condition that Belgium would never have to finance his personal fiefdom. And it never did. Instead, on several occasions Congo made contributions to the Belgian treasury, in addition to bestowing immense wealth on the king and private companies. Belgian capitalism was at the forefront of the industrial revolution in Europe during the nineteenth century, ranking second behind Britain in industrial output per capita (Buelens and Marysse, 2009). Initially Congo lacked the roads, railways, ports, administrative buildings and military posts necessary to realise investments, and the Belgians had wage bills to pay for colonial administrators and the police force. African labour was the key to meeting all of these needs and to producing profits; the Belgians imposed a regime of forced day work, which was the crudest means to capture African labour, and for many, forced labour meant migration (Cordell, 2013).

Two companies, Abir and the Société Anversoise de Commerce au Congo (both founded in 1892), held the rubber monopoly and made enormous profits by severely exploiting Congolese tappers; profits fattened after 1898 when the railway opened between Matadi and Stanley-Pool (even more harshly abused

Congolese workers built the railway: more than 2,000 workers died during its construction) (Buelens and Marysse, 2009, p. 140). Income from Congolese raw materials financed impressive new buildings in Brussels, rapidly expanded the Antwerp harbour, and made the city of Antwerp a more important marketplace than London for the sale of ivory and rubber (Buelens and Marysse, 2009, p. 140). Congo became a continuous source of raw materials and tropical products for Belgium and its trading partners. Belgian colonists complained incessantly about the shortage of Congolese labour, which they attributed in part to the success of peasant agriculturalists who grew and marketed the food needed by industrial and infrastructure workers (Seibert, 2011, p. 384). After the First World War, the colonial government set out to destroy the indigenous economy by abandoning the free market food system: they dissolved local food markets, forced peasants to sell their produce to European dealers at fixed prices, and introduced the forced cultivation of certain crops. These policies and the need for more mine labour had devastating consequences for African agriculture. The burdens on women increased as more men were drawn into the colonial labour force, particularly as migrant workers to distant worksites.

The labour policies of Congo Free State carried over into the colonial period: in place of slavery and tribute, the colonial administration relied on forced labour and forced requisitioning of goods. Abolition changed little; it did not create a free market in labour or goods. The League of Nations adopted a convention condemning slavery and slave labour in 1925, which Belgium signed only in 1962 (Britain signed in 1953); and in 1930 the ILO adopted Convention 29 prohibiting forced labour, which Belgium did not sign until 1944 (Britain ratified it in 1931). Forced labour depressed real earnings since labour was often paid not in cash but in kind (an arbitrary assortment of overvalued goods); it not only lowered wage rates generally but it hit government employees especially hard; and low wages operated as a disincentive to local markets, exacerbating shortages, particularly of food (Northrup, 2007, p. 119).

Jan Vansina's (2010) account of village life under Belgian rule inventories the mechanisms of the steady decline of women's status, not as some by-product of history, but as a result of deliberate Belgian policies that were partly economic and partly ideological. The systematic restriction of women's activities, limiting them to farming and childbearing/child rearing; the denial of meaningful education to girls; the reinforcement of elder men's hold on women at every turn of the industrial wheel, as more men were wanted for colonial commercial and infrastructure projects, private as well as public; the suppression of matrilineal societies and the tampering with customary laws that gave women some rights to divorce and inheritance; the blocking of any possibility of women becoming proletarians, of earning wages for their labour, of entering the modern economy on the same terms as African men – if all this is placed on top of the legacy of the slave trade, domestic slavery and pawnship, the downward trajectory of women's status in Congolese society is unmistakable.

Elder men exercised their hold on women through their control of young men's access to marriage partners; the chiefs' tenacity is explained by the portion of bride price they would receive for marriages they arranged, as well as gifts brought to them by husbands returning from distant worksites. If women left the village and became economically independent in the towns, they might choose their own partners and neglect village obligations, including monetary payments to their elders. This hold on women was dressed up as concern for their welfare, ornamented with tales of the temptations of prostitution and the perils of evil cities. In their conservatism, African elders had the conspiratorial support of missionaries and colonial officials, who also wanted to keep women barefoot and pregnant, down on the farm producing food for the cities and workers on mine sites and plantations (Schmidt, 1990). The Belgians deftly used indirect rule to capitalise on the legitimacy of chiefs in their labour recruitment stratagems. Customary chiefs – many of them appointed by the Belgians who consolidated ethnic groups over and over again – could in turn demand that the colonial powers' enforcement capacities ensure their common subjects' obedience (Veit, 2010, p. 17).

Women's forced labour was critical to colonial rule, as Belgium developed the peasant lands of eastern Congo in which women held acknowledged places in production and reproduction that had been maintained by intricate and sophisticated systems institutionalised in marriage and customary land distribution. European state and private investors turned the densely populated, pastoral eastern provinces into an urbanised and industrialised economy by commercialising agriculture and linking farms and markets through a network of roads that were built and maintained mainly or partly by women (Likaka, 1994). The Kivus became the Belgian Congo's breadbasket, exporting cereals, meat, potatoes and palm oil to Kinshasa and other cities and towns (Vlassenroot and Büscher, 2009). Women grew much of this produce, a good part of it under compulsory cultivation, in addition to producing food for domestic consumption. The exploitation of women persisted even when mechanisation might have relieved them. The production of palm oil and palm seeds was highly labour-intensive but manual production was cheaper than mechanisation. Even when motorised transport became available, and rail and river traffic multiplied, women still transported most goods to market on their heads.

Women's reproductive value was so great to the Belgians (who were always worried about an inadequate labour supply) that the colony promulgated regulations about the maximum percentage of adult male workers that could be extracted from any community in the belief that this measure would halt the demographic decline so noticeable in the 1920s. The Belgians sought to instil their ideas of maternal and child health in Congolese women in order to encourage procreation and decrease maternal and child mortality, but the decline in births did not halt until the 1940s and the population did not begin to grow until after the Second World War (Hunt, 1988).

The colonial educational system was designed to reinforce demands for more productive and reproductive labour from women – more food production under the compulsory crop scheme and more pregnancies to supply a new generation of workers; neither of these activities called for literacy. Unlike other colonial powers in early twentieth-century Africa, Belgium did not directly oversee education, but turned the responsibility over to missionaries (Masandi, 2004).[15] In 1908, 587 missionaries, mostly Roman Catholic, were educating 46,075 students, a tiny fraction of the population; the mainly religious curriculum encouraged conversion, supported colonialism and challenged African cultural values and beliefs (Achberger, n.d.). Education for women emphasised domestic arts and 'feminine work' like nursing, elementary school teaching and infant care, pushing most women deeper into the domestic sphere. By being taught in the vernacular rather than in French, girls were denied opportunities to enter wage labour and qualify for administrative positions. Colonial education dissociated women from salaried work, training only a tiny minority of girls for the few vocational training slots in primary school teaching and auxiliary health care (Mianda, 2002, p. 157).

The effect was to marginalise women from modernisation, and the specificity of girls' schooling was situated in the cultivation of this marginalisation; ideology enabled its maintenance (Masandi, 2004). Catholic education and colonial legislation responded to the needs for more agricultural produce and more babies, and laws restricted wives' freedom to work outside the home. The Belgians assumed that working wives would bear fewer children and that girls' schooling and formal sector employment would repress fertility rates. The Church wanted monogamy to replace polygyny (fertility rates were higher in monogamous marriages), and men to take over more tasks on their individual farms. Colonial administrators needed a larger labour force and employers constantly complained about unmet manpower needs, but tapping the female reserve army for wage labour was passed over in favour of confining women to their roles as farmers and reproducers of the next generation of workers. These policies were riddled with contradictions and disappointment was inevitable (Hunt, 2005). The inherent logic of colonialism clashed with the Belgian model of conservative Catholicism (Masandi, 2004).[16] Nonetheless, women were central to the construction of infrastructure for Congo Free State and the Belgian Congo, and they played a critical role in supplying food for urban populations as well as workers in mines, plantations and factories.

The traditional patrimonial system[17] in eastern Congo revolved around the distribution of access rights to communally held land in return for rents that were redistributed through the system (Van Acker, 2005, p. 79). In these societies, women were assets, not liabilities: they had independent rights to cultivate land and to dispose of its produce; they could also inherit and pass on rights in land and other real property to others (Wilson, 1982, p. 153). The rural agricultural economy of Kivu changed in the colonial period. The Belgian colonial administration established limits and reduced the extent of customary land (Van Acker, 2005, p. 83). It confiscated land to establish national parks and anti-erosion forests. The Belgians also introduced a system of land registration and private ownership, which they used to create plantations for the production and export of cash crops. In 1885 King Leopold II had declared all 'vacant' land (and all wild plants and animals on the land, notably elephants and wild rubber plants) the property of the state (Northrup, 1988, p. 40). Although the colonial administration promised to recognise local land tenure arrangements, it used 'declarations of vacancy' to limit customary tenure to all land not settled or cultivated. 'It therefore subverted the very principle of the social cohesion in place, the customary right to land; non-occupied land was not simply vacant but rather the basis for collective security and social mobility' (Van Acker, 2005, p. 83). The colonial invention of vacancy transformed the meaning of land from possession as a social relation in the village to possession as alienable property on plantations.

Between 1944 and 1957, the Belgians had allocated or sold anywhere from 4.4 to 12.3 million hectares of Congolese land in concessions to a variety of public and private entities; most lots were traded in speculative deals and never developed (Merlier, 1962, pp. 58, 70). This violent expropriation of communal lands destabilised northern Kivu and eventually broke the African agrarian system. Despite growing competition for land in the face of these expropriations, the Belgians decided to introduce another wave of migrant settlers from Ruanda (later Rwanda), the former German territory that it held under League of Nations mandate (Mathieu and Tsongo, 1998). The transplanted chiefs of these settlers were given autonomous chiefdoms in parts of Masisi and Rutshuru that were claimed by the Hunde, creating competition and eventually conflict between the indigenous peoples and the immigrants (Van Acker, 2005, p. 84). Between 1937 and 1955 about 85,000 Rwandans were resettled, and many more came of their own accord following the routes of the 100,000 who emigrated in response to the 1927–1930 famine (Kraler, 2004, p. 13). No mention is made of how these changes affected women's access to land, which traditionally passes through fathers and husbands, but one assumes that limited land availability would have affected all households and made generous allocations to women more difficult, while ethnic competition increased insecurity of tenure. This is a complex story that feminist historians and anthropologists need to complexify further. We want to know whether immigrants and indigenous groups ever intermarried; we wonder whether there was competition among them and whether it prompted an inflated birth rate in a demographic race for land.

Extractive industries in the colonial period

The purpose of the colonial vacant land policy was two-fold: to clear mine sites and to open up to European colonisation 'unoccupied' fertile regions: the dispossessed Africans would serve as reservoirs of labour (Mararo, 1997, p. 510). Twentieth-century plantation agriculture and mining investments differed from nineteenth-century plunder: the maturation period of mining investment was long and development was capital-intensive. The shift in strategy led to changes in labour mobilisation and control, more precise economic planning, direct supervision of the production process, and stricter control over African labour (Roes, 2010). The screen of temporary and freely enacted contracts shielded officials from the realities of forced labour as they transferred the locus of coercion to (new or old) African chiefs, providing strong incentives to ensure a supply of workers commensurate with demand; a chief's failure to deliver was construed as an act of opposition to the colonial state that justified military repression.

The labour force was significant: in Katanga Province where copper mining dominated the economy, the Union Minière du Haut-Katanga (UMHK), one among many mining companies, employed over 15,000 men in 1920; another 6,000 labourers were building the railway from Bukama to Port Franqui, 12,000 more were involved in other infrastructure projects, 9,000 porters transported materials of all kinds, 6,000 worked as domestic servants, 1,700 were enlisted as soldiers in the Force Publique, and 12,000 worked in agriculture to grow the food needed by these 49,700 workers and themselves (Seibert, 2011, pp. 377–378).

Eastern Congo was vitally important to the colony's economy by the late 1920s: it was a major labour pool containing 30 to 40 per cent of the country's population, it supplied a third of the colony's direct tax revenue, and it contributed three-quarters of its ivory exports, 85 per cent of cotton and coffee, 75 per cent of rice, most of the cattle, and nearly all its gold exports (Northrup, 1988, p. 9). During the 1930s, as Katanga and Kasai rose in importance as mineral producers, eastern Congo remained a mining centre, sharply increasing gold production and adding tin.

Eastern Congo's Kilo-Moto gold mines were discovered by Leopold's agents in 1903 and opened over the period 1905–1911. Jules Marchal (1999) has movingly recounted the brutal history of the Kilo-Moto mines. Here it is sufficient to evoke women's contribution and to establish that women were involved in extractive industries from the very beginning of the colonial enterprise. From 1911 to 1931, the government compelled women and children to bring food from villages 35 km away because it did not pay the workers enough for them to purchase food at local produce markets: their allowance was 10 centimes a day. For the food and the 70 km round trip, the government paid the women a 'derisory' sum (Northrup, 1988, p. 89). In 1920, the Kilo mines were using 36,000 porters and the Moto mines used 400 to 500 per month to bring in materiel: women would have been among those porters. In 1929, under a policy of compulsory cultivation that continued to 1959, African producers (women and men) provided 80 per cent of the 16,000 tons of fresh and dried foodstuffs needed to feed the 35,000 people living at the Kilo-Moto mines; prices paid were so low that returns were reasonable only to farmers in the immediate vicinity. Where sales were unprofitable, the government imposed *corvées*, paying only for the food, not women's porterage of it (Northrup, 1988, pp. 146–147). At the mine sites of Forminière (Société internationale forestière et minière du Congo), the company created by a private individual, Jean Jadot, in 1906, which mined diamonds and gold from 1913, caravans of women, some carrying their babies, covered distances of over 50 km to bring provisions to the Kanua mining camps; half the women's pay was in salt or 'trifling' trade goods worth less than a third of the value assigned by the employers (Northrup, 1988, p. 90).

Women also provided sexual services at the mines, organised in the early years by Belgian employers. Recruiters brought female slaves and sold them for 1,200 francs each to the UMHK, which wanted them for their workers (Merlier, 1962, p. 131). In 1915 a state inspector, Maurice de la Kethulle, visited the Kilo-Moto mines and observed that prostitution was troublesome, prompting an effort to employ the women on the mine site farms in the belief that their wages, though not an economic investment, were a remedy for immorality (Marchal, 1999). Marchal quotes a mine manager, Hector Maertens, who protested that it was white workers who turned the wives of African labourers into prostitutes and that the women's work on the farms only perpetuated their sex slavery. Africans who were allowed to bring their wives to their worksites sometimes had to prostitute them to obtain enough to eat (Northrup, 1988, p. 164).

Mines were sites of extreme violence, as this description of their organisation has shown. Behind the cruelty of individual European managers[18] was the brutality of the system, which relied upon a migratory scheme to supply unfree, unpaid or poorly paid labour; upon women forced under *corvée* conscription to bring food and materiel into the camps and build roads to these remote, mountainous locations; the casual use of the *chicotte* on women, children and men; and a disregard of Africans' health that added illness to the accidental injuries sustained in dangerous mine work. No hospital or pharmacy was built at Moto. Death was familiar, desertions were regular occurrences, and resistance was frequent: for example, in 1912 and 1913, rebellions by the Mamvu and Walese in the region between Kilo and Moto were suppressed, resulting in the deaths of hundreds of Congolese (Marchal, 1999).

Sierra Leone: the colonial period, labour and extractive industries

Differing markedly from eastern Congo in its response to the imposition of colonial rule, Sierra Leone could boast a strategic coastal location, a long history of centralised powers, earlier contact with European traders, greater participation in the slave trade, and the employment of slave labour on large plantations that produced crops for export. British colonial rule was layered on top of an already developing regional economy, in which the long nineteenth-century period of slow emancipation produced a free labour market alongside the continuation of pawnship and other forms of servitude. Although there was wide variation across the West African region, and the transition in Sierra Leone to British control of first the colony (1808) and then the protectorate (1896) was repeatedly contested, the country inherited the legacies of individuals of great wealth (including some women), a population of freed slaves who had lived in Europe and the Americas, and the advantages of early access to British education. The combination of the late discovery of minerals and the early use of Freetown as a regional port city, which required workers to build and maintain ports, railways and public works, resulted in the early organisation of trade unions, which were legally recognised in July 1939 (Luke, 1984, p. 13). The first official general strike, led by workmen at the Public Works Department, occurred in November 1892 over wages that had been reduced during the 1880s world depression (Luke, 1985, p. 426).

Women were already important traders and missionaries in the nineteenth century, astonishing the British (White, 1982, p. 20). Many of these women brought cultural backgrounds of independence they had acquired in the New World, which helped them to take advantage of economic opportunities. Some sold produce in their village market or in Freetown, others travelled upcountry to barter European goods for rice that they in turn sold in Freetown. Yet others, based on Sherbro Island, became wealthy on the kola trade, which women dominated in the late nineteenth century (White, 1982, p. 21). Krio[19] women controlled a flourishing trade in the Big Market in Freetown from its creation in 1860 to 1919 (White, 1978). After the First World War, the colonial government turned to British firms and Lebanese middlemen for provisions, because they regarded Krio economic power as a threat and a potential source of nationalist leadership. As Krio power fell, so went the Big Market women traders (White, 1978, p. 27).

The Second World War provided another impetus to market women who, along with other women workers in Freetown, organised in trade unions. The Sierra Leone Market Women's Union was organised in 1940 and led by Mary M. Martyn and Christiana England (Denzer, 1987, p. 445). The Sierra Leone Washerwoman's Union with 300 members was led by Violet Johnson and featured among the 11 trade unions registered in 1942 (Luke, 1985, p. 439). Union women were among the founding members of the Sierra Leone Women's Movement in 1951 (Denzer, 1987, p. 445).

A geological survey in 1926/27 confirmed that a number of minerals, including platinum, gold, iron ore, chrome and diamonds, existed in commercial quantities (Zack-Williams, 1982, p. 78). The colonial government passed the first Minerals Act in 1927, organising and regulating the new industry (Ojukutu-Macauley and Keili, 2008, p. 516). The first diamond was found in 1930 and significant production commenced in 1935 (Smillie, 2000, p. 2). Mining quickly became the major employer in an arrangement that induced Africans to work as hard as possible, since their earnings depended on output. European and African capital operated in the platinum, gold and diamond industries under a system called 'tributing', in which a licence holder employed workers to find ore on his leasehold (Zack-Williams, 1982, p. 78). Tributors were organised in gangs of five under a headman; they sold the minerals to the owner of the mining lease at half price. The system relieved employers of the burden of paying wages to labourers who did not produce, a problem in the relatively poor deposits that were mined.

Women were observed at mine sites at the outset by prospectors such as Katarine Fowler-Lunn (1938, p. 135), who remarked on the compound at the gold mining site in Makong where the labourers slept in

> double mud houses with palm-thatched roofs, twenty-four rooms on each side. Each room housed one laborer and as many wives, children and relatives

as he allowed to live with him. All the women and relatives were out preparing chop or getting firewood for the night, so the streets were deserted.

On her treks, the porters who accompanied her brought women to prepare their meals; mothers carried their infants as well as baskets heaped with pots and pans. 'When we returned to camp at the end of our trek this retinue had been doubled. Some new wives were bought en route, others were following, but came just the same, and no questions were asked' (Fowler-Lunn, 1938, p. 158).

Commonly, women have worked in alluvial mining throughout West Africa: in Cameroon (Chupezi et al., 2009), in Ghana and Niger (ILO, 2007), in Guinea (Sow, 2003), in Mali (Mapeli and Chirico, 2013), and in Sierra Leone (Pijpers, 2011). The British introduced the Sierra Leone Alluvial Diamond Mining Scheme in 1956 to regulate the rush and prevent illicit mining and smuggling; the scheme allowed artisanal miners to participate legally in diamond mining for the first time, essentially breaking the exclusive monopoly previously held by the Sierra Leone Selection Trust (Ojukutu-Macauley and Keili, 2008, p. 516). Before the start of the civil war in 1991, 250,000 people made a living in the mining and quarrying sector with direct and indirect employment accounting for 14 per cent of the country's total labour force. As many as 200,000 men, women and children are currently employed in small-scale gold mining in Sierra Leone (Maconachie and Hilson, 2011, p. 602) and another 200,000–400,000 in diamond mining (Maconachie, 2009).

Sierra Leonean miners were manipulated, and tributing was an exploitative system: the licence holder recruited his labour force and then divided the (usually undervalued) 'winnings' – two-thirds for the licence holder and one-third for the tributors (Zack-Williams, 1982, p. 78). When a gang master was involved, 60 per cent went to the licence holder, 30 per cent to the tributors and 10 per cent to the gang master. The work was undoubtedly strenuous, the conditions were dangerous, and the labourers were underpaid; there were struggles with security forces in the diamond-mining areas, and crime, violence and disorder; there was also a decline in women's status and frequent accusations of witchcraft (Zack-Williams, 1995, pp. 183, 189, 190). But no mention is made of forced or unfree labour.

Violent continuities and discontinuities: Congo/Zaire and Sierra Leone after independence

The post-independence economic and political histories of Congo and Sierra Leone, two countries that bear sad similarities of disastrous mismanagement abetted by western governments and corporations that kept these countries weak and then profited from their powerlessness, have been told by numerous Belgian, British, Congolese, French, Sierra Leonean and other authors; readers are referred to the *Afrique des Grands Lacs Annuaire* and to the extensive bibliographies in the African historical dictionaries series (Fyle, 2006; Kisangani and

Bobb, 2010). The focus of this section is on women's experiences in the 30 years between independence and the civil wars.

Continuities: independent Congo/Zaire

Although Crawford Young (1965, p. 10) saw decolonisation as 'a virtually seamless web', later characterisations of the years 1960 to 1965 viewed the turmoil of the first republic as presaging the violent regime of Mobutu Sese Seko (1965–1997). At independence in 1960 Congo was the second most industrialised country in sub-Saharan Africa, but under Mobutu's rule, foreign-owned firms were nationalised, many European investors were forced out of the country, the economy deteriorated, infrastructure decayed and social services nearly disappeared. The climate of state violence closely followed popular violence, often turning into armed violence (Ndaywel è Nziem, 1998, p. 418). Women had campaigned for independence, and associations like Action féminine congolaise persisted in demanding equality between the sexes (Mianda, 1995, p. 55). Although women's organisations flourished in the immediate post-colonial period, a persistent bias linked all women's associations with prostitution. Women remained invisible. The independent government maintained colonial limitations on women's legal rights (Wilson, 1982, p. 158) and did not grant women the right to vote until 1967. Women's lives, especially in rural areas, continued to worsen in the Mobutist era.

Policies in two sectors – education and land tenure – had the greatest consequence for women. Women's access to land under changing laws is described in Chapter 4 below; the discussion here focuses on education. During the last five years of the colonial period Congo's school system had become one of sub-Saharan Africa's most fully elaborated – and gender-imbalanced (Boyle, 1995, p. 452). Girls' education was far more bounded than boys' and higher education lagged far behind primary schooling. In 1960, no girl or woman was among the several hundred Congolese students attending the two newly established universities or the half-dozen post-secondary institutes, nor were there any women among the 800 cumulative academic secondary school graduates (Yates, 1982, p. 127). The Belgians had succeeded in making it impossible for most women to leave farming for wider opportunities in the new economy. After independence, international pressures for educational reforms and growing demands from Africans for secular schooling led to a breakdown of the long-standing colonial arrangement with the Catholic Church, which controlled and confined the curriculum (Boyle, 1995).

Women in Kinshasa did far better than women in eastern Congo. Despite protracted periods of poor economic performance and short periods of acute economic crisis, women in Kinshasa made considerable progress in acquiring education. By 2004, 65 per cent of women over age 20 had at least some secondary schooling; 34 per cent of women aged 20 and above had reached at least upper-level secondary school; only 8 per cent had no schooling (Shapiro *et al.*, 2011). Enrolment figures are dramatically lower in eastern Congo: in 2010 the percentage of boys and girls admitted to primary school was 46.8 in North Kivu and 48.9 in South Kivu; at the secondary level in North Kivu, 24.1 per cent of girls and in South Kivu, 26.4 per cent of girls were in attendance starting at ages anywhere from 11 to 17 (MICS-RDC, 2010, pp. 150, 154).[20] Of young women 15 to 24 years old, only 47.2 per cent in North Kivu and 48.3 per cent in South Kivu were literate in 2010 (MICS-RDC, 2010, p. 146). For this reason, national literacy figures are misleading: the DRC ranks number 25 in Africa with a national literacy rate of 67 per cent; Sierra Leone – with the same west/east split between the capital and rural areas as Congo – ranks number 47 with a national literacy rate of 35 per cent; literacy in the Western Area of Sierra Leone is 65 per cent.

Discontinuities: independent Sierra Leone

In Sierra Leone, the British, aided by an increasingly well-educated group of Sierra Leonean women, some of whom trained in England and returned as teachers, adopted a different emphasis in their colonial education policy from the Belgians. Belgium[21] favoured primary education and Britain invested heavily in higher education, making Sierra Leone a regional centre for education and training. Fourah Bay College, the subcontinent's oldest, was founded in 1827; Lati Hyde-Forster was its first woman graduate in 1938. In 1962, the year after independence, 9.5 per cent of pupils 16–21 years old were enrolled in college and university in Sierra Leone and that figure rose to 16.5 per cent by 1989; no breakdown by sex is available, but it is known that fewer girls than boys received an education (Banya, 1993).

The issue here is one of long-standing debate: should one invest first in primary education or in higher education? Perhaps one measure of an educational system's achievement is women's participation in politics. The first female holder of political office in Congo was Ekila Liyonda, foreign minister in Zaire in 1987. In Sierra Leone the first woman held office 30 years earlier: Ella Koblo Gulama was the first elected female member of parliament in 1957; she was re-elected in 1962, and Prime Minister Milton Margai made her a cabinet minister in the first independent government. Today an impressive number of women hold influential positions in Sierra Leone, ranging from paramount chiefs, political activists, high court judges, educators, entrepreneurs, businesswomen, cabinet ministers to presidential candidates; women are also represented in the civil service, the legal profession, police force, military, teaching and nursing (Abdullah et al., 2006). Congolese women lag behind: in 2008, 12 per cent of ministers were women and in 2009, 5 per cent of the Senate (upper chamber) and 8 per cent of the National Assembly (lower chamber) were women (UN, 2010). Nonetheless, the difference in female literacy rates between the two countries is striking: 36 per cent of women in Congo are illiterate; almost twice that many women, 62.7 per cent, are illiterate in Sierra Leone.

Illiteracy at these levels amounts to structural violence; it builds unequal power and unequal life chances into the system; it excludes women from the modern economy and the public sphere, relegating them to essentialist aspects of reproduction; and it denies women the power of decision-making. In the literature one finds references to violence in schools (bullying, corporal punishment, teachers' predatory sexual behaviour) or the content of the curriculum (teaching conflict resolution and non-violence). But one doesn't find books or articles about the ordinary, everyday violence of depriving girls and women of a formal education.[22] There are expressions of regret and the commencement of many programmes addressing the unequal achievements of girls relative to boys in access to education, an acknowledgement of the disadvantages uneducated women experience, and inferences that an educated mother is healthier and has healthier children. My premise here is that illiteracy is a type of violence that penetrates and pervades production and social reproduction, themes that are explored in Part II of this book.

Chapter summary

This chapter traces the history of violence against women through slavery, looking at the particular histories of Sierra Leone and Congo and emphasising labour in production and social reproduction. The slave era was a brutal period, one that permanently transformed Africa and Africans and created a diaspora that resonates in all our lives. The slave trade, in its multiple destinations and multifarious purposes, in its enduring consequences for human and physical development, restructured lives at every level from the individual to the international. Slavery reordered class hierarchies, racialised stratification and radically transformed relations between genders and generations. New research shows the profoundly negative consequences of domestic slavery for long-term economic and political development in the former European colonies (Nunn, 2007, 2008). Econometric analyses used to evaluate income growth suggest that indigenous slavery impeded the development of capable and accountable states in Africa (Bezemer *et al.*, 2014).

The story of violence carries on into the colonial period when European administrations made superhuman demands on their subjects' labour in the course of extracting the continent's wealth. In this long saga of unfree, forced and coerced labour, women were as necessary as men, and children were not spared, neither girls nor boys. The demands made upon their time, energy and resources necessarily changed Africans' relations to each other, to their extended families, to their communities and to authority. The continuities from slavery to colonisation and decolonisation have been at once seamless and violent, and the discontinuities were disruptive.

Violence against Congolese women can be traced back to the mid-nineteenth-century Zanzibari slave raids, up through Leopold II's (Congo Free State, 1877–1908) and Belgian colonial rule (1908–1960), through the presidency of Mobutu Sese-Seko (1965–1997) to the present wars and unrest (Laurent-Désiré Kabila, 1997–2001, and his son, Joseph Kabila, 2001–). The economic history of eastern Congo is one of rapid colonial industrialisation, the slow creation of a free labour market (forced labour replaced slavery in 1908), and then swift deindustrialisation under Mobutu. From 1996, the invasions, in which Rwanda was joined by Uganda, Zimbabwe and others, dismantled whatever commercial enterprises were left (with a few exceptions); foreign troops backed by governments and companies removed timber, stockpiles of minerals and herds of cattle; and for a time they controlled production and export (Onana, 2009; Renton *et al.*, 2007, pp. 188–200; United Nations Security Council, 2008).

Women in eastern Congo have been under assault for more than a century, and the attacks are rooted in the need for women's productive and reproductive labour and in the conviction that it is necessary to control women's lives. Violence is a means of control, and the means alter as the political economy evolves. The need to control women also changed, as did the restraining mechanisms used to keep them producing and reproducing. The exploitation of women's productive and reproductive labour developed under new political and economic conditions, but women were not, and are not, passive in the face of these onslaughts.

Notes

1 Belgium became an independent nation in 1830.
2 For the period of the slave and ivory trade on the Congo–Tanzania border see McCurdy (2010); for the colonial period in Congo, see Hunt (1999); for an account of African-American slave motherhood, see Roberts (1997).
3 The definition of slavery in an African context was the subject of inconclusive debates in the 1970s by Igor Kopytoff, Paul Lovejoy, Patrick Manning, Claude Meillasoux, Suzanne Miers, Joseph Miller, Orlando Patterson and others.
4 For a general discussion of the enslavement of women and children in relation to the transatlantic trade, see Lovejoy (2007, pp. 21–28).
5 In Africa, the ratio of enslaved adults to children and of women to men varied over time and according to location (Robertson and Klein, 1983, p. 4). The internal African market absorbed more women and children than men. The European export market purchased male slaves by a margin of two to one. The Muslim market of the Arab world absorbed more female slaves.
6 For a detailed study of motherhood, intimate relationships and women's work in the Jamaican slave system from 1780 to 1838, see Altink (2007).
7 Slavery should be distinguished from other forms of labour such as extra-economic types of coercion like menace, physical or psychological violence, or threats of violence. Because most pawns were women, pawnship – a system in which individuals are held in debt bondage as collateral for loans – is the most important type of slavery in the context of this study. For an extensive discussion of free and unfree labour, see Brass and van der Linden (1997). See also Chapter 1 above.
8 The British Slave Trade Act of 1807 outlawed the slave trade, but not slavery itself; the British Slavery Abolition Act was passed in 1833. Portugal abolished the transatlantic slave trade in 1836; France and Belgium abolished slavery in 1848. The traffic continued until colonial rulers suppressed the traders in the early 1900s.
9 For a review of the literature on indigenous slavery, see Bezemer *et al.* (2014).
10 Smaller in number and longer in years than the Atlantic slave trade, the Indian Ocean trade dates from the ninth century but did not reach eastern Congo till the 1840s.

11 The American Colonization Society founded Liberia in 1822 as a colony for emancipated slaves, and France founded Gabon in 1848 for the same purpose.
12 Martin Klein's (1994) compilation of figures on enslavement in Guinea during the early years of the twentieth century indicates that in some places high proportions of the population were enslaved. The figure may have reached or exceeded 60 per cent in Rio Pongo, Rio Nuñez and the Timbo region of Futa Jalon. He estimates that there were 75,000 enslaved people in the circle of Rio Pongo around the turn of the twentieth century.
13 For a fictional account of this period, see Gurnah (1994).
14 Patriarchy refers to the systems by which the power of older men is perpetuated and implemented.
15 The Catholic Party in Brussels held power for much of the reign of King Leopold II and retained an absolute majority until 1918.
16 It is worth noting that Belgium did not grant Belgian women the right to vote until 1948; in contrast, women could vote in Sierra Leone from 1930.
17 A Weberian concept, patrimonialism is a form of political domination or authority based on personal and bureaucratic power that gives the ruler direct control of administration.
18 Likaka (2009, p. 14) says the experience of this violence is recorded in the names that Congolese villagers assigned to Europeans: Angry Eyes, Hyena, Leopard and Europe's Lion.
19 Krios are descendants of West Indian slaves from the Caribbean, primarily from Jamaica, freed African-American slaves from the United States (Black Loyalists) resettled from Nova Scotia, and Liberated Africans from various parts of Africa. They began arriving in Freetown in 1792 (Northrup, 1995, p. 49).
20 Entry to school was often delayed and children frequently repeated classes so students in their early twenties may still be in secondary school (Shapiro and Tambashe, 2003, p. 29).
21 Herbert Weiss (2012, p. 110) points out that 3,000 Congolese men had attended seminaries by 1960 where they received rigorous intellectual training, which 'put the Congo comparatively quite high in any African colonial education index'. The Roman Catholic hierarchy excluded women from seminaries, and it was still the case at independence that no Congolese had been trained as medical doctors, lawyers or engineers.
22 Today, education is under attack; thousands of educational institutions across dozens of countries and spanning most regions of the world have been bombed, shelled or burned, and students and teachers killed, injured, kidnapped, abducted or arrested by armed forces or security forces, armed non-state groups or armed criminal groups (GCPEA, 2014).

References

Abdullah, Hussainatu J., Aisha F. Ibrahim and Jamesina King (2006) Women's voices, work and bodily integrity in pre-conflict, conflict and post conflict reconstruction processes in Sierra Leone, http://r4d.dfid.gov.uk/PDF/Outputs/WomenEmp/Abdullah_SierraLeoneCountryPaper.pdf, accessed 20 January 2014.

Achberger, Jessica (n.d.) Belgian colonial education policy: a poor foundation for stability, http://ultimatehistoryproject.com/belgian-congo.html, accessed 15 September 2014.

Altink, Henrice (2007) *Representations of slave women in discourses on slavery and abolition, 1780–1838.* London: Routledge.

Banya, Kingsley (1993) Illiteracy, colonial legacy and education: the case of modern Sierra Leone, *Comparative education* 29(2): 159–170.

Becker, Jerome (1887) *La vie en Afrique, ou trois ans dans l'Afrique centrale.* Paris and Brussels: J. Lebegue, 2 vols.

Bezemer, Dirk, Jutta Bolt and Robert Lensink (2014) Slavery, statehood, and economic development in sub-Saharan Africa, *World development* 57: 148–163.

Boyle, Patrick Michael (1995) School wars: church, state, and the death of the Congo, *Journal of modern African studies* 33(3): 451–468.

Brass, Tom and Marcel van der Linden, eds (1997) *Free and unfree labour: the debate continues.* Bern: Peter Lang.

Brown, Carolyn A. (1996) Testing the boundaries of marginality: twentieth-century slavery and emancipation struggles in Nkanu, Northern Igboland, 1920–29, *Journal of African history* 37(1): 51–80.

Buelens, Frans and Stefaan Marysse (2009) Returns on investments during the colonial era: the case of the Belgian Congo, *Economic history review* 62(S1): 135–166.

Chupezi, Tieguhong Julius, Verina Ingram and Jolien Schure (2009) Study on impacts of artisanal gold and diamond mining on livelihoods and the environment in the Sangha Tri-National Park (TNS) landscape, Congo Basin. Yaoundé, Cameroon: CIFOR.

Coquery-Vidrovitch, Catherine (2009) *Africa and the African in the nineteenth century: a turbulent history.* London: M. E. Sharpe.

Cordell, Dennis D. (2013) Interdependence and convergence: migration, men, women, and work in Sub-Saharan Africa, 1800–1975. In *Proletarian and gendered mass migrations*, edited by Dirk Hoerder and Amarjit Kaur, pp. 173–215. Leiden: Brill.

Denzer, LaRay (1987) Women in Freetown politics, 1914–61: a preliminary study, *Africa* LVII(4): 439–456.

Fabian, Johannes (1986) *Language and colonial power: the appropriation of Swahili in the former Belgian Congo, 1880–1938.* Cambridge: Cambridge University Press.

Fowler-Lunn, Katharine (1938) *The gold missus: a woman prospector in Sierra Leone.* London: George Allen and Unwin.

Fyle, C. Magbaily (2006) *Historical dictionary of Sierra Leone.* Lanham, MD: Scarecrow Press.

Gberie, Lansana (2007) Liberia and Sierra Leone: civil wars, 1989–2002. In *Daily lives of civilians in wartime Africa: from slavery days to Rwandan genocide*, edited by John Laband, pp. 195–225. Westport, CT: Greenwood.

GCPEA (2014) *Education under attack 2014.* New York: Global Coalition to Protect Education from Attack, www.protectingeducation.org/sites/default/files/documents/eua_2014_full_0.pdf, accessed 20 January 2015.

Gurnah, Abdelrazak (1994) *Paradise.* London: Hamish Hamilton.

Harms, Robert (1983) Sustaining the system: trading towns along the Middle Zaire. In *Women and slavery in Africa*, edited by Claire C. Robertson and Martin A. Klein, pp. 95–110. Madison: University of Wisconsin Press.

Hochschild, Adam (1998) *King Leopold's ghost: a story of greed, terror, and heroism in colonial Africa.* Boston: Houghton Mifflin.

Howard, Allen (1994) Pawning in coastal northwest Sierra Leone, 1870–1910. In *Pawnship in Africa: debt bondage in historical perspective*, edited by Toyin Falola and Paul E. Lovejoy, pp. 267–283. Boulder, CO: Westview Press.

Howard, Allen (2006) Nineteenth century coastal slave trading and the British abolition campaign in Sierra Leone, *Slavery and abolition* 27(1): 23–49.

Huggins, Chris (2010) Land, power and identity: roots of violent conflict in eastern DRC. London: International Alert.

Hunt, Nancy Rose (1988) 'Le bébé en brousse': European women, African birth spacing and colonial intervention in breast feeding in the Belgian Congo, *International journal of African historical studies* 21(3): 401–432.

Hunt, Nancy Rose (1999) *A colonial lexicon of birth ritual, medicalization, and mobility in the Congo.* Durham, NC: Duke University Press.

Hunt, Nancy Rose (2005) Hommes et femmes, sujets du Congo colonial. In *La mémoire du Congo. Le temps colonial,* edited by Jean-Luc Vellut, pp. 51–57. Tervuren: Musée Royal de l'Afrique central; Gand: Éditions Snoeck-Ducaju et Zoon.

Hunt, Nancy Rose (2008) An acoustic register, tenacious images, and Congolese scenes of rape and repetition, *Cultural anthropology* 23(2): 220–253.

ILO (2007) *Girls in mining: research findings from Ghana, Niger, Peru and the United Republic of Tanzania.* Geneva: International Labour Organisation.

Kisangani, Emizet François and Scott F. Bobb (2010) *Historical dictionary of the Democratic Republic of the Congo.* Lanham, MD: Scarecrow Press.

Klein, Martin A. (1994) The demography of slavery in western Soudan: the late nineteenth century. In *African population and capitalism: historical perspectives,* edited by Dennis D. Cordell and Joel W. Gregory, pp. 50–61. Madison: University of Wisconsin Press.

Kraler, Albert (2004) The state and population mobility in the Great Lakes – what is different about post-colonial migrations? University of Sussex migration working paper 24, www.sussex.ac.uk/webteam/gateway/file.php?name=mwp24.pdf&site=252, accessed 25 September 2014.

Lawrance, Benjamin N. and Richard L. Roberts (2012) Contextualizing trafficking in women and children in Africa. In *Trafficking in slavery's wake: law and the experience of women and children in Africa,* edited by Benjamin N. Lawrance and Richard L. Roberts, pp. 1–25. Athens: Ohio University Press.

Likaka, Osumaka (1994) Rural protest: the Mbole against Belgian rule, 1897–1959, *International journal of African historical studies* 27(3): 589–617.

Likaka, Osumaka (2009) *Naming colonialism: history and collective memory in the Congo, 1870–1960.* Madison: University of Wisconsin Press.

Lovejoy, Paul (1991) Foreword. In *The anthropology of slavery: the womb of iron and gold* by Claude Meillassoux, pp. 7–8. London: Athlone Press.

Lovejoy, Paul (2006) The children of slavery – the transatlantic phase, *Slavery and abolition* 27(2): 197–217.

Lovejoy, Paul (2007) Civilian casualties in the context of the trans-Atlantic slave trade. In *Daily lives of civilians in wartime Africa: from slavery days to Rwandan genocide,* edited by John Laband, pp. 17–49. Westport, CT: Greenwood Press.

Luke, David Fashole (1984) *Labour and parastatal politics in Sierra Leone: a study of African working-class ambivalence.* Lanham, MD: University Press of America.

Luke, David Fashole (1985) The development of modern trade unionism in Sierra Leone, part 1, *International journal of African historical studies* 18(3): 425–454.

MacCormack, Carol P. (1983) Slaves, slave owners, and slave dealers: Sherbro coast and the hinterland. In *Women and slavery in Africa,* edited by Claire C. Robertson and Martin A. Klein, pp. 271–294. Madison: University of Wisconsin Press.

McCurdy, Sheryl A. (2010) Disease and reproductive health in Ujiji, Tanganyika: colonial missionary discourses regarding Islam and a 'dying population'. In *The demographics of empire: the colonial order and the creation of knowledge,* edited by Karl Ittmann, Dennis D. Cordell and Gregory H. Maddox, pp. 174–197. Athens: Ohio University Press.

MacGaffey, Wyatt (2008) Kongo slavery remembered by themselves: texts from 1915, *International journal of African studies* 41(1): 55–78.

Maconachie, Roy (2009) Diamonds, governance and 'local' development in post-conflict Sierra Leone: lessons for artisanal and small-scale mining in sub-Saharan Africa?, *Resources policy* 34: 71–79.

Maconachie, Roy and Gavin Hilson (2011) Artisanal gold mining: a new frontier in post-conflict Sierra Leone? *Journal of development studies* 47(4): 595–616.

Manning, Patrick (1983) Contours of slavery and social change in Africa, *American historical review* 88: 835–857.

Manning, Patrick (1990) *Slavery and African life*. Cambridge: Cambridge University Press.

Mapeli, Katherine C. and Peter G. Chirico (2013) The influence of geomorphology on the role of women at artisanal and small-scale mine sites, *Natural resources forum* 37(1): 43–54.

Mararo, Bucyalimwe (1997) Land, power, and ethnic conflict in Masisi (Congo-Kinshasa), 1940s–1994, *International journal of African historical studies* 30(3): 503–538.

Marchal, Jules (1999) *Travail forcé pour le cuivre et pour l'or: l'histoire du Congo, 1910–1945*. Borgloon: Paula Bellings.

Marchal, Jules (1996) *L'état libre du Congo: paradis perdu. L'histoire du Congo, 1876–1900*. Borgloon: Paula Bellings, 2 vols.

Masandi, Pierre Kita (2004) L'éducation féminine au Congo belge, *Paedagogica historica: International journal of the history of education* 40(4): 479–508.

Mathieu, P. and A. M. Tsongo (1998) Guerres paysannes au Nord-Kivu (République démocratique du Congo), 1937–1994, *Cahiers d'études africaines* 38(2/4): 385–416.

Meillassoux, Claude (1991) *The anthropology of slavery: the womb of iron and gold*. London: Athlone Press.

Merlier, Michel (1962) *Le Congo de la colonisation belge à l'indépendance*. Paris: Maspéro. Reissued as Maurel, Auguste (1992) *Le Congo de la colonisation belge à l'indépendance*. Paris: L'Harmattan.

Mianda, Gertrude (1995) Dans l'ombre de la 'démocratie' au Zaïre: la remise en question de l'emancipation Mobutiste de la femme, *Canadian journal of African studies* 29(1): 51–78.

Mianda, Gertrude (2002) Colonialism, education, and gender relations in the Belgian Congo: the *évolué* case. In *Women in African colonial histories*, edited by Jean Allman, Susan Geiger and Nakanyike Musisi, pp. 144–163. Bloomington: Indiana University Press.

MICS-RDC (2010) *Enquête par grappes à indicateurs multiples en République Démocratique du Congo rapport final, mai 2011*. Kinshasa: Institut national de la statistique and UNICEF.

Miers, Suzanne (1983) Foreword. In *Women and slavery in Africa*, edited by Claire C. Robertson and Martin A. Klein, pp. ix–x. Madison: University of Wisconsin Press.

Miers, Suzanne and Richard Roberts, eds (1988) *The end of slavery in Africa*. Madison: University of Wisconsin Press.

Miller, Joseph C. (2012) *The problem of slavery as history: a global approach*. New Haven, CT: Yale University Press.

Morton, Fred (2009) Small change: children in nineteenth-century East African slave trade. In *Children in slavery through the ages*, edited by Gwyn Campbell, Suzanne Miers and Joseph C. Miller, pp. 55–70. Athens: Ohio University Press.

Mouser, B. (2007) Rebellion, marronage and jihad: strategies of resistance to slavery on the Sierra Leone coast, c. 1783–1796, *Journal of African history* 48(1): 27–44.

Ndaywel è Nziem, Isodore (1998) Du Congo des rébellions au Zaïre des pillages, *Cahiers d'études africaines* 150–152, XXXVIII(2–4): 417–439.

Northrup, David (1988). *Beyond the bend in the river: African labor in eastern Zaire, 1865–1940*. Athens, OH: Ohio University Center for International Studies monographs in International Studies Africa series 52.

Northrup, David (1995) *Indentured labor in the age of imperialism, 1834–1922*. Cambridge: Cambridge University Press.

Northrup, David (2007) Slavery and forced labour in the eastern Congo 1850–1910. In *Slavery in the Great Lakes region of East Africa*, edited by Henri Médard and Shane Doyle, pp. 111–123. Oxford: James Currey.

Nunn, Nathan (2007) Historical legacies: a model linking Africa's past to its current underdevelopment, *Journal of development economics* 83: 157–175.

Nunn, Nathan (2008) The long-term effects of Africa's slave trades, *Quarterly journal of economics* 123(1): 139–176.

Ojukutu-Macauley, Sylvia and Andrew K. Keili (2008) Citizens, subjects or a dual mandate? Artisanal miners, 'supporters' and the resource scramble in Sierra Leone, *Development southern Africa* 25(5): 513–530.

Onana, Charles (2009) *Ces tueurs tutsi: au coeur de la tragédie congolaise*. Paris: Duboiris.

Patterson, Orlando (1982) *Slavery and social death: a comparative study*. Cambridge, MA: Harvard University Press.

Pijpers, Robert (2011) When diamonds go bust: contextualizing livelihood changes in rural Sierra Leone, *Journal of international development* 23(8): 1068–1079.

Renton, David, David Seddon and Leo Zeilig (2007) *The Congo: plunder and resistance*. London: Zed Books.

Roberts, Dorothy E. (1997) *Killing the black body: race, reproduction, and the meaning of liberty*. New York: Pantheon Books.

Robertson, Claire C. and Martin A. Klein, eds (1983) *Women and slavery in Africa*. London: Heinemann.

Roes, Aldwin (2010) Towards a history of mass violence in the État indépendant du Congo, 1885–1908, *South African historical journal* 64(4): 634–670.

Samarin, William J. (1989) *The black man's burden: African colonial labor on the Congo and Ubangi Rivers, 1880–1900*. Boulder, CO: Westview Press.

Schmidt, Elizabeth (1990) Negotiated spaces and contested terrain: men, women, and the law in colonial Zimbabwe, 1890–1939, *Journal of southern African studies* 16(4): 622–648.

Seibert, Julia (2011) More continuity than change? New forms of unfree labor in the Belgian Congo, 1908–1930. In *Humanitarian intervention and changing labor relations: the long-term consequences of the abolition of the slave trade*, edited by Marcel van der Linden, pp. 369–386. Leiden: Brill.

Shapiro, David and B. Oleko Tambashe (2003) *Kinshasa in transition: women's education, employment, and fertility*. Chicago: University of Chicago Press.

Shapiro, David, Mark D. Gough and Roger Bertrand Pongi Nyuba (2011) Gender, education, and the labour market in Kinshasa. http://econ.la.psu.edu/people-documents/d89/David%20Shapiro%20-%20Gender-%20Education-%20and%20the%20Labour%20Market%20in%20Kinshasa.pdf, accessed 20 March 2014.

Shields, Francine (2000) Those who remained behind: women slaves in nineteenth century Yorubaland. In *Identity in the shadow of slavery*, edited by Paul Lovejoy, pp. 183–201. London: Continuum.

Smillie, Ian (2000) Getting to the heart of the matter: Sierra Leone, diamonds, and human security, *Social justice* 27(4): 24–31.

Sow, Nene Ousmane (2003) Women activities in artisanal mining in Guinea, paper presented at the Women in mining conference, Madang, Papua New Guinea, 3–6 August. Available at http://siteresources.worldbank.org/INTOGMC/Resources/336099-11636 05893612/ousmaneguinea.pdf, accessed 6 October 2014.

Thayer, James Steel (1981) The persistence of slavery on the Guinea coast, www. webcote.net/bibliotheque/james-thayer/persistence-slavery-guinea-coast.html, accessed 20 June 2013.

UN (2010) *The world's women 2010: trends and statistics*. New York: United Nations.

United Nations Security Council (2008) Letter dated 11 February from the chairman of the Security Council committee established pursuant to resolution 1533 (2004) concerning the Democratic Republic of the Congo, addressed to the president of the Security Council. New York: United Nations document S/2008/43.

Van Acker, Frank (2005) Where did all the land go? Enclosure and social struggle in Kivu (DR Congo) *Review of African political economy* 103: 79–98.

Vansina, Jan (2010) *Being colonized: the Kuba experience in rural Congo, 1880–1960.* Madison: University of Wisconsin Press.

Veit, Alex (2010) *Intervention as indirect rule: civil war and statebuilding in the Democratic Republic of Congo.* Frankfurt: Campus Verlag.

Vlassenroot, Koen and Karen Büscher (2009) The city as frontier: urban development and identity processes in Goma. London: LSE Crisis States Research Centre Working Paper no. 61.

Vos, Jelmer (2012) 'Without the slave trade, no recruitment': from slave-trading to 'migrant recruitment' in the lower Congo, 1830–90. In *Trafficking in slavery's wake: law and the experience of women and children in Africa*, edited by Benjamin Lawrence and Richard L. Roberts, pp. 45–64. Athens: Ohio University Press.

Weiss, Herbert (2012) The Congo's independence struggle viewed fifty years later, *African studies review* 55(1): 109–115.

Whatley, W. C. and R. Gillezeau (2011) The fundamental impact of the slave trade on African economies. In *Economic evolution and revolution in historical time*, edited by P. W. Rhode, J. L. Rosenbloom and D. F. Wiman, pp. 86–110. Stanford, CA: Stanford University Press.

White, E. Frances (1978) The big market in Freetown: a case study of women's workplace, *Journal of the historical society of Sierra Leone* IV(1&2): 19–32.

White, E. Frances (1982) Women, work and ethnicity: the Sierra Leone case. In *Women and work in Africa*, edited by Edna G. Bay, pp. 19–33. Boulder, CO: Westview Press.

Wilson, Francille Rusan (1982) Reinventing the past and circumscribing the future: *authenticité* and the negative image of women's work in Zaire. In *Women and work in Africa*, edited by Edna Bay, pp. 153–170. Boulder, CO: Westview Press.

Wright, Marcia (1993) *Strategies of slaves and women: life-stories from West/Central Africa*, London: James Currey.

Yates, Barbara A. (1982) Colonialism, education, and work: sex differentiation in colonial Zaire. In *Women and Work in Africa*, edited by Edna Bay, pp. 127–152. Boulder, CO: Westview Press.

Young, Crawford (1965) *Politics in the Congo: decolonization and independence*. Princeton, NJ: Princeton University Press.

Zack-Williams, Alfred (1982) Merchant capital and underdevelopment in Sierra Leone, *Review of African political economy* 25: 74–82.

Zack-Williams, Alfred (1995) *Tributors, supporters and merchant capital: mining and underdevelopment in Sierra Leone*. Aldershot: Avebury.

Part II

Violence in production and social reproduction

3 Gender and the use of force in production

There were a lot of rumors about diamonds in Angola. My husband decided to interrupt his [medical] studies to go to Angola. I tried to convince him to continue his studies and to give me the permission to go in his place. He finally accepted ... I travelled from Kinshasa to Tembo, a diamond town on the border with Angola.... The carriers [who accompanied us] contacted villagers in possession of diamonds [and] returned with a list of goods which these people wanted in return for their diamonds.... As quickly as possible we returned to Congo. It happened frequently that the villagers themselves betrayed us and informed armed men of our presence. They would come and confiscate all of our goods.... Personally, I suffered a great deal during another ambush. Four soldiers raped me and left with all the goods I had brought along. That is why during those days many women tried to marry soldiers in order to get protection.

(De Boeck and Plissart, 2014, p. 212)

The relations of production encompass the social relationships people enter into in order to produce and reproduce material life; these production relations constitute the economic structure of every society, whether slave, mercantile or capitalist. The processes of production, the women and men whose labour power is necessary for production, and the violent practices of those who employ and manage workers in neoliberal capitalist regimes are the focus of this chapter. Gender roles and relations are of theoretical concern and production relations in the extractive industries are of concrete interest. A third dimension is what happens to women as workers under wartime conditions. The chapter illustrates all of these themes by exploring the cumulative impacts on women of productive regimes transformed by violent conflict. The mining sector of the Democratic Republic of Congo – where conflict continues in the east – and Sierra Leone – where fighting ended in 2002 – is compared with that of Tanzania, which has not experienced armed conflict on the mainland. The analysis centres on how war affects women's livelihoods, their expectations and opportunities, their risks and responsibilities. Also considered is how armed conflict disorganises the economic structure of society, upsets the usual hierarchies of genders and generations, and opens doors to the trafficking of girls and women, as well as the smuggling of illicit minerals, weapons and drugs.

Wars occasionally create a political power vacuum (as in the appearance of failed states), but they do not give rise to an economic vacuum: the formal economy may be ruined but an informal one rises in its place. Civilians (and often combatants) must find ways to survive in the context of a dramatic increase in risk and uncertainty, political instability, violence and economic decline (Korf, 2004). Violent economies comprise many categories of violent actors – conflict entrepreneurs (looters, organised criminals, military managers, political entrepreneurs), conflict opportunists and conflict dependants (Jackson, 2005, pp. 160ff.). The new wars,[1] discussed in Chapter 1 above, ended state monopolies on violence; rebel leaders and the governments they seek to overthrow equally wield force and power, and war profiteers and international criminal networks use violence in parallel trade to link up with legitimate international businesses. The violent economic regimes spawned by these new regionalised wars have opened another phase in gender and the use of force in production.

Social relations of production

Globalisation is changing the social relations of production by globalising labour markets, making work more flexible and informal and systematically weakening the bargaining power of workers; chronic economic insecurity is the result, and the binary division of labour markets into formal or informal is no longer adequate to describe people's working lives. Guy Standing (2009) argues that *labour* has exchange value and is usually remunerated, whereas *work* consists of many activities that are productive or reproductive: most work has use value and is done out of necessity because we are obliged to do it. In other words, we all work and we engage in labour when we can get paid for our work. Women working in limestone quarries in Tanzania typically spend eight hours quarrying, six hours searching for other means to support their families, four hours in domestic chores (finding water and firewood, breastfeeding), and six hours asleep (Kinabo, 2003, p. 317). Women are frequently besieged by demands on their time and must combine several unrelated tasks (Standing, 2013). Self-employment and casual wage labour are expanding in many countries, at the expense of regular stable wage employment. Women's share of employment is rising, and their relative rate of unemployment has fallen, but in this era of globalisation their social or economic situation is not necessarily improved.

States and markets are socially constructed institutions. Labour markets in general are highly gendered institutions operating at the intersection of the productive and reproductive economies (Elson, 1999, p. 611). Men are often concentrated in formal, more closely regulated occupations, and women consigned to more precarious informal and casual jobs (Barrientos *et al.*, 2004), what the IMF is now calling unstructured employment. Increasingly, all workers, but women more than men, are likely to experience temporary jobs, lower pay, precarious subcontracting, excessive overtime, denial of rightful benefits, higher unemployment and extreme levels of health risk. One explanation for this discrimination is women's position at the fulcrum of the work/family nexus: women's paid employment is precarious in part because of their domestic duties and the consequent insecurity underlies their lack of power on the labour market. Women's paid work and their inescapable obligations at home condition each other, as does the (learned) compulsion to meet the needs of others. This mutual relationship of paid and unpaid work contains the moment of structural violence; direct force, laws and religious dictates maintain structurally coercive and hierarchical relationships at home and in the workplace (Bennholdt-Thomson, 1988) and regulate women's wealth or poverty.

Another explanation for persistent discrimination in women's employment lies in the structure of labour markets, in the practices, perceptions, conventions and networks that are bearers of gender (Elson, 1999). Social stereotypes associate masculinity with having authority over others in the workplace (being the 'boss') and with what is men's work and what women's work (Elson, 1999, p. 611). The content of women's and men's work varies across cultures: in most of Africa men were the weavers and women the spinners of thread, whereas in Latin America the weavers were indigenous and rural women. Also, remuneration for work changes when tasks migrate from the home to the commercial sector (commonly, unwaged housewives cook the family's food and well-paid male chefs prepare gourmet restaurant meals). The content of women's and men's work also changes in times of armed conflict, as we shall see.

Gendering in the global division of labour is strategic: from the period when foreign firms employed men to grow cash crops at below subsistence wages, relying on the subsidies of women's unpaid household production and farming, to the internationalisation of manufacturing, which disproportionately employs a low-wage female workforce (Sassen, 2010, p. 29). Currently, it is human trafficking and smuggling that employ strategic gendering.

Underlying reasons for continuing gender discrimination link to neoliberal policies of structural adjustment that increase women's burdens at home by reducing government funding of welfare. Government budgets weighted in service of debt repayment invoke austerity in cutting health, education and social benefit programmes (Sassen, 2000), and women themselves must supply the care work needed in the breach. Austerity and adjustment programmes are also behind rising unemployment and the bankruptcy of many smaller, national, market-oriented firms (Sassen, 2000, p. 513). Young male high school graduates in Zimbabwe perceive themselves as the 'sacrificed generation' because the collapse of the economy meant that they could not translate their education into jobs (Moyo, 2014). Women laid off from formal and public sector jobs are forced to make disadvantageous choices to ensure household survival: to engage in subsistence food production, informal work, emigration or prostitution. Exposure to unpatrolled violence increases as women move away from the formal sector, and the dangers of being caught up in human trafficking and smuggling rise.

The use of force

Violence is a factor of modern production because it supports distribution and is a dynamic in competition (Cockayne, 2010, p. 189); it is available to business as a resource and it necessarily influences the structure of labour markets. Violence enables the capture of women's and children's labour power and it can change the social relations of production rapidly. One school of thought holds that violence receded as capitalist labour relations took hold; another that coercion continued into the last quarter of the nineteenth century in England with the police powers of the state enforcing employers' prerogatives in fixing the length of work contracts (Gerstenberger, 2014). In Africa over the course of the twentieth century, forced labour moved from the public sector, where colonial governments used their political and military powers to exact work from their subjects, to the private sector, where private security guards (or the national army) enforced disadvantageous employment conditions and where government agents mandated to protect workers often ignored infractions. Governments also used their power in service to the private sector: when Congolese businesses were unable to recruit voluntary labour, they enlisted the colonial government's Force Publique to dragoon workers.[2] Among the sectors most concerned are domestic work, agriculture, construction, extraction, manufacturing and entertainment.

The use of force in the suppression of labour unions is familiar to historians of labour relations everywhere; when unions prevailed, they protected their members from the worst violence inflicted by private armies and state militias. Globalisation has increased the complexity of labour organising, not only because past models of industrial-based unionising do not match current needs for cross-border alliances with workers in outsourced and subcontracted jobs, but also because companies avoid their legal obligations to workers by replacing permanent jobs with contract and temporary work. Firms routinely deny precarious and casual workers the rights of permanent employees. Workers' associations in flexible and informal work are rare: SEWA (Self Employed Women's Association), a trade union registered in India in 1972, is an exception. The current assault on workers' organisations comes not only from national and transnational corporations but also from nongovernmental organisations proposing livelihood solutions to poverty and unemployment. Livelihood studies have all but replaced labour studies, shifting emphasis from collective to individual solutions.[3] Yet collective action and collective voice are keys to resolving the challenges in the global labour process (Standing, 2014, p. 977).

Livelihood approaches to economic development were initially promoted by the administration of Prime Minister Tony Blair through the Department for International Development (DFID), the UK's development cooperation agency, as New Labour's attempt to design a poverty alleviation policy based on the 'Third Way' between socialism and capitalism (De Haan, 2012).[4] These programmes, which include microfinance activities directed mainly at women, are problematic for reasons other than their individualistic focus on self-help private sector activities. Livelihood approaches emphasise a range of assets, merging spheres of production and consumption. The state profoundly influences liveli-hoods: laws determine access to resources; public policies influence market con-ditions; state-sanctioned violence renders assets insecure and depresses local economies; and levels of repression influence more powerful groups to steal the poor's assets (Bebbington, 2010, p. 7). One critical analysis of microcredit uses the concept of accumulation by dispossession, a recasting of the term primitive accumulation and a set of processes by which new subjects are brought into the structure of capitalism in exploitative and often violent ways (Keating *et al.*, 2010).

Connected to the social relations of production and the use of force is the renewed discussion in Marxist circles of primitive accumulation. As originally understood, primitive accumulation was a two-fold process: the accumulation of original (or primary) capital, which entailed the destruction of pre-industrial social organisation and the absorption of its workforce, and the plunder of land and raw materials, which involved the dispossession or enslavement of people through colonisation and capture (Wilson, 2012, p. 202). Current interpreta-tions of primitive accumulation stress the continuing nature of this historical process (De Angelis, 2001; Harvey, 2005). Unfree production relations result in a type of primitive accumulation or accumulation by dispossession, as well as in violent labour relations and what Saskia Sassen (2010, p. 26) describes as the increasingly degraded use of people as sex workers, as workers who are used and disposed of, as providers of body organs. Nancy Hartsock (2006) argues that 'Primitive accumulation is very clearly and perhaps at its very core a gendered set of processes, a moment which cannot be understood without central atten-tion to the differential situations of women and men' (quoted in Keating *et al.*, 2010, p. 154). A new version of primitive accumulation has surfaced in pro-grammes promoted by international organisations that are designed to empower women economically: microfinance is a strategy to alleviate poverty through the extension of small loans for the purpose of giving groups start-up capital for small enterprises. Financialisation (the growth of the financial sector as a share of gross domestic product and an important factor in the growth of income inequality), the renegotiation of the social contract, the rise of new ideological formations and a transformation in social reproduction drive the new accumula-tion to which microcredit lending contributes (Keating *et al.*, 2010, p. 153).

The social relations of microfinance

The social relations among members and relatives of microcredit associations are of concern here, rather than the merits of microfinance schemes (on which the literature is voluminous). Two facets of this question are relevant to the use of force: first, the relations among members of microcredit groups, particularly in regard to repayment of loans, and second, the gender relations between the women who receive microloans and the male decision-makers in their house-holds. Although the euphemism for networks and norms of association is social capital, in fact microcredit groups are substitutes for financial collateral, which is the basis for the selection of loan beneficiaries and loan disbursal and recovery. The reason for forming microcredit groups is to produce economic agents who will facilitate monitoring, repayment and fiscal discipline; cooperation is not the aim and, in many instances, violence and conflict are the results (Geleta, 2014).

Advocates of microcredit schemes claim that individual women are empowered by the loans, but sceptics find significant problems created in the social relations of groups, including a rise in women's violence against women. In Ghana, where World Vision, a Christian humanitarian organisation, charges 20 per cent interest on its loans and requires joint liability as a condition of borrowing, women who are unable to pay monthly interest fees face moral coercion, verbal abuse, aggression and physical assault from female group members (Ganle et al., 2015). This Ghanaian study documents the painful experiences of women who often must borrow from friends and moneylenders in order to avoid defaulting; they dread the social pressures and shame that come with the group's violent confiscation and sale of their personal assets and household items including cooking pots, often in a public place such as the market, in order to compel them to pay.

Other studies document an increased rate of male violence against women who have taken microcredit loans, and World Bank staff, who 'virtually ignored the problem for fear of provoking conflict in the community', eventually acknowledged the issue (Bott et al., 2005, p. 39). Research in Bangladesh found a significant pattern of women surrendering the money to husbands or other male guardians to invest directly in the men's businesses; some husbands, unwilling, as opposed to unable, to supply weekly instalments, resorted to violence when their wives begged them for the money (Goetz and Gupta, 1996). Some men in Bangladesh and Bihar (India) use violence to force their wives to borrow from microfinance institutions against their will in order to obtain money to expand their own businesses (Hunt and Kasynathan, 2001). In Cameroon, the microfinance industry provides a pretext for husbands to coerce their wives into providing cash for their families; with men less willing to support family needs, women must shoulder additional responsibilities for their household activities (Mayoux, 2001).

The violence of microcredit schemes takes place at the level of a household or small group of borrowers. The violence of armed conflict may be confined geographically to an area smaller than a nation-state, but it usually affects a broad swath of society. The armed conflict of the new wars is often regional in that it crosses borders. New wars transform the use of force in social relations of production and reproduction by rescaling violence to a wider plane. The next section gives an overview of how war transforms gender relations in this liminal arena.

Gender roles in wartime

The literature on women's wartime experiences has grown in the past decade, and we now know more about the many ways that armed conflict victimises women. The wartime loss of competent and legitimate nation-state apparatuses resonates profoundly in women's lives. Weak as the rule of law was at times in conflict zones or even in spaces of relative stability in African countries at war, women still had recourse to statutory or customary law or, in other circumstances, to religious law (predominantly Islamic and Christian). In militarised societies, as private and voluntary sectors supplant the state, these alternatives – statutory, customary or religious authorities – lose their power and legitimacy as arbiters of social justice.

The combined pressures of disorder, rising criminal activity and globalisation necessarily changed old social relations – either loosening or strengthening them. Military recruitment (by state and non-state forces) has broken – some would say transcended – many family, clan and ethnic ties. And although many women recognise the constraints of those ties, others have noted that those communities offered women protection (however irksome at times). It may also be that insecurity and self-provisioning strengthen social and cultural ties in ways that make life more difficult for nonconforming women. Violence is often used as a means to maintain, change or expand cultural forms. But women are not only victims of these pressures. We know from the literature on war that some women stepped out of their homes for the first time, not just to support – or oppose – war efforts, but also to undertake new kinds of work and leadership roles (Meintjes *et al.*, 2001).

In wartime women enter the civilian labour force in significant numbers (World Bank, 2011). One explanation of women's greater participation in the workforce during armed conflict is the 'added worker effect', which refers to an increase in the labour supply of married women when their husbands die, or are unemployed or absent (World Bank, 2011, p. 61). A study of women's work and the Maoist People's War found that Nepali women who lived in areas with high conflict intensity were more likely to engage in employment than comparable women in regions of low conflict intensity (Mennon and Rodgers, 2015).

War transforms gender assignments, sometimes permanently. During both world wars the content of women's work changed dramatically. In Britain, massive recruitment of civilians for the total war effort of the First World War introduced women's paramilitary organisations; women assumed clerical and transport functions that had been exclusively men's work; and, in far greater numbers, women replaced men in industrial jobs producing munitions (Woollacott, 1998, p. 126). In the Second World War, in addition to factory work in the arms industry, women played significant roles in resistance movements; for example, in the French Resistance women assumed new tasks like clandestine propaganda, intelligence collection and courier services (Schwartz, 1989, p. 127). After the war, most of the 20 million women recruited for war work in the United States left the factories to the demobilised men, but many continued working and found (poorly paid) employment in clerical and service jobs. In the Soviet Union, with so many men dead or disabled and the infrastructure in ruins, women remained in the workforce.

War also provides opportunities for women that would be considered criminal or unsavoury in other circumstances, but in Sierra Leone, for example, rebel camps became an opportunity and alternative, offering a better life for many women because looting was a ready means to acquire undreamed-of possessions. Trading in rebel zones occasioned real benefits as well as such risks as road accidents and being ambushed. When the UN imposed sanctions on arms and oil in 1997, women found black-market trading and smuggling across the Guinea border extremely lucrative (Abdullah *et al.*, 2010, p. 41).

The observation that the gendered division of labour is less differentiated in war economies[5] appears to contradict the widely held opinion that masculinisation accompanies the militarisation of society. Military culture relies on sexism and notions of femininity to reinforce aggressive ideals of masculinity thought necessary for warfare. Yet, as Cynthia Enloe (2000, p. xi) notes of the high percentage of women in fighting forces, 'even a thoroughly patriarchal regime may subvert the orthodox sexual division of military labor in order to maintain itself in power'. Few countries draft women (as of 2013 only eight did so: Bolivia, Chad, Cuba, Eritrea, Israel, Mozambique, North Korea and Sudan).[6] However, almost every rebellion against colonial power and for emancipation in the second half of the twentieth century mobilised women (Algeria, Guinea Bissau, Mozambique and Zimbabwe, to name just a few).

The use of compulsory or forced labour in armed conflict is not limited to conscription, however, and the common use of unfree[7] labour in wartime restructures labour markets. The Third Reich forced some ten million women and men to work in Germany and occupied Europe (Nathan Associates, n.d.). The assignment of millions of prisoners of war and concentration camp prisoners to work in private factories apparently fell into the range of normal management strategies, showing that extreme brutality can be reconciled with the operation of advanced industrialised production (Gerstenberger, 2014). Forced labour debases labour markets by undercutting wages that would normally rise in the context of a labour shortage. Although it cuts labour costs and can be a cost-saving strategy of multinational companies that resort to it, forced labour also disadvantages legal enterprises by creating unfair competition.

Forced labour is not solely the prerogative of legitimate governments at war: rebel armies use it extensively. In Sierra Leone, the RUF, the rebel group that started the war in 1991, used civilians throughout the conflict as a workforce: thousands of civilians were captured, abducted and held as slaves used as forced labour, mainly for diamond mining but also for other tasks such as farming and carrying looted goods, weaponry and ammunition (Kamara, 2009).

In the context of the new wars, the gendered division of labour within and outside fighting forces appears to be less discriminate than in pre-war society. Among civilian populations in war zones, women left on their own must manage households and farmsteads (in effect becoming the boss and doing men's work). In military bush camps, captured youths are forced to do all and any kind of work that is necessary to maintain camp life; even sex work is imposed on captive boys and girls (Mazurana *et al.*, 2002, p. 109). An interesting parallel seems to exist in the world of diamond trafficking, which, though characterised by extreme machismo, nevertheless has a considerable number of active women participants (De Boeck, 2000, p. 213).

Studies of female fighters in civil wars, including the DRC (Verhey, 2004) and Sierra Leone (Coulter, 2009), are increasingly available. During the six-year conflict from 1998 to 2004 in Congo young girls were actively involved as fighters in the armed forces. Armed groups throughout the towns and villages of the eastern provinces forcibly recruited thousands of girls under 18 years old (Verhey, 2004). Some also joined by choice, stating in a few cases that patriotic values inspired them. In other instances girls joined because they wanted to escape problems at home or because joining was seen as the only opportunity to obtain food and material goods. A majority of the girls served multiple roles simultaneously in the armed forces. The prevailing assumption that girls were used as 'wives' and did not serve in active combat roles is incorrect (Verhey, 2004, p. 10). As in many other conflicts it is hard to estimate how many female fighters were part of the armed forces in the DRC. A reported 12,500 girls were in the armed groups, and girls were estimated to make up 40 per cent of all children in such groups (Save the Children, 2005). In 2007 the DRC internal affairs minister reported that 130,000 fighters had been disarmed in the disarmament, demobilisation and reintegration (DDR) process, including 2,610 women and 30,200 children (whose gender was not disclosed) (IRIN, 2007).

Impact of new wars on households

Studies of the impact of structural adjustment programmes on households point the way to examine the impact of new wars on families (Overa, 2007; Sparr, 1994). New wars flourish under restructured national and global economies, taking advantage of loosened trade and financial regulations to create shadow import-export businesses. Households struggle with the effects of devalued currencies, privatisation of common assets, loss of state support and new types of precarious labour markets. Although the ILO launched discussions about the need to safeguard children from the worst forms of work and the imperative to provide decent work for young women and men, governments have been reducing their workforce and weakening protective work laws under pressure from the international financial institutions. Militias forcing civilians to work in the new wars know there is no recourse to government protection. New wars also affect households by justifying austerity budgets (even as military allocations soar) and by siphoning civilians into the armed forces, taking personnel away from such government work as monitoring industrial sites and manufacturing practices. As well, austerity budgets reduce health services at a time when women must care for injured, disabled and elderly relatives; and cuts in education budgets affect mothers bringing up their children on their own and sometimes caring for orphans, too. What might have been expanded opportunities for paid work in health and education services is once again unpaid care work in the home.

Armed conflict both sanctions and assists the use of violence as well as the commoditisation of certain goods and services not usually available – for example forced labour, sexual servitude, and illegal minerals, wildlife and agri-cultural products (Cockayne, 2010, p. 189). In conflict zones, human beings may be traded as if they were ivory or coltan or palm oil. By disorganising society, by upsetting the usual hierarchies of genders and generations, armed conflict removes traditional family protections and opens portals to the traffick-ing of girls and women. And once those routes are established and traffickers recruited into criminal networks, the gates are very difficult to close. The viol-ence of armed conflict persists in social relations of production long after the truce is signed by diminishing the value of labour, as in Congo (Jackson, 2003, p. 32), and by destroying the infrastructure of the economy that was the basis of productivity, as in Angola. Jelmer Vos (2014) speculates that self-employment in the informal economy is the new norm in post-war Angola, reversing an earlier trend towards labour commoditisation; wage labour, widespread under colonialism, has become less common since independence. The reduction of formal sector employment and the resulting growth of self-employment in the informal sector have therefore also led to a reversal of traditional gender roles (Vos, 2014, p. 382).

This discussion of gender roles in wartime provides a context for the investi-gation of resource extraction. The next section presents an overview of labour relations in mining and a snapshot of women's activities, before turning to the specifics of resource extraction in the armed conflicts of Sierra Leone and Congo.

Production relations in the extractive industries

There are few more apposite examples of violent labour relations than the extractive industries. Consider the cruel history of mine accidents and miners' occupational illnesses the world over.[8] Stories of miners' strikes that were met with armed force attest to the antagonism between miners and mine owners: recent examples from Africa include the toll of more than 70 shot dead in June 2004 at Anvil's silver mine, Dikulushi, DRC; the October 2010 shooting of 13 miners at the Chinese-owned Collum Coal Mine in Sinazongwe, Southern Province, Zambia; and the deaths of 38 miners at Lonmin's Marikana platinum mine in South Africa, August 2012. For all that, the use of brutality in the mining sector is poorly researched. M. I. A. Bulmer (1975) recognises the nature of capitalist exploitation of human labour – the mutually opposed interests of capital and labour – in primary mineral extraction and specifies that exploita-tion arises from the system of production. But one rarely finds studies of man-agers' responsibility for violent mine environments or of violence as a strategy of mining capital; instead there are innumerable studies of violent clashes between/among workers.[9]

The use of 'disciplinary' violence to induce black Africans to work harder was widespread and 'a standard aspect of the nineteenth-century racial colonial order in South Africa' (Moodie, 2005, p. 549). Floggings with rawhide whips were regularly administered on Congo's Kilo-Moto gold mines; mine managers

duly recorded each lash and reported quarterly to the Belgian colonial authorities.[10] But beyond individual bosses' brutality, 'assault was entrenched in the
structure of production itself' (Moodie, 2005, p. 550). The force used in mining
is manifest in the violent organisation of mine work, in low rates of pay and
payment systems for extractive work, as well as in mine owners' abuse of their
power to control workers and suppress trade unions.

One contributing factor to mine violence is the geographically fixed, often
isolated location of mines in areas with low population density; this combination leads to the need to import workers, a common basis of mining operations.
Migrant workers inevitably are more dependent on their employers than locally
embedded workforces, and they experience some degree of compulsion: 'All the
way from slavery to vaguely felt and undefined "forced" labour, the mine and
the plantation tend to get similar reputations with respect to the status of their
labour forces' (Bulmer, 1975, p. 61). Language barriers may handicap migrant
workers' training, and lack of immunity to diseases in the new environment may
affect their health. Inability to follow instructions and declining health contribute to violent management. By recruiting workers from other countries,
mine owners could forestall unionisation; migrants competed with locals for
jobs, which deterred worker organising, reduced demands for better living and
working conditions, and provoked tensions and social clashes (Global Health
Watch, 2014, p. 233). Because extraction is usually limited to a single mineral
and displaces other productive activity such as fishing and farming, both the
local community and the mine workforce become dependent on international
export commodity market prices for extractives, a peculiar form of precarity in
the absence of international contacts.

Many South African gold mines conform to this description of geographical
fixity, isolation in areas of low population density and an imported workforce.
T. Dunbar Moodie (2005) argues convincingly that high levels of underground
violence in South African gold mines from 1913 to 1965 can be explained only
partially by general cultural factors such as masculinity or race, social factors
such as corporal punishment in schools, political factors such as state support for
whites, or spatial factors such as the dangers of working underground. 'All are
relevant and important as background conditions, but for a complete explanation [of deeply entrenched industry-wide violent work practices underground],
attention must also be paid to production relations in the workplaces themselves', particularly organisation at the point of production where assault was
institutionalised as a form of labour control (Moodie, 2005, p. 547). The ultimate purpose of the use of force was to cheapen labour: the long-term survival
of the South African gold mining industry depended on a reliable supply of
cheap black labour from which to squeeze maximum profits (Moodie, 2005,
p. 563). Mining capital preferred violence to monetary incentives to extract
hard labour.

Relations of production in large-scale mining, often deep underground,
organised by transnational corporations, are different from work relations in
small-scale and artisanal mines. All three settings attract transient young

workers from beyond the local community whose after-hours activities spill over into the villages surrounding the digs. Young adventurous women as well as men migrate to the mines, despite the pits' bad reputation for lawlessness and violence. Without banks or savings facilities, theft is common, and most men spend their earnings on drugs, alcohol, gambling and sex (Jackson, 2003). The impact of this influx on existing communities can be dramatic – increased prostitution, trafficking and personal insecurity. In his novel about post-war Sierra Leone Ishmael Beah (2014) relates what happens when a foreign company opens a rutile mine near the fictional village of Imperi: more bars in town, more drunks harassing young women, public urination, drunk driving. From this beginning, the situation deteriorates into months of nightly brawling, harassment and rape; the police intervene, always on the side of the company, and arrest not the workers who cause the disruptions but the villagers who defend their families. As breadwinners disappear, desperate wives and daughters prostitute themselves, eventually in competition with sex workers who converge on the town from other parts of the country.

Mining promises quick riches and this illusion undermines and devalues women's work in farming. Mines may be zones of danger where rape, prostitution and violent assault expose women to mental, emotional and physical harm including increased risk of AIDS and other sexually transmitted infections, but mine sites are also locales of opportunity that draw women for some of the same reasons they attract men.

Women's activities in mining

In South Africa, as almost everywhere in underground mining before the 1970s, the labour force was male. Myths about women bringing bad luck to underground work are to be found in every mining culture (for example, Bolivia (Nash, 1993), Burkina Faso (Werthmann, 2009), the United States (Guerin-Gonzales, 2006)). ILO convention 45 of 1935 concerning the employment of women in underground work in mines states clearly, 'No female, whatever her age, shall be employed on underground work in any mine'. Seventy countries ratified the convention. In 1967 Sweden 'denounced' it (the official ILO term), the first of 28 countries to do so.[11]

Not only were women excluded from underground work, African families were rarely allowed to accompany migrants to industrial mine sites (see Jane Parpart's 1986 study of the Zambian copper industry for a rare exception). In the struggle to control labour, the Belgians came to the conclusion quite early that family accompaniment was good policy: from 1928 (with an interruption due to the Great Depression), the Union Minière du Haut-Katanga (UMHK) switched from migrant labour to family settlement at the mines (Dibwe dia Mwembu, 1993, p. 106).[12] Not all Belgian mining operations applied this policy, however; a quite different approach prevailed at the Kilo-Moto gold mines of eastern Congo (see Chapter 2 above for details).

Although African women were not found working underground, they were and are prominent in alluvial (stream bed) artisanal mining, especially of gold and diamonds. Today on average 30 per cent of the world's artisanal miners are women; the percentage is highest in Africa, ranging from 40 to 50 per cent. Artisanal miners are subsistence miners, many of whom work independently and autonomously; they are to be distinguished from employees of small-scale mines who generally use hand tools. It is estimated today that artisanal miners account for 80 per cent of global sapphire mining, 20 per cent of gold mining and up to 20 per cent of diamond mining (World Bank, 2013). This artisanal mining is really informal work by another name. Traditional African practices contrast sharply with European methods of mining, in regard not just to different levels of technology and mechanisation, but in labour relations and class and gender divisions. Traditional African mining was customarily a family affair, often practised by farmers in the dry season. As a family activity or one pursued mainly by women, artisanal mines have not been violent settings in sub-Saharan Africa. In the colonial period, no strict gender division of labour existed on the mines and, according to Raymond Dumett (1999), it is highly likely that more women than men participated in mining operations in any given year. Women's critical roles in mining in West Africa in the last quarter of the nineteenth century bear little relation to artisanal mining today in terms of social relations of production. Long-standing artisanal mining sites seem to have been free of conflict until markets created a 'rush' (for example, the gold rush in Brazil's Amazon) and either large corporations (for instance, Barrick Gold Corporation in Tanzania's Bulyanhulu gold fields) or the state (Zimbabwe in the Marange diamond fields[13]) or non-state armed forces (like the Revolutionary United Front in the diamond region of Sierra Leone) decided to occupy the sites and control the labour force.[14]

It matters to women whether corporations or militaries move in to take over artisanal sites: corporations tend to replace independent artisanal miners with wage labour, often forcing women out with variations of myths about women working underground (described above) or the excuse that skilled workers are needed to operate the machinery. Of course women can acquire such skills as readily as men.[15] Corporations introduce armed guards because industrial mining operations, whether underground complexes or vast surface mines, require important capital investment in machinery and equipment as well as infrastructure (electricity, roads, airports). Such investments must be protected, and there is a marked spiral of violence accompanying mining companies' increased use of private security (Aoul et al., 2000).[16] In Papua New Guinea, where mineral-extraction operations often employ large security forces, these private security contractors have often themselves been accused of disproportionate violence, including numerous examples of sexual and other assault (Economist Intelligence Unit, 2014).

Militaries that take control of mine sites often use existing artisanal workforces of men and women to work for them, subjecting them to brutal, near-slave working conditions. In these militarised and masculinised settings, payment for the work is arbitrary. Congolese women seeking work in the profitable Angola–Congo diamond trade risked rape, theft, betrayal and capture, as the epigraph at the head of this chapter recounts (De Boeck and Plissart, 2014, p. 212). UNITA soldiers, formerly in control of some Angolan diamond sites, forced unprotected women – those not attached to Angolan men – to transport sacks of sand, which divers hauled up from the river, to designated areas where these sacks were sifted. The women's compensation was one sack for every ten they transported, and the soldiers allowed them to keep any diamonds their sack contained. Sifting or washing the sand was a preferred assignment, and those women were considered lucky because they could steal the diamonds they found by throwing them back in the water; the trick was to recuperate the diamonds at day's end, but if supervisors who monitored unauthorised off-hours access to the sites caught them, they could be arrested or shot and killed (De Boeck, 2000, p. 213).

Many Congolese women ignored the advice of the men in their lives and travelled periodically to Angola, sometimes for long stays, where most earned money working around the illicit trade in diamonds, often in sex work. Observing the labour arrangements at mine sites, Congolese women perceived the need for a protector to be so great that they married Angolan soldiers in temporary unions of convenience. The women didn't regard these marriages as real but as strategies that, when successful, gave them economic power and freedom. Filip De Boeck (2000, p. 229) compares these women's tactics to those men have used for centuries – cementing marriages and alliances to enlarge their social and resource networks by exchanging products (formerly game, palm wine, rubber and slaves, nowadays diamonds). The contrast with Tanzanian women's freedom to negotiate unions from a variety of choices at gold mining sites is strong; new configurations are emerging of polygamy, monogamy and promiscuity that are different from prostitution and are sexual/conjugal relationships between men and women varying in degree of sexual and material commitment (Bryceson *et al.*, 2013, p. 34). The difference in part lies in the militarisation of extractive work in Congo, which introduces high levels of violence.

The World Bank and its backers argue that unregulated resource extraction in the artisanal mining sector creates competition and conflict; that revenues from legal and illegal exploitation of natural resources finance conflicts, turning diamond and gold fields into threats to political order (Bannon and Collier, 2003). Advocates for artisanal miners claim that their criminalisation serves to justify further violence (Le Billon, 2006); that these workers are wrongly associated with criminality and state fragility; that as producers they try to disperse economic risk by balancing alternate types of resources; and that, in a context of transitioning from war to peace, regulation will generate more violence and military exploitation (Raeymaekers, 2013).

The social relations of production, the globalisation of labour markets, the use of force and forced labour all come together in studies of extractive industries. The next part of this chapter turns to three case studies of women's participation in the mining sector to illustrate the impact of the use of force in production on gender and generational relations: the Democratic Republic of Congo depicts violence in the mines in an era of on-going conflict, and Sierra

Leone exemplifies violence at mine sites persisting years after conflict has ended.[17] The third case study of artisanal mining in Tanzania, a country that has not seen armed conflict on the mainland, demonstrates some of the opportunities for women in this sector in the absence of open armed violence.[18]

Mining: Congo

An estimated 500,000 adults – half of them women – are working as artisanal miners in Congo; perhaps 20 to 40 per cent (100,000–200,000) are underage girls and boys (Kushner, 2013). Many miners are from communities that lost crops and farmland, cattle and pastures in the first and second Congo wars. In villages near mine sites, tree felling and pollution from unregulated mining have destroyed farms, sources of drinking water and firewood, propelling women into the mining sector (Braeckman, 2006). At the height of the conflict, mines frequently changed hands, and successive groups of combatants inherited the civilian artisanal workforce when they took over these areas.

In addition to activities directly related to mining, women perform support and service work at mine sites in restaurants, markets and kiosks. This concentration is not surprising because women run only 18 per cent of small businesses in Congo, where discriminatory provisions in the Family Code require married women to obtain spousal authorisation to enter into any obligation including performing salaried work and starting a business.[19] Income from mining activities varies according to the location of the mine, the market for the mineral involved and the particular task. Currently, four times more artisanal workers are engaged in gold mining than in tin, tantalum and tungsten combined (IPIS, 2013), so the focus here is on women in gold mining.

Women in gold mining

Gold mining has a long history in eastern Congo going back to Belgian rule when the police forcibly recruited men to work the mines and women to supply food to the workers. Women hiked up to 50km a day to and from these remote mine sites: they were not paid for the food or for the transport of it on their heads. Women's situation in gold mining is not much better today: they may receive (meagre) pay but the risk of violence is even greater. And there is more uncertainty because artisanal miners do not have the technology to locate profitable deposits, though experienced shaft owners may have better information.

Small-scale gold mining is currently a principal survival strategy for a majority of the population in the Kivus, serving as a substitute source of income for people who have lost their primary livelihoods (Geneen and Byemba, 2008–2009). Of this population 70 per cent is rural; their economy was based in agriculture and long-distance trade, not mineral exploitation; and historically there was no fighting around the mines (Johnson, 2009). But the Congo economy changes rapidly in response to outside forces, and in the course of the wars, mines became contentious sites of control.

The rush for gold was an indirect result of international efforts to help end fighting in eastern Congo. Mining had drawn farmers off the land when world market prices for coltan peaked between 1999 and 2001, a period of intense struggle in the second Congo war. NGOs opposed the sales of coltan, necessary for electronics like cell phones, because rebel militias in control of mines were using the profits to obtain arms. NGOs lobbied the US Congress to pass the Dodd–Frank Act in 2010: section 1502 requires certification that Congo minerals do not come from conflict zones. An unintended consequence was that many companies, wary of being fined by the US for purchasing tainted minerals, supplied their needs elsewhere; the slump in sales put many coltan, tin and tungsten miners out of work (Raeymaekers, 2013). Hence the switch from coltan to gold, a mineral that is far less easily traced.

Some women who sell food at the markets around the camps also buy and sell gold, but most women working at the mine sites fall into the hierarchy of workers extracting gold (for a complete description, see Geneen, 2011, pp. 200ff.). Men who extract the rock are at the beginning of the supply chain; they may be individual diggers or groups of diggers who employ women on an ad hoc basis to pulverise the stones to extract the gold. The women work without a contract, and are thus at risk of non-payment or accusations of theft (Geneen, 2011). Some women admit that they hide stones in their underclothes.[20]

With the price of gold so high – in 2015, US$1,200 per ounce, down from US$1,800 in 2011 – no grain can be lost. After the rock is crushed the remaining sand is sifted again and again. Three categories of workers are involved. The first is a team of four to six men to rework the sand to extract gold dust; according to Sara Geneen's 2009 fieldwork, they might earn $9 to $30 a day. Next is a group called *mamans bizalus* who are paid to wash, work and crush a quantity of sand once more to find any remaining gold dust; they can earn $3 to $6 a day. A third category of mainly women and children gather the leftovers to pound, wash and sift the waste yet again; these *mamans toras* might earn $1 to $3 a day (Geneen, 2011, pp. 205–206). The work pulverising stone is physically demanding and many suffer from pulmonary diseases including tuberculosis due to the harsh conditions; these daily rates of pay are well above the national poverty line of 78 cents.

Women's reproductive health is affected by the environmental impact of mining. A process commonly used to extract gold, called amalgamation, uses mercury, which can result in sterility, breast milk contamination and oestrogenic disruption, damaging to pregnant and breastfeeding women. Women, sometimes with infants in their arms or toddlers clinging to their skirts, perform this task. The women combine mercury with gold-laden silt to form a hardened amalgam that picks up most of the gold metal from the silt. The amalgam is then heated over an open flame to evaporate the mercury, leaving small pieces of gold. Women and children inhale this gaseous mercury during the burning process.

Chronic mercury poisoning, known familiarly as mad hatter disease, results from prolonged exposure to mercury vapours. The neurotoxic effects include neuropsychiatric symptoms such as irritability, emotional instability, depression and fatigue. Other adverse effects include damage to the nervous, digestive and immune systems, and to lungs, kidneys, skin and eyes. Discarded mercury also settles into surrounding streams and lakes, where fish absorb and transform elemental mercury into methylmercury. A dangerous neurotoxin, methylmercury can be transferred from pregnant woman to fetus and produce permanent damage to the fetal nervous system, a condition known as Minamata disease. This type of mercury pollution from small-scale mining has been found in Lake Victoria and its surrounding communities (Campbell *et al.*, 2003). Although researchers have carried out many studies measuring mercury in blood in other countries, none has documented mercury-related disease in gold mining communities in Congo – or in Sierra Leone.[21]

Mining: Sierra Leone

Because of the importance of diamonds to the civil wars in Sierra Leone and Liberia, the literature on diamond mining is voluminous.[22] Gold mining, which has received less attention, is an activity that artisanal miners see as an alternative source of income when diamonds fall in value; when diamond diggers have destroyed their farmland, poor farmers turn to gold panning for higher income. The early history of mining in Sierra Leone is described in Chapter 2 above. Artisanal and small-scale mining is Sierra Leone's second largest employer after agriculture and provides a living for some 200,000 to 300,000 individuals. A high degree of mobility characterises the activity, which often takes place in confined spaces where hygiene is poor, a combination of factors that facilitated the spread of Ebola in 2014. Tight border controls implemented to halt the dispersal of the virus made mining activities difficult, and many operators abandoned mining altogether. Before the crisis, artisanal gold mining provided a steady and reliable income for women who constitute 90 per cent of artisanal gold miners. Gold revenue helped purchase household essentials, including food, clothes, school fees, schoolbooks and medical care (Maconachie, 2014).

A study of Sierra Leone during the conflict found that one of the ways in which violence affected extractive industries was through a form of technical regression: contraction in output, skills that atrophy through neglect, disruption of production through the flight of employees, unreliability of transport and fear of looting (Collier and Duponchel, 2013). Technical regression amounts to reversion to pre-industrial production practices that are inefficient. Faced with no electricity, a lack of supplies, stolen equipment and limited ability to repair machines, workers may switch to manual operations. A return to peace renders these practices useless, and workers find that they are not aware of new technological demands. Workers lose skills indirectly through the effects of technical regression on income and demand. Paul Collier and Marguerite Duponchel (2013) found the decline in skills long-lasting in areas where the conflict was more intense.

Throughout the 1990s, conflict made mine work even more improvised and precarious and remuneration for work unpredictable. Soldiers and militia cycled through the mines with increasing frequency, alternating work on the battlefield and in the pits as control of the mines changed hands (Hoffman, 2011, pp. 41–42). More inexperienced artisans entered the mining sector temporarily, often working in exchange for food and basic medical care, selling whatever they might find at very low prices to the patrons who supplied them with equipment and support. During the war, mining was less an occupation than a fleeting opportunity. Daniel Hoffman (2011, pp. 41–42) explains how wartime conditions further destabilised the labour practices of the resource economies, turning young men into 'just in time' production workers 'based on whatever opportunities presented themselves: mining, timber cutting, tapping rubber, or war fighting'.

Mining: Tanzania

Tanzania has become one of Africa's main gold producers, the third largest after South Africa and Ghana (Spiegel, 2009, p. 3080).[23] Like the DRC and Sierra Leone, Tanzania has seen the expansion of combined legal-illegal import-export trade. Even in the absence of armed conflict, illegally exploited and marketed commodities like gold enter legal circuits as a result of liberalised trade and finance rules. In 1995 the estimate was that half of the gold produced was smuggled out of the country, which would lead one to expect high levels of violence around the mines. Violence has erupted at Bulyanhulu, originally an artisanal gold mine that was bought by Barrick, a Canadian company that had the miners forcibly evicted in 1996 (Lissu, c.2002); security guards at that mine were accused of further violence in 2011 and 2013. Chachage Seithy L. Chachage (1993, p. 97) describes environmental and health problems in the mining camps but not violence, despite the presence of the 'traditional' Sungu Sungu[24] defence groups.

In the 1990s, grinding, crushing and recovery of gold were done with rented equipment and hired labour (mostly older men). Others were hired to pound the rock, the most highly paid labour process; within a gold field there could be up to 20 groups of 4–15 workers to do this job. The pounded product was sieved and then pounded again, a process performed by children who were a source of cheap labour. Gold recovery from sand was done by sluicing and amalgamating with mercury. Tailings were sold for regrinding and rewashing, a job undertaken indoors by women in mining and surrounding villages (Chachage, 1993, p. 95). Once a camp was established, within weeks there followed a chain of entrepreneurs – second-hand clothes dealers, tailors, beer sellers, prostitutes and service workers who ran food stalls, kiosks and hotels (Chachage, 1993, p. 96). Many mining camps were highly organised, and some claim holders erected living quarters in order to attract a permanent labour force.

This scene shifted dramatically after Tanzania changed its regulations in 1998 and 1999, providing small-scale miners with an opportunity to own mining claims by issuing primary mining licences (Jønsson and Bryceson, 2009). Many women began to migrate, not only to provide trade and services to the relatively moneyed miners, but also to finance mining operations. Some women have become wealthy from backing mining operations or running bars, hotels and shops (Fisher, 2007). Not all women are successful: among the poorest are those who manually crush rocks or reprocess tailings, and impoverished or elderly women commonly tell stories of extreme hardship and non-payment for labour.

Among the advantages of living in a nation at peace is the ability of mine workers to organise and to benefit from prevailing law and order. The Tanzanian Women Miners Association (TAWOMA) aims to improve women's participation in mining; it lobbies for support and the advancement of women miners through identification of training and technical needs and by conducting training, developing database collateral to guarantee funds, and facilitating the marketing and establishment of mining databases and libraries (Kinabo, 2003a). TAWOMA has argued that members should be allowed to use their primary mining licences as collateral and has asked the government to give this message to banks, but so far, as one critic complained in a news media interview, a lot of the banks are relentlessly hesitant at providing loans to women miners (Andrew, 2008; Spiegel, 2009, p. 3080).

The contrast with the DRC is palpable; as fighting has become more sporadic women have moved into mining areas in South Kivu to pursue economic opportunities, but the Congolese are not effectively protected by health and safety laws in the mines, and the women lack supportive social networks in these mining areas. In the most extreme cases in South Kivu, women are subject to coercion, intimidation and sexual violence. Female miners face the double risk of being rural women in a war zone and of working outside any legal framework in precarious social, economic and environmental conditions (Heller and Perks, 2013). In 2013 the Congolese government, with the support of the World Bank and the European Union, created not an independent trade union but RENAFEM, Women in Mining DRC. The association unites women active all along the mining value chain – from small-scale miners to academics to businesswomen to government officials. Through this national network, provincial focal points work with local women's groups to disseminate laws on the participation of women in mining, to provide technical grants to build ancillary women-led businesses around mines, and to support maternal and child care so that women can work freely in the mining sector.

Women's livelihoods in conflict zones

Although not all transactions that pass through the shadow economy in conflict zones are illegal, criminal activities have infiltrated at all levels and have come to dominate deals in Sierra Leone and eastern Congo. The existence of armed conflict encourages certain forms of organised crime to flourish under the guise of political struggle; on the other hand, the wars in Sierra Leone and Liberia engaged highly irregular forces that lived largely by plunder, making it reasonable to consider such wars as a form of crime. Predatory corruption is pernicious when public officials grab public resources such as land or minerals directly or indirectly through private factions; petty corruption exists when basic public services are sold instead of provided by right (Khan, 2006). The extraction of protection money from citizens affects in particular poor women who depend heavily on services like water and electricity to conduct business in towns. Also, the currency of corruption is frequently sexualised – women and girls are often asked to pay bribes in the form of sexual favours (UNIFEM and UNDP, 2010).

In addition to diamonds, cocaine is trafficked, money is laundered and people are smuggled out of Sierra Leone (UNODC, 2015). Illegal logging, a multimillion-dollar trade involving powerful politicians, is laying waste to the country's forests despite laws and bans (Samura, 2011). Women in Sierra Leone and Liberia are increasingly involved in smuggling large quantities of cannabis across borders (Vorrath, 2014). The operation of illegal markets facilitates corruption, which is used systemically by organised crime. High-level corruption filters down to daily life when women must make informal payments to access medical care and school services (Chêne, 2010). In Sierra Leone, women and children entitled to free care routinely pay for health services (Pieterse and Lodge, 2015).

Some say that distinctions between formal/informal and official/unofficial are meaningless in Congo since the government is involved in extra-legal export of commodities and in some cases supports illicit companies that operate openly (Weijs *et al.*, 2012). A confidential UN report estimated that 98 per cent of the gold produced in Congo in 2013 – with an estimated value of $400 million – was smuggled out of the country; nearly all of it was traded in Uganda (Charbonneau and Nichols, 2013). Not all of these gold sales pay for weapons, and since the passage of US and Canadian legislation tracking so-called conflict minerals in 2010, armed groups no longer raise funds from the sale of tantalum, tin and tungsten (Wolfe, 2015). The core of the arms trade shifted to traffic in a variety of commodities, for example palm oil and cattle (a single cow can sell for up to $500).

Theodore Trefon (2009, p. 16) gives this example of the creative use of predatory administrative power in Congo: municipal hygiene services are responsible for public health issues, but they overlap with municipal environmental services, which are responsible for the cleanliness of public space; this deliberately designed ambiguity facilitates the harassment of service users. When agents from both services approach a market woman selling chickens, she has no idea whose requirements she should respect or indeed which agent is real and which false.

Cross-border trade

Internal problems are magnified by opportunities for private gain at border crossings. Because the wars of 1996–1998 and 1998–2003 followed decades of Mobutu's disastrous rule, by the beginning of the twenty-first century the country's physical infrastructure was so destroyed, decayed or corrupted that eastern Congo was effectively cut off from Kinshasa, which had once been its primary economic partner. In the period of Zairianisation, which began in 1973, the focus of the Kivus' commercial activity pivoted from the west to the east; trade became trans-border, markets were regionalised and exchange was globalised. The most extensive change occurred in agriculture, for which women provide most of the labour. In colonial times, eastern Congo boasted huge palm oil plantations, the industries that transformed palm nuts into oil, and the production of rice, sugar, coffee and tea. All of that was gone by the end of the second Congo war.

Today trade is the primary means of subsistence for the majority of Congolese on the borders of Burundi, Rwanda, Tanzania and Uganda. Much of the coffee exported from Rwanda is grown in the Kivus and moved from Goma to Kigali and thence to Kampala, Nairobi and the port of Mombasa (Weijs *et al.*, 2012, p. 14). For Congolese traders, 75 per cent of whom are women, small-scale commerce is the main activity (male traders have access to more capital and higher earnings). In a not always successful effort to avoid paying informal tariffs and enduring physical harassment, as 90 per cent of traders do at the Goma border, many Congolese women resort to smuggling, using unpatrolled tracks (Raeymaekers, 2009). At the Goma/Gisenyi crossing between Congo and Rwanda, this small-scale cross-border trade in agricultural goods is the principal source of income and principal means of subsistence for about 22,000 people, the majority of them women (Kimanuka and Lange, 2010). Although they have interests in common, women traders from the two cities are in competition and distrust each other. The competition created by the Rwandan women's practice of itinerant trading vexes Congolese women traders. Rwandan women claim that their Congolese competitors chase them from the market, that the Rwandans do not have their own markets in Goma, and that Congolese customs services and other persons in Goma harass them when they cross the border (Kimanuka and Lange, 2010).

In West Africa, urban demand from Conakry, Freetown and Monrovia drives cross-border flows of local rice, gari (processed cassava), palm oil and groundnuts, with Sierra Leone supplying the Guinean market, and Guinea at the centre of regional markets in Côte d'Ivoire, Liberia, Mali and Senegal (Bauer *et al.*, 2010). Local market women are key players in the Sierra Leone palm oil trade; Kpelle women specialise in groundnuts.

Trafficking and smuggling of women and girls

During armed conflict, cross-border trafficking of women is thought to be common because of impunity, lawlessness and dysfunctional state institutions and border controls as well as the generally high level of violence during wars (Wölte, 2004). It is also the case that neoliberal rules of finance and trade have enabled international criminal organisations to gain entry to conflict zones and operate with near-impunity. The trafficking of women and girls through and from war zones controlled by warlords already engaged in war-related dealing in small arms and drugs with criminal organisations represents a profitable expansion of their activities. The global profits from human trafficking in 2005 were US$32 billion (ILO, 2014). Women and girls are at risk of being trafficked when their livelihoods are destroyed and they are forced to leave their homes; internally displaced persons and refugees are particularly susceptible to being trafficked.

The US Department of State (2013) ranks Congo as a Tier 3 country, which means that its government does not fully comply with minimum standards of the US Trafficking Victims Protection Act. The Department of State alleges that the DRC is a source, destination and possibly a transit country for men, women and children subjected to forced labour and sex trafficking. The majority of this trafficking is internal, and armed groups and rogue elements of government forces outside government control in the country's eastern provinces perpetrate much of it. Some Congolese girls are forcibly prostituted in brothels or informal camps, including in markets and mining areas, by loosely organised networks, gangs and brothel operators. Some girls in Bas-Congo Province are reportedly coerced into prostitution by family members or transported to Angola's sex trade. Congolese women and children have been exploited within the country in conditions of domestic servitude, and some migrate to Angola, South Africa, the Republic of Congo and South Sudan, as well as East Africa, the Middle East and Europe, where they are exploited in sex trafficking, domestic servitude or forced labour in agriculture and diamond mines. Pub owners in Bisie, North Kivu, are said to lure young girls from their families and home villages with false promises of legitimate employment near the mines, and then refuse to pay them for the work they perform (Free the Slaves, 2011, p. 17). Instead, the girls are told that their 'pay' is in the form of being given a venue in which to have sex with men for money. Some pub owners take the money directly, some give a portion of the money back to the girls, but they all use the girls' presence and implied sexual availability to attract customers to their establishments.

Sierra Leone is a source and destination country for men, women and children subjected to forced labour and sex trafficking (US Department of State, 2014). Victims come mainly from rural provinces and are recruited to urban and mining centres for sex work and prostitution, domestic servitude and forced labour in artisanal diamond and granite mining, petty trading, portering, rock breaking, street crime and begging. Trafficking victims may also be found in fishing and agriculture or subjected to sex trafficking or forced labour through customary practices such as forced or arranged marriages. Brima Acha Kamara (2008, p. 171) writes that parents are exploiting their own sons and daughters, sending young children out to work instead of to school, allowing girls to be taken out of the country to work as maids in Lebanon where they are sexually abused, or forcing them into early, often polygamous, marriages. This exploitation is directly attributed to the war, to family displacement and the breakup of the extended family network, which was a source of support.

In contrast, there is less transnational than internal trafficking in Tanzania, which is usually facilitated by family members, friends or intermediaries who offer assistance with education or finding lucrative employment in urban areas. The exploitation of young girls in domestic servitude continues to be Tanzania's biggest trafficking problem, though cases of child trafficking for commercial sexual exploitation are increasing along the Kenya–Tanzania border (US Department of State, 2013a).

Conclusions: livelihoods under duress

This chapter has considered gender and the use of force in production from several perspectives: a theoretical view of gender relations in production and reproduction, a contextualised account of gender in labour markets, and empirical observations on the utility of force in production. One premise is that the violence of social production is structural, built into management systems because it serves a purpose: it increases productivity and profits. Examples are drawn from the microfinance industry: women who participate in microfinance schemes experience violence that can be traced directly to the strategies of lenders and the deliberate manipulation of women's position in the household and community. Microfinance illustrates the crossover of productive and reproductive activities – the manner in which 'income-generating' activities exploit household resources – and how violence in the sphere of production permeates the sphere of reproduction.

Structural violence in production is generally associated with gendered labour markets. Close examination reveals how the underlying ideology of separate spheres for women's and men's activities rationalises work assignment; the next chapter discusses the ways in which policies determining social relations of reproduction, based on the same assumptions, maintain discrimination against women in labour markets (because women's inescapable obligations at home condition the terms of their paid labour).

Abundant evidence confirms that war transforms gender roles in ways that belie the stereotypes of women's work and men's work. At the same time the political chaos of armed conflict deprives women of customary mechanisms of protection and recourse in case of injury. When women assume the tasks normally assigned to men in their society, whether by choice or by force, they seem to exchange shelter that has become unsafe for agency that is uncertain and unpredictable – or they lose all control over their lives. Protracted armed conflict appears to create patterns of exploitation that are refined over time, and the practices that prove the most profitable become normalised in the post-conflict period. Examples of these dilemmas are drawn from the mining sector. Because extractive industries were critical to the wars in Congo and Sierra Leone, and because women are prominent in mining in both countries, violence in mineral production is discussed at length in this chapter, both the structural violence of the organisation of work and the personal violence that women endure. The war economies of Congo and Sierra Leone are contrasted with Tanzania where evidence suggests that Tanzanian women find more opportunity in the mines with less risk of violence.

These civil wars, protracted over more than a decade in Sierra Leone and two decades in eastern Congo, profoundly altered livelihoods – not just the ways in which women and men earn their living, not only their occupations and employment, but also the social, community, legal, political, security and economic environments in which people work. Dispossession – as in loss of control of one's labour power, in forced labour arrangements or in the forfeit of one's assets – is the hallmark of modern primitive accumulation. The chapter concludes with a review of women's lives in conflict zones, focusing on criminal activity and corruption, cross-border trade and trafficking and smuggling of women and girls. What emerges from these pages is a portrait of the cumulative impacts on women of violent production regimes that are compounded by armed conflict, enabled by neoliberalism, enmeshed in international criminal networks, abetted by legitimate corporations, and condoned by complicit governments, both women's own states and those of the international community.

Violent economies depend for their existence on a very long human supply chain that crosses national borders and circles the globe. They ensnare poor men, women and children in remote rural regions and urban slums. They co-opt government workers in tax and customs offices and in the police and military. They attract politicians (including heads of state) and self-styled rebel leaders. They engage pilots and pimps, bank tellers and terrorists, jewellers and judges. They lure small entrepreneurs and large company executives. And they even tempt UN peacekeepers sent to patrol armed conflicts. At the very end of this supply chain are the consumers – you and me. We are the buyers of mobile phones, bearers of gold chains and fiancées with diamond rings.

Notes

1 New wars is the term used to describe international or civil wars that involve so many transnational connections that it is difficult to support distinctions between internal and external, aggression and repression, and local and global. See Chapter 1 above for a full discussion of the term.
2 Until 1951, southern states in the US profitably leased convicts to private businesses, matching arrest rates, predominantly of African-Americans, to local labour needs (Blackmon, 2008).
3 For a comprehensive review of the concept of livelihoods, see De Haan (2012). A livelihood comprises people, their capabilities and their means of living, including food, income and assets. Tangible assets are resources and stores, and intangible assets are claims and access. A livelihood is environmentally sustainable when it maintains or enhances the local and global assets on which livelihoods depend and has net beneficial effects on other livelihoods. A socially sustainable livelihood can cope with and recover from stress and shocks and provide for future generations (Chambers and Conway, 1991, p. i).
4 For information on the Third Way, see Jary (2002).
5 Military conscripts in the US armed forces from the Second World War to the Vietnam War regularly performed kitchen duties and other 'women's work'.
6 The ILO exempts compulsory military service from the 1930 Forced Labour Convention, even though conscripts are not free to decline enlistment and draft dodging and desertion are often punished severely. Child soldiers are considered unfree labour.
7 See Chapter 1 above for a detailed discussion of unfree labour.

8 Even today mining remains the most hazardous occupation in most countries when the number of people exposed to risk is taken into account (ILO, n.d.).

9 For a vivid description of the supervisory abuse, faction fights and gang activity that South African mine workers were exposed to and participated in, see Kynoch (2011).

10 See Chapter 2 above for details of use of the *chicotte*.

11 www.ilo.org/ilolex/cgi-lex/ratifce.pl?C045. The US was never a party to this convention.

12 According to Higginson (1989, p. 108), the UMHK initially brought women to the mines for the men to marry in order to keep new recruits working, but the workers regarded these women as prostitutes.

13 The government of Zimbabwe took over the rights to Marange via the Zimbabwe Mining Development Corporation in 2006, but seven private entities partnered with the Zimbabwe government under the affiliate Zimbabwe Mining Development Corporation to operate the diamond fields as of February 2014. For more information see www.globalwitness.org/sites/default/files/library/Zimbabwe_Diamonds_debate_House_of_Commons_17_July_2012.pdf, accessed 28 February 2015.

14 On the Amazon gold rush, see www.reuters.com/article/2009/04/16/us-brazil-gold-idUSTRE53F0HD20090416, accessed 8 February 2012. On Sierra Leone's blood diamonds, see Smillie (2010). There are numerous examples of evictions. Bulyanhulu Gold Mine is an underground gold mine in the Shinyanga Region of Tanzania, operated by African Barrick Gold. In 1996 the Tanzanian Police forced an estimated 400,000 small-scale miners from their land on behalf of the Kahama Mining Corporation, a subsidiary of Barrick Gold, a Canadian company, to make way for the development of the Bulyanhulu mine (Lissu, c.2002). Currently the most blatant example is that of the Marange diamond fields where Zimbabwe police and private security guards employed by mining companies shot, beat and unleashed attack dogs on poor, local, unlicensed miners (www.hrw.org/news/2011/08/30/zimbabwe-rampant-abuses-marange-diamond-fields). For a comprehensive report on Zimbabwe, see PAC, Diamonds and Clubs www.pacweb.org/Documents/diamonds_KP/Zimbabwe-Diamonds_and_clubs-eng-June2010.pdf, accessed 8 February 2012.

15 In US coal mines, women are known to handle machinery more safely than men do (Moore, 1996).

16 Roger Moody (2005) discusses the insurance policies for political risk that large companies carry thanks to bilateral agencies like the US Overseas Private Investment Corporation and international agencies like the World Bank's Multilateral Investment Guarantee Agency; when projects fail, however, insurance is rarely paid to compensate mine workers and local people for injury, death, loss of arable land or poisoning of vital water supplies.

17 See Chapter 1 above for a brief history of the conflicts in the DRC and Sierra Leone.

18 Mainland Tanzania has been free of armed civil conflict; there was violence in Zanzibar in 1964 and again in 2001, and Tanzanian forces invaded Uganda in 1979.

19 Authorisation is also required to go to court in a civil case and to buy or sell property. Banks generally require co-signature/approval of husbands if women are to obtain loans. The Family Code requires proof of marital status and this affects the ability of all women to obtain employment because it is difficult to obtain identification papers in conflict zones. Neighbouring Rwanda, by contrast, has no such regulations, and women in that country run more than 41 per cent of the small businesses (IFC, 2008, p. 3).

20 Women who smuggle gold across the Ugandan border told me that they hid nuggets in soiled sanitary napkins.

21 For a comprehensive review of health impacts among individuals in the artisanal and small-scale gold mining community, see Gibb and O'Leary (2014).

22 Before the 1990s war the mining sector contributed 70 per cent of foreign exchange earnings, 20 per cent of the GDP and 15 per cent of fiscal revenues. Since 2002

economic returns from mining have remounted and by 2010 accounted for almost 60 per cent of export revenues (Natural Resource Governance Institute, n.d.).

23 Prospecting began in the 1930s and after a hiatus of nearly 50 years production soared to 39,012 kg in 2012 from 300 kg in 1995 (Chachage, 1993). For a history of gold mining in Tanzania, see Chachage (1995).

24 Sungu Sungu were state-sponsored vigilante groups (Fleisher, 2000).

References

Abdullah, Hussainatu J., Aisha F. Ibrahim and Jamesina King (2010) Women's voices, work and bodily integrity in pre-conflict, conflict and post-conflict reconstruction processes in Sierra Leone, *IDS bulletin* 41(2): 37–45.

Andrew, F. (2008) Women mineral dealers want licenses to guarantee bank loans, *Guardian*, 25 November 2008, www.ippmedia.com/ipp/guardian/2008/11/25/127045.html, accessed 18 February 2009.

Aoul, Samia Kazi, Émilie Revil, Bruno Sarrasin and Bonnie Campbell with the collaboration of Denis Tougas (2000) Towards a spiral of violence? The dangers of privatising risk management of investments in Africa. Mining activities and the use of private security companies. Montreal: Working Group on Human Rights in Congo/Kinshasa, Development and Peace, MiningWatch Canada.

Bannon, Ian and Paul Collier, eds (2003) *Natural resources and violent conflict: options and actions*. Washington, DC: World Bank.

Barrientos, Stephanie, Naila Kabeer and Naomi Hossain (2004) The gender dimensions of the globalization of production policy. Geneva: International Labour Office, working paper 17.

Bauer, Jean-Martin, Laouali Ibrahim, Salif Sow and Amadou Moctor Konaté (2010) Cross-border trade and food security: Liberia and Sierra Leone. Rome: World Food Programme.

Beah, Ishmael (2014) *Radiance of tomorrow*. New York: Farrar, Straus and Giroux.

Bebbington, Anthony (2010) Social movements and poverty in developing countries, UNRISD civil society and social movements programme paper 32, October. Geneva: United Nations Research Institute for Social Development.

Bennholdt-Thomson, Veronika (1988) The future of women's work and violence against women. In *Women: the last colony*, by Maria Mies, Veronika Bennholdt-Thomson and Claudia von Werlhof, pp. 113–129. London: Zed Books.

Blackmon, Douglas A. (2008) *Slavery by another name: the re-enslavement of black Americans from the Civil War to World War II*. New York: Doubleday.

Bott, Sarah, Andrew Morrison and Mary Ellsberg (2005) Preventing and responding to gender-based violence in middle and low-income countries: a global review and analysis. Policy Research Working Paper 3618, World Bank Gender and Development Group, Washington, DC. http://econ.worldbank.org/external/default/main?pagePK=64165259&theSitePK=477960&piPK=64165421&menuPK=64166093&entityID=000112742_20050628084339, accessed 12 March 2012.

Braeckman, Colette (2006) Running on empty, *Index on censorship* 3: 29–34.

Bryceson, Deborah Fahy, Jesper Bosse Jønsson and Hannelore Verbrugge (2013) Prostitution or partnership? Wifestyles in Tanzanian artisanal gold-mining settlements, *Journal of modern African studies* 51(1): 33–56.

Bulmer, M. I. A. (1975) Sociological models of the mining community, *Sociological review* 23(1): 61–92.

Campbell, L. M., D. G. Dixon and R. E. Hecky (2003) A review of mercury in Lake Victoria, East Africa: implications for human and ecosystem health, *Journal of toxicology and environmental health*, part b, 6: 325–356.

Chachage, Chachage Seithy L. (1993) New forms of accumulation in Tanzania: the case of gold mining. In *Mining and structural adjustment: studies on Zimbabwe and Tanzania*, edited by Chachage Seithy L. Chachage, Magnus Ericsson and Peter Gibbon, pp. 72–108. Research Report 92. Uppsala: Nordiska Afrikainstitutet.

Chachage, Chachage Seithy L. (1995) The meek shall inherit the earth but not the mining rights: mining and accumulation in Tanzania. In *Liberalised development in Tanzania* edited by Peter Gibbon, pp. 37–108. Uppsala: Institute for African Studies.

Chambers, Robert and Gordon R. Conway (1991) Sustainable rural livelihoods: practical concepts for the 21st century. IDS discussion paper 296. Brighton: Institute of Development Studies, www.ids.ac.uk/publication/sustainable-rural-livelihoods-practical-concepts-for-the-21st-century, accessed 7 February 2015.

Charbonneau, Louis and Michelle Nichols (2013) Exclusive: Congo's army accused of abuse as rebels regroup in Rwanda: U.N. experts. United Nations. 16 December, www.reuters.com/article/2013/12/17/us-congo-democratic-un-idUSBRE9BF1GJ20131217, accessed 12 October 2014.

Chêne, Marie (2010) Overview of corruption and anti-corruption in Sierra Leone. Transparency international, www.u4.no/publications/overview-of-corruption-and-anti-corruption-in-sierra-leone/, accessed 20 January 2014.

Cockayne, James (2010) Crime, corruption and violent economies. In *Ending wars, consolidating peace: economic perspectives*, edited by Mats Berdal and Achim Wennmann, pp. 189–218. Abingdon, UK: Routledge for International Institute for Strategic Studies.

Collier, Paul and Marguerite Duponchel (2013) The economic legacy of civil war: firm-level evidence from Sierra Leone, *Journal of conflict resolution* 57(1): 65–88.

Coulter, Chris (2009) *Bush wives and girl soldiers: women's lives through war and peace in Sierra Leone*. Ithaca, NY: Cornell University Press.

De Angelis, Massimo (2001) Marx and primitive accumulation: the continuous character of capital's 'enclosures', *Commoner* 2: 1–22, www.thecommoner.org.

De Boeck, Filip (2000) 'Des chiens qui brisent leur laisse': mondialisation et inversion des catégories de genre dans le contexte du trafic de diamant entre l'Angola et la République démocratique du Congo (1984–1997). In *Chasse au diamant au Congo/Zaïre*, edited by Laurent Monnier, Bogumil Jewsiewicki and Gauthier de Villers, pp. 209–232. Paris: L'Harmattan, Cahiers africains 45–46. Text available in English in *Changements au féminin en Afrique noire* edited by Danielle de Lame and Chantal Zabus, pp. 87–114. Paris: L'Harmattan, 1999, volume I: anthropologie.

De Boeck, Filip and Marie-Françoise Plissart (2014) *Kinshasa: tales of the invisible city*. Leuven: Leuven University Press.

De Haan, Leo J. (2012) The livelihood approach: a critical exploration, *Erdkunde* 66(4): 345–357.

Dibwe dia Mwembu, Donatien (1993) Les fonctions des femmes africaines dans les camps des travailleurs de l'Union Minière du Haut-Katanga (1925–1960), *Zaïre-Afrique* 272: 105–118.

Dumett, Raymond E. (1999) *El Dorado in West Africa: the gold-mining frontier, African labor, and colonial capitalism in the Gold Coast, 1875–1900*. Athens: Ohio University Press.

Economist Intelligence Unit (2014) Crime without punishment. 18th November, http://country.eiu.com/article.aspx?articleid=972495081&Country=Papua%20New%20

Guinea&topic=Economy&subtopic=Forecast&subsubtopic=The+domestic+economy, accessed 18 March 2015.

Elson, Diane (1999) Labor markets as gendered institutions: equality, efficiency and empowerment issues, *World development* 27(3): 611–627.

Enloe, Cynthia (2000) *Maneuvers: the international politics of militarizing women's lives.* Berkeley: University of California Press.

Fisher, Eleanor (2007) Occupying the margins: labour integration and social exclusion in artisanal mining in Tanzania, *Development and change* 38(4): 735–760.

Fleisher, Michael L. (2000) Sungusungu: state sponsored village vigilante groups among the Kuria of Tanzania, *Africa* 70(2): 209–228.

Free the Slaves (2011) The Congo report: slavery in conflict minerals. June, www.free-theslaves.net, accessed 2 December 2013.

Ganle, John Kuumuori, Kwadwo Afriyie and Alexander Yao Segbefia (2015) Micro-credit: empowerment and disempowerment of rural women in Ghana, *World development* 66: 335–345.

Geleta, Esayas Bekele (2014) Microfinance and the politics of empowerment: a critical cultural perspective, *Journal of Asian and African studies* 49(4): 413–425.

Geneen, Sara (2011) Constraints, opportunities and hope: artisanal gold mining and trade in South Kivu (DRC). In *Natural resources and local livelihoods in the Great Lakes region of Africa: a political economy perspective*, edited by A. Ansoms and S. Marysse, pp. 192–214. London: Palgrave Macmillan.

Geneen, Sara and Gabriel Kamundala Byemba (2008–2009) 'Qui cherche, trouve'. Opportunités, défis et espoirs dans le secteur de l'or à Kamituga, *Afrique des Grands Lacs*, pp. 183–214. Paris: L'Harmattan.

Gerstenberger, Heide (2014) The political economy of capitalist labor, *Viewpoint magazine* 2 September, http://viewpointmag.com/2014/09/02/the-political-economy-of-capitalist-labor/, accessed 7 December 2014.

Gibb, Herman and Keri Grace O'Leary (2014) Mercury exposure and health impacts among individuals in the artisanal and small-scale gold mining community: a comprehensive review, *Environmental health perspectives* 122(7): 667–672.

Global Health Watch (2014) *Global Health Watch 4*. London: Zed Books.

Goetz, A.-M. and R. Sen Gupta (1996) Who takes the credit? Gender, power, and control over loan use in rural credit programmes in Bangladesh, *World development* 24(1): 45–63.

Guerin-Gonzales, Camille (2006) From Ludlow to camp solidarity: women, men, and cultures of solidarity in U.S. coal communities, 1912–1990. In *Mining women: gender in the development of a global industry, 1670 to 2005*, edited by Laurie Mercier and Jaclyn J. Gier, pp. 296–324. New York: Palgrave Macmillan.

Hartsock, Nancy (2006) Globalization and primitive accumulation: the contributions of David Harvey's dialectical Marxism. In *David Harvey: a critical reader*, edited by Noel Castrée and Derek Gregory, pp. 167–190. New York: Blackwell.

Harvey, David (2005) *A brief history of neoliberalism*. Oxford: Oxford University Press.

Heller, Katherine C. and Rachel Perks (2013) Extractive industries in fragile settings present opportunities and risks for women, 7 October, https://collaboration.worldbank.org/groups/gender-issues-in-fragile-situations, accessed 20 May 2015.

Higginson, John (1989) *A working class in the making: Belgian colonial labor policy, private enterprise, and the African mineworkers, 1907–1951*. Madison: University of Wisconsin Press.

Hoffman, Daniel (2011) Violence, just in time: war and work in contemporary West Africa, *Cultural anthropology* 26(1): 34–57.

Hunt, J. and N. Kasynathan (2001) Pathways to empowerment? Reflections on microfinance and transformation in gender relations in South Asia, *Gender and development* 9(1): 42–52.

IFC (2008) IFC smart lessons: creating opportunities for women entrepreneurs in conflict-affected countries. Washington, DC: International Finance Corporation.

ILO (2014) *Profits and poverty: the economics of forced labour.* Geneva: International Labour Office.

ILO (n.d.) Mining: a hazardous work, www.ilo.org/safework/areasofwork/hazardous-work/WCMS_124598/lang-en/index.htm, accessed 6 December 2015.

IPIS (2013) Analysis of the interactive map of artisanal mining areas in eastern DR Congo. November, www.ipisresearch.be/publications_detail.php?id=428, accessed 1 October 2014.

IRIN News (2007) Africa: integration of ex-combatants 'still a challenge', 18 June, www.irinnews.org/Report.aspx?ReportId=72779, accessed 20 June 2014.

Jackson, Stephen (2003) Fortunes of war: the coltan trade in the Kivus. In *Power, livelihoods and conflict: case studies in political economy analysis for humanitarian action,* edited by S. Collinson, pp. 21–36. London: Humanitarian Policy Group report 13, February.

Jackson, Stephen (2005) Protecting livelihoods in violent economies. In *Profiting from peace: managing the resource dimensions of civil war,* edited by Karen Ballentine and Heiko Nitzchke, pp. 153–182. Boulder, CO, and London: Lynne Rienner.

Jary, David (2002) The global third way debate: review article, *Sociological review* 50(3): 437–449.

Johnson, Dominic (2009) Minerals and conflict in eastern DRC, Pole Institute discussion paper, July, www.pole-institute.org/site%20web/echos/echo114.htm, accessed 1 November 2014.

Jønsson, Jesper Bosse and Deborah Fahy Bryceson (2009) Rushing for gold: mobility and small-scale mining in East Africa, *Development and change* 40(2): 249–279.

Kamara, Brima Acha (2008) The challenges of trafficking in women and children in Sierra Leone. In *Global trafficking in women and children,* edited by Obi N. I. Ebbe and Dilip K. Das, pp. 163–174. Boca Raton, FL: CRC Press.

Kamara, Joseph F. (2009) Preserving the legacy of the special court for Sierra Leone: challenges and lessons learned in prosecuting grave crimes in Sierra Leone, *Leiden journal of international law* 22(4): 761–777.

Keating, Christine, Claire Rasmussen and Pooja Rishi (2010) The rationality of empowerment: microcredit, accumulation by dispossession, and the gendered economy, *Signs: journal of women in culture and society* 36(1): 153–176.

Khan, Mushtaq H. (2006) Determinants of corruption in developing countries: the limits of conventional economic analysis. In *International handbook on the economics of corruption,* edited by Susan Rose-Ackerman, pp. 216–244. Cheltenham: Edward Elgar.

Kimanuka, Celestin and Maria Lange (2010) *The crossing: small-scale trade and improving cross-border relations between Goma (DR Congo) and Gisenyi (Rwanda).* London: International Alert.

Kinabo, Crispin (2003) Women and small-scale mining in Tanzania. In *The socioeconomic impacts of artisanal and small scale mining in developing countries,* edited by Gavin M. Hilson, pp. 313–324. Lisse: A. A. Blakema.

Kinabo, Crispin (2003a) A socio-economic study of small-scale mining in Tanzania. In *The socio-economic impacts of artisanal and small scale mining in developing countries,* edited by Gavin M. Hilson, pp. 291–311. Lisse: A. A. Blakema.

Korf, Benedikt (2004) War, livelihoods and vulnerability in Sri Lanka, *Development and change* 35(2): 275–295.

Kushner, Jacob (2013) In Congo, lure of quick cash turns farmers into miners, NPR 28 March, www.npr.org/2013/03/28/175577518/in-congo-lure-of-quick-cash-turns-farmers-into-miners, accessed 13 March 2015.

Kynoch, Gary (2011) Of compounds and cellblocks: the foundations of violence in Johannesburg, 1890s–1950s, *Journal of southern African studies* 37(3): 463–477.

Le Billon, Philippe (2006) Fatal transactions: conflict diamonds and the (anti)terrorist consumer, *Antipode* 38(4): 778–801.

Lissu, Tundu A. M. (c.2002) Tanzania: human rights advocacy and the Bulyanhulu gold mine, www.eli.org/sites/default/files/docs/advocacytoolscasestudies/casestudy.tanzania.final.pdf, accessed 30 June 2015.

Maconachie, Roy (2014) Ebola's catastrophic consequences on Sierra Leone's small-scale mining sector, *Guardian*, 4 November, www.theguardian.com/sustainable-business/2014/nov/04/ebola-sierra-leone-small-scale-mining-sector-catastrophic-consequences, accessed 18 March 2015.

Mayoux, L. (2001) Tackling the down side: social capital, women's empowerment and microfinance in Cameroon, *Development and change* 32(3): 421–450.

Mazurana, Dyan E., Susan A. McKay, Khristopher C. Carlson and Janel C. Kasper (2002) Girls in fighting forces and groups: their recruitment, participation, demobilization, and reintegration, *Peace and conflict: journal of peace psychology* 8(2): 97–123.

Meintjes, Sheila, Anu Pillay and Meredeth Turshen, eds (2001) *The aftermath: women in post-conflict transformation*. London and New York: Zed Books.

Mennon, Nidhiya and Yana van der Meulen Rodgers (2015) War and women's work: evidence from the conflict in Nepal, *Journal of conflict resolution* 59(1): 51–73.

Moodie, T. Dunbar (2005) Maximum average violence: underground assaults on the South African gold mines, 1913–1965, *Journal of Southern African studies* 31(3): 547–567.

Moody, Roger (2005) *The risks we run: mining, communities and political risk insurance.* Utrecht: International Books.

Moore, Marat (1996) *Women in the mines: stories of life and work.* New York: Twayne.

Moyo, Otrude N. (2014) Surviving structural violence in Zimbabwe: the case study of a family coping with violence. In *Ordinary violence and social change in Africa*, edited by Jacky Boju and Marjam de Bruijn, pp. 84–100. Leiden: Brill.

Nash, June (1993) *We eat the mines and the mines eat us: dependency and exploitation in Bolivian tin mines.* New York: Columbia University Press.

Nathan Associates (n.d.) Forced labor under the Third Reich, part one, www.nathaninc.com/sites/default/files/Pub%20PDFs/Forced%20Labor%20Under%20the%20Third%20Reich,%20Part%20One.pdf, accessed 2 August 2015.

Natural Resource Governance Institute (n.d.) Sierra Leone extractive industries, www.resourcegovernance.org/countries/africa/sierra-leone/extractive-industries, accessed 18 March 2015.

Overa, Ragnhild (2007) When men do women's work: structural adjustment, unemployment and changing gender relations in the informal economy of Accra, Ghana, *Journal of modern African studies* 45(4): 539–564.

Parpart, Jane (1986) The household and the mine shaft: gender and class struggles on the Zambian copperbelt, 1926–64, *Journal of southern African studies* 13(1): 36–56.

Pieterse, P. and T. Lodge (2015) When free healthcare is not free. Corruption and mistrust in Sierra Leone's primary healthcare system immediately prior to the Ebola outbreak, *International health*, 23 April, doi:10.1093/inthealth/ihv024.

Raeymaekers, Timothy (2009) The silent encroachment of the frontier: a politics of trans-border trade in the Semliki Valley (Congo–Uganda), *Political geography* 28: 55–65.

Raeymaekers, Timothy (2013) Fair phone = fair trade?, *Liminal geographies*, www.timoth-yraeymaekers.net/2013/06, accessed 20 January 2014.

Samura, Sorious (2011) Sierra Leone: timber! *Aljazeera*, November 26, www.aljazeera.com/programmes/africainvestigates/2011/11/20111123134340348960.html, accessed 20 January 2013.

Sassen, Saskia (2000) Women's burden: counter-geographies of globalization and the feminization of survival, *Journal of international affairs* 53(2): 503–524.

Sassen, Saskia (2010) A savage sorting of winners and losers: contemporary versions of primitive accumulation, *Globalizations* 7(1–2): 23–50.

Save the Children (2005) Forgotten casualties of war: girls in armed conflict. London: Save the Children UK.

Schwartz, Paula (1989) *Partisanes* and gender politics in Vichy France, *French historical studies* 16(1): 126–151.

Smillie, Ian (2010) *Blood on the stone: greed, corruption and war in the global diamond trade.* Ottawa: Anthem Press.

Sparr, Pamela, ed. (1994) *Mortgaging women's lives: feminist critiques of structural adjust-ment.* London: Zed Books.

Spiegel, Samuel J. (2009) Socioeconomic dimensions of mercury pollution abatement: engaging artisanal mining communities in sub-Saharan Africa, *Ecological economics* 68(12): 3072–3083.

Standing, Guy (2009) Global employment: two reports in search of the problem, *Devel-opment and change* 40(6): 1319–1337.

Standing, Guy (2013) Tertiary time: the precariat's dilemma, *Public culture* 25(1): 5–23.

Standing, Guy (2014) Understanding the precariat through labour and work, *Develop-ment and change* 45(5): 963–980.

Trefon, Theodore (2009) Public service provision in a failed state: looking beyond preda-tion in the Democratic Republic of Congo, *Review of African political economy* 119: 9–21.

UNIFEM and UNDP (2010) Corruption, accountability and gender: understanding the connections. New York: United Nations.

UNODC (2015) Sierra Leone. Dakar: United Nations Office on Drugs and Crime regional office for West and Central Africa, www.unodc.org/westandcentralafrica/en/sierra-leone.html, accessed 20 July 2015.

US Department of State (2013) *Trafficking in Persons Report.* Washington, DC: Office to Monitor and Combat Trafficking in Persons, www.state.gov/j/tip/rls/tiprpt/coun-tries/2013/215442.htm, accessed 12 January 2015.

US Department of State (2013a) Tanzania, *2013 Trafficking in Persons Report*, www.state.gov/j/tip/rls/tiprpt/countries/2013/215632.htm, accessed 12 January 2015.

US Department of State (2014) Sierra Leone, *2014 Trafficking in Persons Report.* Wash-ington, DC: Office to Monitor and Combat Trafficking in Persons, www.state.gov/j/tip/rls/tiprpt/countries/2014/226810.htm, accessed 20 July 2015.

Verhey, Beth (2004) Reaching the girls: study on girls associated with armed forces and groups in the Democratic Republic of Congo. London: Save the Children UK and the NGO Group: CARE, IFESH and IRC.

Vorrath, Judith (2014) From war to illicit economies: organized crime and state-building in Liberia and Sierra Leone. Berlin: Stiftung Wissenschaft und Politik (German Insti-tute for International and Security Affairs).

Vos, Jelmer (2014) Work in times of slavery, colonialism, and civil war: labor relations in Angola from 1800 to 2000, *History in Africa* 41: 363–385.

Weijs, Bart, Dorothea Hilhorst and Adriaan Ferf (2012) Livelihoods, social protection and basic services in Democratic Republic of the Congo. Secure Livelihoods Research Consortium working paper 2. London: Overseas Development Institute.

Werthmann, Katja (2009) Working in a boom-town: female perspectives on gold mining in Burkina Faso, *Resources policy* 34: 18–23.

Wilson, Tamar Diana (2012) Primitive accumulation and the labor subsidies to capitalism, *Review of radical political economics* 44(2): 201–212.

Wolfe, Lauren (2015) How Dodd–Frank is failing Congo, *Foreign policy*, 2 February, http://foreignpolicy.com/2015/02/02/how-dodd-frank-is-failing-congo-mining-conflict-minerals/, accessed 20 July 2015.

Wölte, Sonja (2004) *Armed conflict and trafficking in women*. Eschborn, Germany: Deutsche Gesellschaft für Technische Zusammenarbeit (GTZ) GmbH, www.gtz.de.

Woollacott, Angela (1998) Women munitions makers, war, and citizenship. In *The women and war reader*, edited by Lois Ann Lorentzen and Jennifer Turpin, pp. 126–131. New York: New York University Press.

World Bank (2011) *World development report 2011*. Washington, DC: World Bank.

World Bank (2013) Artisanal and small-scale mining, www.worldbank.org/en/topic/extractiveindustries/brief/artisanal-and-small-scale-mining, accessed 20 January 2015.

4 Violence in biological and social reproduction

One day I had a miscarriage while at work. They put the cassiterite load in my bag and told me I could carry it on my back because it was 25 kilograms. After a few steps, my friends came running and told me there was blood running down my legs. I had started to feel pain and had to stop to see. Some people had come to help me. They weighed the package, which, contrary to what they had told me, weighed 70 kilograms. Nobody cared for me. The owner of those minerals didn't even pay me because I had not yet washed the ore. So, I sold some of my clothes to get treatment. After I recovered, I went back in the mines. There was nothing else I could do. [Claudine, working at the cassiterite Zola Zola mine, Nzibira, South Kivu, DRC]

(Rothenberg, 2014, p. 13)

This chapter presents the argument that violent economies, which are economies warped by war and armed conflict and incorporate violence as a factor of production, not only shape women's productive activities but also condition social reproduction. Social reproduction encompasses all the ways that societies reproduce themselves from day to day and from generation to generation. General economic, political, social and cultural contexts influence patterns and strategies of reproduction (the influence works in both directions). Day-to-day reproduction encompasses the reproduction of the necessities of household survival – labour, food, shelter and daily life. Taken together, these two dimensions of social reproduction – general contexts and daily endurance – make up what has come to be called the demographic regime.[1] In this construction, the household mediates between broad economic structures and individual decision-making concerning migration, labour force participation, consumption and fertility (Cordell, 2013).

The concept of social reproduction is clearly wider than that of the social determinants of health and encompasses far more than women's sexual and reproductive health or reproductive health services (WHO, 2008). We begin with general considerations of social reproduction defined very broadly, place the relations of social reproduction in historical context, and then discuss violence in biological and social reproduction. This analysis opens up several sets of specific questions about social reproduction in connection with resource extraction in Congo, Sierra Leone and Tanzania: questions about the use of women's reproductive labour to finance and prosecute conflicts, how women's wartime food production and marketing support their households and are transformed by conflict, and how women manage social reproduction in relation to agents of the state (regular or irregular). Finally, to understand better how armed conflict warps and constrains women's options, the situations in Congo and Sierra Leone are contrasted with resource extraction in relatively peaceful Tanzania.

Definitions and uses of social reproduction

Feminist economists have shown how women's reproductive work (in the sense of the regeneration of societies) contributes to men's productive work.[2] The heart of the argument for the value of women's reproductive work lies in the paradigm that the basis of surplus value production is located in the labour of daily and generational reproduction (Caffentzis, 2002). In this model, non-market relations produce value in one of three ways: by generalising the commodity form (for example, the commoditisation of intimacy through sex work, surrogacy contracts and sales of oocytes); by generalising the social-exchange relation to include relations of reciprocity and redistribution as well as market exchanges (for instance, volunteerism and work in the non-profit sector); and by assigning value to the work needed to produce and reproduce labour power (in effect, the effort to create and nurture workers). This last is the hard core of social reproduction; it encompasses pregnancy and childbirth, breastfeeding and child rearing, housework and care of the sick and elderly.

The first approach, which explains social reproduction through a generalisation of the commodity form, suggests that capitalism does not really divorce production from reproduction because it opportunistically seizes every chance to commoditise relations in both spheres, in social as well as economic relationships (Caffentzis, 2002, p. 4). Ray Bush (2007, p. 191) takes as a hallmark of capitalism its ability to induce relations between people to take the form of relations between things – a process of alienation from one's community and one's humanity. A major target for agents of capital is the transformation of labouring households, of people's ability to produce, reproduce and sustain life. Capitalism's recurrent attempt to promote commoditisation is like a campaign for control over the processes and results of fertility. Central to the process of enacting or realising fertility are women's knowledge, their time and their bodies – in addition to labour and land (Turner and Brownhill, 2001, cited in Bush, 2007, p. 192). Queer theory has also re-examined social reproduction under capitalism; for Rosemary Hennessy (2006, p. 389), social reproduction takes place through the making, exchange and consumption of commodities. Mail order zygotes for surrogacy and prepared food – everything from frozen organic baby food to refrigerated fresh meals for dogs – illustrate the commercial transformation of social reproduction.

The second approach to social reproduction sees commodity exchange as a special case of more general relations of social exchange. In this version, social reproduction rests on relations of reciprocity and redistribution as preconditions for market exchanges (Caffentzis, 2002, p. 10). Policy-makers see non-profit organisations as the mediators between production and reproduction, giving capitalism a human face. Non-profits – and nongovernmental organisations (NGOs) more generally – were critical to neoliberal strategies to shift the costs of social reproduction from the public to the private sphere. Currently, new actors from the private sector are exposing the failures of NGOs to provide services and insisting that commercial entrepreneurs can do better. Social services, which governments had provided following decades of workers' struggles for those benefits in the nineteenth and twentieth centuries, are being switched to individual responsibility (women's unpaid work) or into the private sector (voluntary, but increasingly corporate) or, where the private sector fails to meet people's needs, into the informal economy (for example, privately employed undocumented and unlicensed childcare workers). Isabella Bakker and Stephen Gill (2003, p. 19) call this the reprivatisation of the governance of social reproduction, which can be seen in the privatisation of previously socialised institutions associated with provisioning for social reproduction.

Michel Foucault (1981, p. 94, cited in Caffentzis, 2002, p. 12) agrees: relations that are not commoditised condition the possibility of capitalist exchange; but Foucault also believes that power relations are essential to social reproduction, defining power as relationships of force in production, in families, groups and institutions, and in the bases for cleavages that rupture the social body. George Caffentzis (2002, p. 13) argues that Foucault's theory of bio-power fails to explain crises of social reproduction because for Foucault crisis and discontinuity are permanent conditions of social reproduction. But, Caffentzis argues, if crisis is everywhere, if it is yet another name for power, then it becomes the norm in a society where war is so common that it needs no special explanation. Yet radical ruptures and massive social cleavages do require explanation.

The third approach to social reproduction rests on the argument that value is created not only by the work needed for the production of commodities, but also by the work needed to produce and reproduce labour power; thus the unwaged also produce value (Caffentzis, 2002). What is so interesting about this approach is its ability to explain violent gendered power relations between productive and reproductive workers. For example, West African migrant workers in Paris regarded annual births as their wives' work because the French government paid an allowance for each child. The men bound their wives by a very short leash: every morning as they left home for their jobs, they gave their women just enough money to meet that day's household needs – so that the women would not run away (Turshen *et al.*, 1993). 'A network of "informal," but determining, often violent power relations among workers themselves is inscribed in this money with "strings attached"' (Caffentzis, 2002, p. 15).

There is also another conflict within capitalism that the labour power approach (a way of looking at social reproduction that seems both apt and accurate) brings out: the conflict between the needs of capitalist production and the demands of those whose work is centred in the arena of the social reproduction of labour power. This conflict can lead to major crises of reproduction appearing as dramatically falling (or rising) birth rates, urban riots or agrarian revolts. One of capital's laws is to make the reproduction of labour power completely dependent upon the wage form and hence to keep the reproducers of labour both invisible to and controlled by the system. That is the reason for the relentless attack on any guarantees of subsistence, especially to those who reproduce labour power. The labour power production approach posits the antagonism between circulation/production and accumulation/reproduction as essential to the existence of capitalism (Caffentzis, 2002, pp. 15–16).

Social reproduction is thus both essential, since it creates the next generation of workers while sustaining the current workforce, and unremunerated because capitalists deem this reproductive work as non-productive. Almost all of the ideology surrounding motherhood and housewifery turns on the illusion that women are marginal to the process of social production. Housework becomes invisible, the status of women dependent, and employers and the state talk incessantly about the importance of stable families (Caffentzis, 2002, p. 14). Against this political stance it is not difficult to project the use of force in biological reproduction.

Violence in biological reproduction

Biological reproduction is a subject of millennial concerns, figuring in the fifth of the UN Millennium Development Goals with a target of reducing the maternal mortality ratio (deaths of women in childbirth) by three-quarters between 1990 and 2015. None of the countries featured in this book reached that target. Maternal mortality ratios in Congo and Sierra Leone are among the highest in the world, the percentage of women attended by trained personnel in childbirth among the lowest. The estimated maternal mortality ratio during the civil war in Sierra Leone was 1,800 deaths per 100,000 live births in 2000, a ratio that has improved and in 2010 stood at 890 deaths per 100,000 live births (Commonwealth Foundation, 2013). The figures for the DRC are 1,000 per 100,000 live births in 1990, rising to 1,100 per 100,000 live births during the civil war in 2000, and falling to 730 per 100,000 live births in 2013 (UN MDGs, 2015). The decline in mortality ratios in Tanzania was slow even in the absence of armed conflict: from 529 per 100,000 live births in 1996 to 433 in 2012 (UNDAP, 2014, p. 20). The figures for these three countries are two to four times as high as the global ratio of 210 deaths per 100,000 live births in 2013. Nowhere does the UN discuss this loss of life in terms of the violence of biological reproduction, and the UN defines social reproduction narrowly in terms of cultural constraints on women and girls.

Violence is exercised in societies in which life expectancy is twice as high in the upper as in the lower classes. Direct attacks, as when one person kills another, are not the only demonstrations of violence, as Johan Galtung (1969, p. 177) observes:

Inequality shows up in differential mortality rates between individuals in a district, between districts in a nation, and between nations in the international system – in a chain of interlocking feudal relationships. They [the lowest-ranking actors] are deprived because the structure deprives them of chances to organize and bring their power to bear against the top dogs, as voting power, bargaining power, violent power – partly because they are atomized and disintegrated, partly because they are overawed by all the authority the top dogs present.

The relationships between economic violence and human reproduction are many and complex. Nancy Rose Hunt (2008), in a haunting article about the history of rape in Congo, writes about finding repeated periods of low fertility that corresponded with violence in production: the 'red rubber' period of King Leopold II's forced extracted of rubber (1885–1908), and the Belgian colony (1908–1960), which practised a form of *corvée* or forced labour.

The foremost expression of violence in social reproduction is what happens to women in wartime. We assume that violence profoundly affects women's health in pregnancy and childbirth and that war impacts childbearing and child rearing, based on studies in Europe of the demographic changes wrought by the Second World War (Hill, 2004; Stein *et al.*, 1975). There is far less information for African civil wars, outside refugee camps (Bitar, 1998). Health services may be damaged or destroyed, left without supplies, deserted by frightened health workers and inaccessible because of heavy fighting, leaving women in labour without recourse to skilled assistance. War disrupts markets, and food insecurity may affect half or more of the population just when pregnancy and lactation make additional demands on the body. These physiological factors alone suggest that war endangers reproduction. The damaging effect of repeated population displacement leads one to expect falling birth rates in violent conflicts: the breakup of families, the disruption of formal and informal support networks in pregnancy and childbirth, and the physical burdens of carrying a child when on the run all tend to diminish the capacity and desire to procreate. Also there is some evidence that displacement related to conflict correlates with high rates of divorce (Laliberté *et al.*, 2003).

Violent conflicts may provoke contradictory reproductive desires in men and women – women may not wish to bring children into the world under these circumstances and men may wish to replace children lost because of war; and these contradictions may extend to differences between older and younger generations. The most vivid study of these opposing views was carried out by Jok Madut Jok (1998) in Sudan. His investigations among the Dinka in an emergency relief centre in what is now South Sudan, where war raged intermittently for 40 years, led him to conclude that families desire many children to replace the infants lost to war. But the recalcitrant young Dinka women who agree to conceive only reluctantly thwart family desires; as many as 35 per cent terminate pregnancy, resorting to unsafe clandestine abortion and risking infertility, infection or death. War creates a pronatalist environment, putting pressure on women, affecting their reproductive choices and resulting in the phenomenon known after the Second World War as the post-war baby boom. There is little feminist analysis of the phenomenon (Powell, 1987). Demographers have published almost no research on this development in the aftermath of other wars, although scattered observations suggest it might be widespread; surely it is complicated by war's outcomes (who was victor/who lost), by ethnic rivalry (desire to boost numbers) and by the reassertion of masculinist ideologies.

We have very little evidence about demographic trends during conflict. Of the three demographic parameters – fertility, mortality and migration – we have limited information on mortality (body counts are manipulated for propaganda purposes), approximate figures on migration (drawn from UN registration of refugees and internally displaced people), and almost nothing on fertility (and limited birth registration). We do not know how societies differ in terms of personal and political pressures to replace children who die during wars – or even produce fighters for long-term conflicts. Conventional micro-economic theory would have us believe that couples delay births in response to the uncertainty that typically follows the outbreak of war, the overthrow of political regimes, changes in the prevailing social order, sudden declines in income or increased unpredictability about future earnings. Temporary drops in fertility have been reported, sometimes followed by a fertility rebound as the severity of the conditions that precipitated the decline abate (Lindstrom and Berhanu, 1999). A review of 13 social crises from the seventeenth-century English Civil War to the fall of communism in Eastern Europe in the late twentieth century found marked falls in fertility arising from deferred female marriage, declining marital fertility, or both (Caldwell, 2004). A study of fertility trends around the time of the Khmer Rouge regime, under which one-quarter of the Cambodian population died, found a one-third decline of fertility during this regime, followed by a substantial baby boom after the fall of the Khmer Rouge (Heuveline and Poch, 2007).

Wars are of different types – from genocide, international battles and civil conflicts to terrorist attacks – and it seems logical that demographic trends would not respond in the same way to all campaigns. A subtle analysis of the impact of genocidal conflict on fertility in Rwanda found that women living in clusters with a higher proportion of sibling deaths were more likely than those living in clusters with a lower proportion of sibling deaths to marry later and have children later (Jayaraman *et al.*, 2009). The authors speculated that age at marriage was probably affected by changes in age structure and sex ratio following the genocide and by the breakdown of kinship in the case of women who lost their siblings. Delayed marriage may have contributed to a marked decline in fertility in Eritrea during the late 1990s period of military conflict with Ethiopia; more likely the overall decline was due to a fall in fertility within marriage (Blanc, 2004; Woldemicael, 2008). Although military conflict may not initiate a sustainable overall transition from high to low fertility, it might prompt short-term fertility changes among certain social groups or modify an on-going decline. One other study bears mention: based on evidence for higher total fertility in poorer countries during conflict, Urdal and Che (2013) postulate that armed conflict may contribute to high fertility levels through increased social insecurity, loss of reproductive health services including family planning, and lower female education.

One reason for the lack of data on fertility is the failure to collect vital and health statistics during conflict, a consequence of the breakdown of state services: already very low levels of birth registration fall even lower. In Congo fewer than one-third of births were registered in 2007; in Sierra Leone the figure was just over half in 2012. DRC law provides for free birth registration, but there is an administrative cost and the system is open to abuse from under-paid civil servants who administer it (World Vision, 2009). So even though most public services cannot be accessed without a birth certificate, most births are not registered.

The low priority assigned to biological reproduction in government budgets reflects a wider problem with appreciating the significance of social reproduction. To understand the status of the order of importance assigned to maternal and child health, we need to know the antecedents – the historical context – of the classic division of productive and reproductive labour as it evolved from the pre-industrial household to the modern workplace and the form that it took in colonial Africa.

The historical context of the division of labour

Socialised production in common workspaces, instituted with the advent of the industrial revolution in Europe, eclipsed households, which had been the centre of production and reproduction. Not only did factory work take production out of the home, but also services associated with social reproduction were gradually socialised (meaning they were commercialised, as in the introduction of restaurants), while biological reproduction, child rearing and other aspects of human reproduction remained in the home. The division of labour originally referred not to gender assignments but to the separation of work processes into several tasks, a basic organising principle of the assembly line for the purposes of saving time and reducing costs. Both women and men worked in factories and in the nascent service industry: productive labour was not the preserve of men. The reality of working-class lives in industrialising and urbanising Europe was that whole families – women, children, men and aged parents – worked for wages (formally or informally) and often continued to produce saleable commodities at home in order to survive (Humphries, 1991).[3] Only the wives and daughters of the new bourgeoisie or the old nobility were able to eschew the labour market; ironically these were the very women who could afford to hire wet nurses to suckle their infants and could thereby be freed from at least one requirement of child rearing. Gender entered the division of labour because most activities of biological and social reproduction were still tied to the home: childcare, laundry, housekeeping and so on were not socialised under capitalism until the late nineteenth century, although wealthy households employed servants privately to do this work.[4]

In modern times social reproduction, like population dynamics, has con-
formed to capitalist economic cycles. The narrative of social reproduction is the
tale of habits, routines and ordinaries; it is also the report of a dramatic shift in
the relative productive and reproductive contributions of women and men.
Clues to this historic reallocation of labour can be found in studies of the transformative period of the industrial revolution in England. In her study of prole-
tarianisation in late eighteenth- and early nineteenth-century England, Jane
Humphries (1990) demonstrates the significance of common rights to the livelihoods of women and children who were the primary exploiters of common
resources. She shows how the loss of those rights in the period of the enclosures
led to changes in women's economic position within the family. Before families
were swept into the urban workforce, women's income from the use of the
commons more than supplemented the casual labour of men. The loss of
common rights to enclosures, as landlords pushed peasants off the land and into
the cities, increased women's dependence on men. Nineteenth-century labour
laws further circumscribed women's income by limiting their opportunities for
better-paid work, and public policy delayed education for poor girls to the last
quarter of the nineteenth century, which curtailed their ability to contribute in
a growing industrial society.

The situation in nineteenth-century England may be compared with that in
many parts of colonial Africa where semi-proletarianisation took the form of the
husband/father working for wages, often in distant commercial enclaves, while
the wife/mother and children added to family subsistence by exploiting traditional rights to rural resources. European expropriation of African commons
through the marketisation and acquisition of land dispossessed women of these
resources – an uneven process that was most intense in settler colonies. This
spatial dispossession diminished and sometimes destroyed the collective spaces
of family life. Women traditionally depended on men for access to land use
rights, but now their reliance extended to remittances of wages. There were
other parallels between women's status in metropole and colony.

Despite the arguments of Mary Wollstonecraft, John Stuart Mill and others
for women's education and equality with men, the legal and moral standards of
nineteenth-century Britain, even before Queen Victoria's retrograde influence,
held women inferior to men, fit only to occupy the separate sphere of domesticity. The class inflection of this discriminatory attitude became increasingly
obvious as the industrial revolution enrolled more women in the waged labour
force. Although a 1772 ruling abolished slave holding in England and Wales, no
parallel act raised free women's status to that of men until the Equal Franchise
Act of 1928.[5] Missionaries and colonists carried their belief in the sexual division of labour to Africa.

British colonisation of West Africa began in 1787, when 400 Africans and
60 Europeans, mostly women, arrived at the foot of the Sierra Leone Mountains
in the company of a chaplain (Hole, 1896, p. 17; Land and Schocket, 2008);
this early settlement failed, but it was soon followed by others that did succeed.
The first two missionaries of the Church Missionary Society (CMS) went to

Sierra Leone in 1804 with their English wives (Harnes, 2014). The CMS, evan-gelical missionary agents of the Church of England, considered western ways of living in virtuous families as a key objective of imperial outreach: the Christian home embodied ideals for women of marriage, homemaking and motherhood, and the Church used it an example to the 'heathen' (Harnes, 2014). Through-out the nineteenth century colonisers and missionaries preached these middle-class ideals of womanhood, teaching Africans these models along with the catechism that incorporated the binary view that men's labour was productive and women's labour reproductive, that men belonged in the public sphere and women in the private domain.[6] The irony was that European women, though of the middle classes, lived in Africa with servants (paid for by missions) they could not afford at home; this attendance enabled some of them to assist their husbands in their work.[7]

The Belgians did not differ significantly from the British in their views of women; the difference was religion: Catholic priests were celibate. In Congo, nuns filled the adjunct roles of teachers and nurses. African women rarely quali-fied to assist them. It was claimed:

> The female gender, hardly liberated and still very imperfectly in a type of servitude which has chained or dulled the will of the black woman over centuries to make them appear little able to practice the position of teacher in an environment in which she will not be under close supervision and in which she will miss guidance and frequent advice.
>
> (quoted in Briffaerts, 2014, p. 38)

The missionaries' vision of the role of women within a Christian family (and consequently in a Christian marriage) did not deviate from Catholic conserva-tism; it included the moral duty to bring children into the world and to fulfil household duties. 'If we want to ensure numerous Catholic descendants in the future – we must now dedicate ourselves to the formation of good Catholic mothers' (quoted in Briffaerts, 2014, p. 38). The Belgians assumed that women would stop working once they had children, and they used this belief to justify their decision not to employ married mothers.

By the time of the Berlin Conference of 1884–1885, at which the major European powers negotiated and formalised claims to territory in Africa, Euro-peans had developed an ideology of ideal femininity to wedge the installation of the capitalist mode of production into colonial Africa. They used this ideal to justify paying low or no wages to women and children and to rationalise exter-nalising the costs of social reproduction. Missionary work sometimes conflicted with demands on colonial administrators to meet immediate labour require-ments: Europeans entertained demographic dreams of African women producing babies every year and contributing to rapid population growth, but they also expected women to work in the fields throughout their pregnancy. The colo-nists' need for labour was so great a priority that not only were men recruited (or compelled) to work in new industries, plantations and building sites, often far from home, but women also had to produce food and provide other kinds of services in and around their villages. Both men's and women's productive activities interfered with reproduction in eastern Congo to such an extent that levies of village manpower had to be capped.[8]

Colonial practice embodied the material indivisibility of production and reproduction, while maintaining that theoretically women's place was in the home. The British eventually codified the ideological split of production from social reproduction in colonial statutory law and rewrote customary law to suit their needs, embedding in it derogatory attitudes towards African women (Chanock, 1985). Among new provisions, the privatisation of communal land gave men new powers as head of household and weakened women's claims to land use rights. After independence, most African countries maintained, often with little modification, parts of customary law, called family law or personal law, which touch the lives of all women (Turshen, 2010). In Sierra Leone for instance, the constitution adopted in 1991 prohibits discriminatory laws, but customary law is exempt and women were not protected in matters of marriage, divorce and inheritance until the laws changed in 2007.

The common binary characterisation of production and reproduction is false for other reasons that intersectional analyses reveal. For example, the duality obscures the racist realities of slavery. In the slave regimes discussed in Chapter 2 above, the productive work of black women and men was interchangeable – men often did 'women's work' and vice versa – and even reproduction was subsumed under production (human beings bred for sale and profit). In the 1980s feminist historians describing women's labour in domestic slavery in Africa exposed the hypocrisy of capitalist ideologies of race and gender (Robertson and Klein, 1983): what women could and should do, what suited women best and what was harmful to their physical and mental health were different for European wives and African slaves.

European ideas of a woman's place took hold in Africa and reshaped many traditions such as female paramount chiefs in Sierra Leone and women long-distance traders in Congo. These ideas, adapted and transformed, are still serviceable in the neocolonial era. Multinational companies hire women as unskilled labourers in a temporary workforce on the assumption that they are more docile than men towards authority and that their primary interests remain in family and home. In effect the companies are recruiting 'femininity' as related to a set of meanings and are shifting the gender stereotype away from home and traditional family production; the new, reconstituted femininity is a set of characteristics – dexterity, docility, tolerance and low pay – that could apply to women or men (Hennessy, 2006). Capital thus accumulates profit by both transgressing and deploying the norms of civil society.

The political ecology of violent social reproduction

Most comparative research aimed at developing a gender perspective on social reproduction previously focused on welfare policies. In these studies the social norm was the male worker and the female caregiver, and policy-makers planned welfare programmes for dependent women at home. Some European states designed social policies to help women function in their dual roles as paid and unpaid workers, for example by providing childcare arrangements to assist working mothers. Since the 1990s the market has come to be the primary source of welfare services. Although neoliberal economic policies are everywhere pushing more and more women into the workforce, families are called upon to take greater responsibility for meeting their own needs by organising care at home or paying out of their own pocket for commercial services. Other social policies – for example, many cash transfer programmes in Latin America where states share welfare responsibility with families – emphasise child wellbeing, although some place heavy responsibility on mothers for good parenting and child rearing practices such as regular medical care and school attendance. These conditional grant programmes presuppose the existence of health and education services, and they do not take women's waged work into consideration.

Day-to-day reproduction encompasses the daily regeneration of workers so they can return to work the next day; women must provide cooked meals, clean clothing, bath water, emotional comfort and sex to fulfil the conditions of reproduction (Robertson and Klein, 1983, p. 9). Reproductive violence in daily life occurs when the cost of food and water rise (in terms of labour and cash exchanges), when water and electricity supplies are intermittent in towns and non-existent in rural areas, when crime-ridden residential areas lack physical security, when slum landlords extort rent or municipalities make squats insecure, when there is no protection from fires or mudslides or floods, when transport to and from shops and workplaces is inadequate and unsafe and costly. Low wages and measly payments for crops drive this violence.

Analysts usually frame the interaction of the reproductive and productive spheres in terms of employers' gender discrimination (based on women's inescapable duties at home) or violations of women's reproductive rights. The litany of employers' reproductive abuses includes requirements for virginity and pregnancy tests, forced contraceptive use and sterilisation, pregnancy as a cause of dismissal from work (still an issue in the United States[9]), denial of reproductive health services, and demands for sexual services. These analysts consider violence when the topic is domestic violence, family violence and intimate partner violence, and they may include instances when this violence tracks into the workplace. Yet for Bennholdt-Thomson (1988, p. 113), 'It is precisely this mutual relationship [of paid and unpaid work] that contains the moment of structural violence'. She discerns a circular trajectory: violence (for example, the force of law and religious ordinances) maintains the low status of women, which in turn determines domestic labour, and housework duties govern paid employment.

The violence of social reproduction extends well beyond this limited list of employers' abuses. Poverty requires people to sell not only their labour power on a daily basis but their bodies, their health and their dignity. At the level of extreme poverty, a pregnancy can precipitate descent to absolute poverty and lead to death, suicide, madness, beggary or total dependence (Verhaegen, 1990, p. xxi). Extreme hunger mobilises all a person's energy, isolates her from her group and imposes its own code of conduct: eat at whatever price including violence towards one's kin (Verhaegen, 1990, p. xxiii).

The ways in which violence in production has repercussions in the sphere of social reproduction stem from the organisation of work – work being all of the labour that human beings undertake every day in countless settings. Heterogeneous societies organise workers according to their race, sex and class. Lindisfarne and Neale (2013) see class as prior, causal and the motor for social change; they argue that those in power manipulate gender, just as they control race, to support class inequality. Evidence for Lindisfarne and Neale's position comes from both current and historical events. For a current example: Cambodian women workers told investigators that they were afraid to have children because the insecurity of short-term contracts on which they work, sometimes as short as one month, meant that if they became pregnant, they risked losing their job, which they could not afford (Tolson, 2014). In another study, Melissa Wright (2006, p. 39) discovered differences in surveillance of male and female factory workers in China, where employers' concern about pregnancy interrupting two-year work contracts justified invasive medical procedures for women workers.

Why do some social scientists see production and reproduction as antagonistic: why is motherhood a constraint on labour force participation? Lewis (1982, p. 264), in a study of the incompatibility of motherhood and labour force participation, found that education has a far greater impact on desired family size than employment status among women in Abidjan, Côte d'Ivoire. Fertility does not keep women from working; she found no evidence that women are voluntarily limiting their family size in order to work. On the contrary, she concluded that lack of employment opportunities kept some women out of the labour force.

For historical testimony of gender manipulation to support class inequality we turn to studies of slave plantation economies, which adapted reproduction to the exigencies of production, the diverse labour regimes dictated by different crops and technologies, and the available supply of labour. Richard Dunn (2014) describes twice as many deaths as births among slaves on a sugar plantation in Jamaica in the late 1700s to early 1800s: plantation agents told investigators that to increase the survival of new-borns they lightened the work burdens of pregnant slave women. But they also punished women who miscarried, blaming them for the deaths of their infants; they sent these women to the workhouse or solitary confinement.[10] Jamaican planters in that era did not want births because they could purchase fresh supplies of slaves for less than the cost of raising young children. The ratio of births to deaths was reversed on a Virginian tobacco and grain plantation in the mid-1800s; this plantation bred slaves for sale and became one of Virginia's many slave exporters to other states.[11] Over the course of the nineteenth century abolitionists succeeded in interrupting the transatlantic slave trade, reducing imports of new slaves. In Virginia, some planters responded to the demands of the expanding American slave economy by organising high levels of births.

Hennessy (2006, p. 389) believes that capitalism does not require any particular cultural values to assemble its labour force and accumulate surplus value. It carves out a modernising path that is fundamentally amoral, pursuing profit by tracking down surplus labour however and wherever it can. It co-opts traditional cultural forms or symbolic values that civil society has upheld for generations or dissolves and replaces them by new subjects and new norms. In African societies that were somewhat homogeneous, the organising principle of workers was less according to race, sex and class than position in a hierarchy that extended from the king or chief down to slaves. Rank and age dictated domination and submission and conferred authority to assign work. Labour supplies determined farm size in the absence of mechanisation, yet there is no evidence to support a claim that slave populations increased through genetic reproduction. Claude Meillassoux (1983, pp. 51–52) argues that slave women's fertility was lower than expected and that they aborted their pregnancies or killed their infants at birth, presumably because 'the conditions of existence of slave women and the social climate within which they lived did not encourage them to procreate or to keep their children'.

Enslavement was by definition a violent process (discussed in detail in Chapter 2 above); Frantz Fanon and Walter Rodney have said the same of colonialism. Colonial conquest was concurrent with the spread of capitalism and immediately attended by a preoccupation with African birth rates, inextricably linked to concerns about labour supplies. The histories of politics and production are thick with accounts from the conquerors and colonisers of Africa, with (often caustic) critiques written by Africans themselves, and with voluminous research by students of African affairs. The history of what Fernand Braudel (1977, p. 4) calls material life is not as well developed, perhaps because, as he says, 'it is not noble or magisterial, that is, exalted history'. The modern African history of ordinary violence – recurrent mental or physical aggression occurring between closely related people – is just beginning to be written (Bouju and de Bruijn, 2014).

Neoliberalism and the conditions of social reproduction

Social reproduction is intimately tied to human security, but neoliberal governance frameworks do violence to human economic and social rights by prioritising and privileging the needs of capital (Bakker, 2004). Two aspects of social reproduction are germane to this discussion of violence: the provision of care and the reproduction of the labour force. Care, it is argued, is a social good that sustains and reproduces society and underpins all development progress. Yet women perform the vast majority of care work at home for free. This gender division of labour has profound implications for women's daily lives and their status in society. Care impacts the institutions of family, state and market, which all stand to lose if arrangements for care are unsustainable. Ideally care work should be divided fairly between the sexes as well as between households and the state, which plays a critical role in negotiating the public/private boundaries of production and reproduction and policing the limits of citizenship (Bakker, 2003, p. 82). Neoliberal fiscal policies shift the risks of economic structural adjustment down to communities and households, forcing economically and socially vulnerable women to absorb the shocks. It is questionable whether this gender order is stable or will result in social dislocations as an increasing number of financial crises mark the global economy.

Current conditions of social reproduction in Africa can be described as substandard, a reflection on highly unequal societies with a majority of the population living in poverty. Lack of jobs is the main contributor to these conditions, a consequence of the failure of the neoliberal development model to create decent work. Wealth continues to leave the continent in the forms of capital flight and human exodus, debt repayment and natural resource outflows. In an era of abusive transfer pricing and tax havens, national treasuries do not benefit from the collection of taxes and royalties that could be budgeted to pay for social services. Yet the need for social protection is great: the World Bank (2014) estimates that at the end of 2011, 70 per cent (616.6 million) of the sub-Saharan African population (874.8 million) subsisted on less than US$2 a day. While only 28 per cent of the global population is covered by comprehensive social protection, the figure in sub-Saharan Africa is one-third of that: a mere 8 per cent of the African labour force is potentially eligible for contributory or non-contributory benefits (ILO, 2014, p. xxii). Fewer than 20 per cent of Africans aged 60 and above have access to any form of pension; in most countries that figure is under 10 per cent (Kalusopa *et al.*, 2012). Public social security expenditure (excluding health expenditure) in sub-Saharan Africa is 2.8 per cent of GDP, the lowest in the world (Omilola and Kaniki, 2014, p. 33). An estimated 80 per cent of Africans are excluded from access to adequate health care.[12]

In industrial countries, personal income taxes, payroll taxes and corporate taxes are the main sources of national revenue. But in African countries, where 80 per cent of the population lives on less than $2 a day, few pay income tax; only 20 per cent of the labour force is employed in the formal sector (Goldberg, 2012) and payroll tax collections are of course low; corporations use accounting tricks like transfer pricing, and tax avoidance is common. As a result, governments have little money to support a social protection floor – the set of basic social security guarantees that should ensure access to essential health care and to basic income security. Given that an employer's purpose is to maximise profitability and productivity, it is not surprising that social insurance arrangements, such as unemployment insurance, contributory pensions and medical aid, are only as generous as workers can negotiate; but only a quarter of the 20 per cent of formally employed African workers are organised in trade unions (Kalusopa *et al.*, c.2011, p. 26). Unions play a central role in the administration of formal social security schemes through tripartite bodies composed of government, organised labour and employers in countries such as Ghana, Kenya, Sierra Leone and Zambia.

These figures hide the even more drastic scenario for African women, whose participation rate in formal employment is lower than that of men. Nine in ten rural and urban workers have informal jobs in Africa and most of them are women and youth (African Development Bank, 2013). Not only are workers in the informal sector without employer social protection, but also public social security schemes exclude the informal sector (Omilola and Kaniki, 2014, p. 36). Within this picture, effective provision of maternity protection shrinks to minuscule proportions: only 28 per cent of women in employment worldwide – and only 15 per cent of women in Africa – are effectively protected through maternity cash benefits, which provide some income security during the final stages of pregnancy and after childbirth; the absence of a regular income forces many women to return to work prematurely (ILO, 2014, p. xxiii). The African data are particularly striking, given the high fertility rates and the high proportion of children in the population (children under 15 make up 42 per cent of Africa's population) (ILO, 2014, p. 13).

African women in need of social protection must fall back on the extended family system that is traditionally responsible for the care of children, the aged and the infirm. The circularity of this logic is inescapable: since the vast majority of care work is a female responsibility, in effect women have recourse to themselves. Entrepreneurial women in the informal sector have evolved unofficial arrangements for social protection. Mutual funds and communal levies are common traditional forms of sharing risks. Traditional savings mechanisms (called *likelembas* in Congo, *osusu* in Sierra Leone) provide income that can be used in times of illness, unemployment or pregnancy. However, most of these arrangements focus on specific events and do not offer broad coverage. The schemes thus provide very little protection for individuals and families facing recurring crises. And even these fragile schemes fall apart once violent conflict erupts, communities are scattered and there is no longer the mutual trust on which shared savings are premised, which is especially true in civil wars when neighbour turns on neighbour. In the next section we consider the depredations wrought by armed conflict on the circumstances of social reproduction.

Social reproduction in wartime

After physical assault and personal injury, the most depressing effect of violence on social reproduction in conflict zones is food insecurity, not just the immediate disruption of markets and supplies as agricultural production dwindles leading to hunger and malnutrition, but also the long-term alteration of the production of crops resulting from changes in land use patterns and land rights (Jackson, 2005, p. 157). The focus on food places people's daily suffering in the foreground (Shepler, 2011, p. 44); food insecurity diminishes individual capacity for labour (Jackson, 2005, p. 156), both productive and reproductive. When fighting, lack of security, ruined roads, absent transport, landmines and fear combine to limit routine movement, cultivation regresses to less labour-intensive techniques and to crops that have low nutritional value as well as low market value (Jaspers and O'Callaghan, 2010). Rural households may prefer root crops that they can leave in the ground during periods of insecurity over more lucrative fruits or vegetables that need to be harvested when ripe and are easily looted (Rockmore, 2012). Homesteads must calculate how much of the crop they will lose to armed combatants. In Congo, the CNDP regularly collected 10 kg of beans, sorghum or corn per household per harvest to feed its soldiers, and in Shabunda, South Kivu, women were routinely forced to hand over as much as 50 per cent of the fuel wood or foodstuffs they transported between their fields and the marketplace (Laudati, 2013). Unsafe conditions affect the financing and purchase of supplies needed for farming as well as the sale of produce (Vlassenroot and Raeymaekers, 2008). The intensification of farming on plots close to homesteads leads to soil degradation and poor harvests. Food insecurity affects social reproduction for the entire household, but the focus here is on women who are the majority of farmers, first on the immediate effects of conflict on their nutritional status and then on the long-term consequences for their access to farmland.

In Congo, between 1996 and 2004, general food production decreased by 12 per cent, vegetable production dropped by 42 per cent and cereal production by 33 per cent (Vlassenroot et al., 2006). The DRC as a whole is a food-deficit country that imported up to 30 per cent of its food needs in 2012 (Weijs et al., 2012, p. 7). A large part of the population remains food insecure and dependent on food aid. The immediate effect of food insecurity is seen in high rates (over 50 per cent) of anaemia[13] in pregnant women; more generally, almost 20 per cent of women have a body mass index below what is considered normal, evidence of chronic malnutrition (Ministère du Plan et Macro International, 2008, p. 27). Although the capacity of famine to curtail procreation has long been documented, the negative effects of hunger and malnutrition on conception and live births are less well established (Stein et al., 1975).

A similar state of affairs has been documented in Sierra Leone. Seven years after the end of the civil war, Sierra Leone was ranked among the five countries with the highest global hunger index score, underlining the critical nutrition problems that people continue to face (Denney et al., 2014). Susan Shepler (2011, p. 44) describes what the people ate during the conflict while hiding in the bush; people lived on what they could eat raw – bananas and bush yams – as they were unable to light a cooking fire for fear of attracting attention. This diet differed from what rebels ate (stolen meat every day) and what politicians ate (foreign aid-donated food, and everything to excess). She interviewed a woman in Rogbom in 2001 who said, 'When the rebels took over our village, life was very hard. They made us work for them. We were totally cut off from the market. Try to imagine: we didn't even have salt to cook with!' (quoted in Shepler, 2011, p. 44). Sierra Leone is a notably fertile country in which it is not easy to create a famine. During the long civil war, farmers suffered from loss of crops to soldiers who regularly pilfered or expropriated produce, yet for a long time security problems were more conspicuous in the headlines than nutritional problems. In 2013, 50 per cent of rural women had anaemia, meaning their diets were deficient in iron and B vitamins; the highest rates (70 per cent) were found in Pujehun District (Statistics Sierra Leone, 2013).

Land use rights are of particular concern to women in wartime as they may lose their rights with the death of the men through whom access is secured or if, in the aftermath of war, land is privatised and male heads of household become the titleholders and decide to sell. Where access to land is the main driver of local conflict, as it was in Congo, rebels regard land as an asset and local claims as obstacles. As a result, war amplifies the effects of limited access to land (Vlassenroot and Raeymaekers, 2008, p. 165). Land or property disputes related to inter-communal grievances are often expressed through the language of indigenous land rights; these conflicts, which are frequently inter-generational, challenge customary authority and result in violent population displacement.

In Sierra Leone, two main land tenure systems exist, one rooted in customary laws and tradition, which consider women to be perpetual minors, and the other based on the statutory freehold system, which is largely applied in urban areas (ActionAid, 2012). Few women own land, and they generally have less access to land than men through inheritance, gifting, renting and purchasing (Sturgess and Flower, 2013). Both discriminatory traditions and lack of judicial recourse are traceable to the lack of a strong protective legal framework (Tarawallie, 2013). Currently, women are losing the land they work due to land grabs, which are a new threat with the post-war influx of multinational corporations. Between 2009 and 2013, foreign investors are thought to have leased more than 20 per cent of the country's total arable land for large-scale industrial agriculture (Tarawallie, 2013). Belgian and French investors have secured prime farmland for rubber and oil palm plantations, despite local opposition (Oakland Institute, 2012).

Land rights arrangements in Congo are more complicated, as one might expect, and in many parts of the eastern provinces, land has been a source of conflict for many years. Before the colonial conquest, stratified patriarchal social structures, which regulated access to land on the basis of communal territorial ownership, marked large parts of the region. Those patriarchal social structures controlled women's access to land through their male guardians. Although colonialism introduced changes that institutionalised the link between ethnic identity and land access within the political structures of the state, it also intensified local competition for land with the importation of a Rwandan labour force. The effect was to politicise and exacerbate conflicts over disputed access to land (Vlassenroot and Huggins, 2004).

The Belgians introduced a double system of property rights that led to manipulation and expropriation. Next to the customary system they implemented a statutory system for white settlers, which enabled the *colons* to establish their plantations. After independence, the confusion of coexisting customary and statutory land access systems was exacerbated by President Mobutu's introduction in 1966 of the Bakajika land law nationalising all land; he reinforced state ownership in 1973 and discarded customary law, which meant that most peasants no longer had any legal rights to land occupied under customary rules.

Traditional authorities, who already held positions of political or economic power, could appropriate any land not yet titled, and they became the privileged intermediaries for the sale of land (Vlassenroot and Huggins, 2004).

Rural women are among the principal agricultural productive forces in the DRC, where they contribute as much as 50 per cent to the agricultural sector and ensure 75 per cent of production in the subsistence economy, yet they suffer discrimination regarding their access to land and control of resources (Women for Women, 2014). Married women obtain access to land through their husbands; divorced and unmarried women must depend on the disposition of their brothers. In the *Bwassa* system, women may lease land (typically paying US$100 for half a hectare) under a shared farming contract that requires them to work two days a week without pay for the plot's owner (Women for Women, 2014, p. 5).

Since the official end of the war, no government efforts to resolve the land crisis in eastern Congo have considered women's rights. Despite the government of Sierra Leone's stated policies and legislation, women still have limited opportunities to own land and land reform has made slow progress. A National Land Policy expected to revolutionise land ownership, use and management in Sierra Leone was drafted in 2014.

Social reproduction and resource extraction

The foregoing analysis opens up a number of specific questions about social reproduction and resource extraction in Congo, Sierra Leone and Tanzania: questions about reproductive labour in conflict zones and peaceful places, about wartime food production and marketing, and about agents of the state (regular or irregular) in relation to social reproduction. Chapter 3 above contains a general description of women's productive activities in mining in the three countries; here attention turns to women's reproductive activities in mining. No single description of social reproduction fits all mine sites since they vary so much in scale and organisation. In apartheid South Africa, male miners were prohibited from bringing their wives to large-scale, corporate installations; they lived in single-sex hostels and relied for the services of social reproduction on 'mine marriages' (homosexual relationships, see Harries, 1990), on extramarital relationships with local village women or on prostitutes (Campbell, 1997). Artisanal and small-scale prospectors lived in their villages or, if they were migrants, in temporary accommodation like guesthouses. At the artisanal mining projects considered here, small villages spring up to house and service the workers, who often move from site to site searching for better returns on their labour. The key to the expansion of mine site villages is the miners' need for services and their ability to pay for them.

The account of sexual experimentation in Tanzanian mining areas by Deborah Fahy Bryceson, Jesper Bosse Jønsson and Hannelore Verbrugge (2013, p. 37) is striking: they find large-scale migration of women who are in search of a better standard of living as well as personally advantageous cohabiting arrangements that fall outside traditional constraints; 'removed from a rural sense of propriety and communal concerns, women gain autonomy in decision-making over their body and feel less circumscribed about sex'. Women's economic activities around Tanzanian mine sites include alcohol sales (barmaids, restaurant bar managers, brewers); trade (cloth, food); mining; services (pharmacists, hair stylists); and farming. Women's economic standing varies with the commitment of men they become attached to: women on their own have the lowest annual income while married women have the highest; in between are women with boyfriends and in polygamous marriages (Bryceson *et al.*, 2014, p. 92).

In the Tanzanian case it appears that both women and men regard reproductive activities, not excluding sexual relationships, as an integral part of their productive lives. In Congo and Sierra Leone, women's reproductive contributions are more severely used and abused by men (and sometimes other women). During intense periods of conflict, fewer Congolese or Sierra Leonean women in their reproductive prime voluntarily migrated alone to the mines where they ran the risk of contracting sexually transmitted infections (including HIV) and becoming targets of violence.

Most of what we know about the uses and abuses of women's reproductive labour in armed struggle comes from testimony before truth and reconciliation commissions and reports of interviews with women and girls who were abducted and forced to serve one side or the other during conflict. From the *décennie noire*, the 1990s period of Islamist insurgency in Algeria, came this account:

> In the terrorists' camp, I lived in hell. I awoke at dawn to start cleaning, washing, cooking, fetching firewood and water. I nursed the sick and served the wives of the terrorists, the legal ones they called 'free women'. Every night the terrorists visited me, taking their turns. They forced me to have sex several times a night. During my six months' captivity I was raped by about 50 dirty, stinking, brutal, violent men.... The rest of the night, to keep me from running away, they bound my wrists and ankles with wire and took away my clothes.
> (Chréa Mériem, March 1998, as told to Belloula, 2000, p. 115)

There is another side to these stories that reveals the attractions of war to adolescent girls and boys – the excitement, adventure, an idealistic cause like community defence, the chance to run away from home and escape life-binding traditions, travel to new places, the camaraderie, and chances for undreamed-of power conferred by the possession of firearms. Chris Coulter (2009) writes about this aspect of some girls' experiences with the RUF rebels of Sierra Leone: they joined up and lived better lives – more food, nice clothing (all looted) – than in their poor villages. Not everyone was a victim lacking agency; when men were away, women were in charge of their compound and sent information, supplies and even soldiers on mission. In Congo, wives of FARDC soldiers have been known to loot humanitarian sites, to be the principal traders in the hemp trade in both South and North Kivu and responsible for trading their husbands' illegally caught fish at local Ituri markets (Laudati, 2013). The binary of victim/

perpetrator is often false, especially in civil conflict, which is much more com-plicated than that.

We know less about the experiences of women and girls in villages occupied by combatants, whether irregular militia or government brigades. Reports to the UN Security Council following its resolutions on the wars in Congo repeatedly describe the control exercised by armed groups over natural resource exploitation, but always in terms of the income derived from sales of minerals and from multiple forms of taxation on the local community; the UN's purpose was to document the way in which the natural resource trade enabled armed groups to survive. Although the UN (2008) acknowledges that troops looted food stocks, they do not describe women's unpaid forced labour such as the pounding, grinding and cooking of cassava, making it into bread (Laudati, 2013). The journalist Colette Braeckman (2004) described the gold mining village of Kamituga in South Kivu, which was under the control of RCD Goma: while the diggers were men, it was women who pulverised the rock to expose the gold flakes. Women received $1 per day for this work in 2004, and they could earn a second dollar if they prostituted themselves at night. Braeckman (2004) wrote of girls pregnant at 13 and delivering by Caesarean section because the immature pelvis is too small for vaginal birth; she also noted that no HIV programme existed in the community. She quoted a market trader in Bunyakiri, where Mai Mai combatants confronted RCD soldiers:

> When we pass through the soldiers' barricades, whether or not we agree to be paid, we will be raped by one lot or another…. It's because of this that we don't dare go to the fields, that our pastures are abandoned.
>
> (Braeckman, 2004, p. 15)

Because extreme rape was one of the horrible experiences of atrocities commit-ted during the civil war in Sierra Leone, feminists in the global North were alert to reports of an epidemic of rape coming from Congo; they linked rape to illegal mining of coltan that funded the wars, noting that the highest rates of rape occurred in the mining districts of the eastern provinces (Peterman *et al.*, 2011). Many claims have been made about the relationship of rape to illegal mining in Congo. Eve Ensler (2011), founder of the V-Project, asserts a link between the two as follows:

> Extraction and transportation of these minerals are labor-intensive pro-cesses and the armed groups in eastern Congo use sexual violence as a bru-tally effective (and cheap) weapon of terror for controlling the civilian population, gaining compliant labor, and maintaining access to the mines and trade routes.

The specific example V-Day gives is this:

> In the infamous Bisie mines of Walikale controlled by the 85th Battalion of the Congolese army, soldiers guarding the sites steal ore from the miners

and intimidate rival tradesmen. They force civilians to dig minerals for them, set up roadblocks, collect illegal taxes from the local diggers, rape women and torture their husbands if they resist.

(Ensler, 2011)

Paul Kirby (2012, p. 188) calls this extractive sexual violence, which he describes as

a more limited instrumentalist violence deployed as part of resource extraction strategies, and co-existing in war economies with parallel structures of taxation, relying partially on rape as part of a package with other forms of violence to coerce civilians into cooperation.

Villagers were working these mine sites before the conflict started and women were an important part of the local labour force in both direct production of minerals and in reproductive activities that allowed the mines and miners to function. The influx of armed troops intent on exploiting these situations to pocket at least half of the output placed women and their households in danger. Those who did not or could not flee were caught up in forced labour. Acts of rape were possibly more dependent on military discipline than on any strategic plan to coerce labour (Baaz and Stern, 2013). The Kivus are a node in a regional network of political identities, and in a recurring sequence armed groups recycle through the districts with too little oversight from any central authority.

Poor women, desperate to earn money that will enable them to feed their families, find themselves endangered in whatever work they undertake in conflict zones. The epigraph at the head of this chapter describes the lengths to which women must go to survive (Rothenberg, 2014, p. 13). Rebel groups engage in a diverse range of activities beyond mineral extraction, which include trade in cannabis, charcoal and timber, the collection of arbitrary taxes, theft of cattle and generally looting the population (Laudati, 2013). For example, the CNDP controlled the lucrative charcoal trade in Virunga National Park; the UN (2008) estimated, on the basis of interviews with Kingi market traders, that the CNDP collected $36,000 per month by charging charcoal porters a $5 tax (nearly 30 per cent) for every 30 kg bag. The charcoal market in Goma is valued at $30 million a year since Rwanda passed a law forbidding charcoal production. Virunga park rangers, trying to protect gorillas and their habitat, have run afoul of the army for attempting to shut down charcoal production. Women who make charcoal are caught in the crossfire, and in 2007 rangers arrested about 50 women involved in making charcoal in the park (Lovgren, 2007). Nearly all the charcoal from Virunga National Park was sold to the wives of high-ranking FARDC officers within the 22nd Sector (Laudati, 2013).

The FARDC, as an arm of the state, is not just a predatory force; the examples above show that military and civilian actors do cooperate. The competition between soldiers and civilians may be unequal, but the poverty of the rank-and-file and their immediate commanders forces them to interact with the larger society of eastern Congo. The next section explores further what part the state plays in social reproduction, which has been warped by conflict, and how gender roles have changed under neoliberal rules.

The role of the state in social reproduction

In negotiating the public/private boundaries of production and reproduction, a state that relinquishes to the private sector its obligations to fulfil UN human rights conventions on social provisioning in effect mediates women's workloads and labour time as well as their reproductive lives. Herein lies the violence of social reproduction and its inevitable link to production. Violent war economies aggravate and amplify all the consequences.

States cannot easily resist the demands of neoliberal capitalist requirements that are facilitated by the General Agreement on Trade in Services (GATS) of the World Trade Organisation (WTO); GATS seeks progressively to liberalise the provision of public services in health care and education (Smith *et al.*, 2003). With its goal of opening services to market forces and facilitating competition, GATS exploits post-war chaos.[14] The agreement gives capital rights to enter and exit new markets and territories in the unproven belief that enhanced market competition will lead to increased efficiency and growth (Bakker and Silvey, 2008, p. 23). In reality the WTO is shifting the risks of structural adjustment and socio-economic restructuring downwards to the subnational and local levels of government (often without increasing the resources or capacity of local administrations to assume new tasks) and down to communities and households, particularly economically and socially vulnerable women who are the system's implicit shock absorbers (Bakker, 2003, p. 82). Women suffer in poor households that are marginalised and excluded when water, utilities, health care, public transport and other public services become subject to market-determined user fees.

All three of the states considered here have poor records of social provisioning, despite being signatories to the UN Convention on Economic, Social and Cultural Rights that guarantees the right to an adequate standard of living. The wartime record of Congo and Sierra Leone is even poorer, judging by the statistics cited earlier of hunger, malnutrition and high mortality. Experts from the global North usually attribute those poor records to mismanagement (read corruption), while they portray the colonial record as a positive contribution to people's wellbeing. Yet it was principally the appalling colonial history of these conflict-laden regions and their wretched post-independence political economy that accounts for the poor social service infrastructure and the deficiently trained social service workforce.

When the Belgians left Congo in 1959, each of the 135 territories with 50,000–150,000 inhabitants had a rural medico-surgical centre, a surgical section, a maternity ward and a prenatal and infant welfare advice centre; each was also served by two western doctors, one of whom was responsible for visiting scattered rural dispensaries. Also in 1959, there were 3,041 hospitals equipped with 86,599 beds; the medical staff included 5,663 Africans and 2,722 non-Africans, including 703 non-African doctors (the averages of both beds and doctors per 100,000 inhabitants were well above African standards at the time). Note that not one single Congolese had qualified as a physician. Following the turmoil of independence, the UN sought to remedy the failure of Belgium to educate and train Congolese professionals, and the WHO recruited an important contingent of doctors, many from Haiti (Jackson, 2014). Services began to decline in the 1970s; by the mid-1990s less than 20 per cent of the population had access to health services (Kisangani and Bobb, 2010, p. 214). By 2012 there were only 290 district hospitals (0.430 per 100,000 people), 11 provincial hospitals (0.016 per 100,000 people) and 1.1 doctors per 100,000 inhabitants. Congo had now fallen well behind its neighbours.

The gap is partially and poorly filled by the informal medical sector – a mishmash of quackery, adulterated medications and the turning of hospitals into markets where the ill must purchase items individually at inflated prices – the services and materiel of care that the state has failed to provide. Ndaywel è Nziem (2002, pp. 143ff., my paraphrase) gives this description of the Cliniques universitaires de Lovanium in Kinshasa in the mid-1990s, once government support ceased:

> The facility was too far from the popular part of town – it took three buses to get there – and it was surrounded by a slum filled with people in need of health care but too poor to pay for the services at the *cliniques*. It has to be said that the staff didn't help the situation – the doctors (who earned between $30 and $50 per month) and nurses (whose monthly salary was between $3 and $13) opened private fly-by-night offices in their homes and recruited patients from the population they examined at the *cliniques*. Worse, some took money invested by private companies for the care of their workers and built palatial private residences in the city or they bought more wives. None could afford to give up an affiliation with the *cliniques* or the university, despite rarely attending or practising. The female nurses helped turn the *cliniques* into a marketplace. Every item patients needed was for sale at the hospital. In addition, the nurses prepared food at home and sold it to staff and patients – everything from homemade jams and beignets to jewellery, cosmetics and baby clothes.[15]

Ndaywel è Nziem (2002, p. 168) goes on to say that people who didn't pay the full bill were not allowed to withdraw corpses from the morgue for burial and women who gave birth were not permitted to leave the hospital. He laments this dehumanisation of the medical system: the gallop for profit to the detriment of the sick, the competition between staff members so damaging to solidarity and collaboration, and the practice of turning patients away – towards one's own private practice.

Deterioration from within has been met by destruction from without. Armed attacks on hospitals continued long after the supposed end of hostilities. In 2013 the UN documented 42 incursions in eastern Congo in which medical supplies and equipment were looted, affecting health care in North Kivu and Orientale Province. They attributed 17 cases to ADF, nine to FARDC, three to FRPI and two to M23. The UN urged the national army to take disciplinary measures against FARDC elements that attacked hospitals, as stipulated in the directive of 3 May 2013.[16]

The situation is, if anything, worse in Sierra Leone, which had an inferior health structure to begin with.[17] The insidious effects of internal corruption, coupled with the 1980s World Bank conditional loan policy that imposed user fees on public services, fostered mistrust among patients and low morale among staff. After more than a decade of war, and despite promises of foreign aid to rebuild, the combination reduced health care to such an extent that the country was unable to respond to the 2014–2015 Ebola epidemic. Fees demanded of patients at every health facility and for every procedure deliberately discouraged women from seeking the health care they needed, which accounts in part for Sierra Leone's high ratios of maternal mortality. On 27 April 2010 the government launched an initiative to provide free health care services for pregnant women, lactating mothers and children under five years old. Expectations were high, but the broken health system was ill prepared for the overwhelming demand, and the resources allocated were inadequate (Amnesty International, 2011, p. 5).

> The launch of the Free Care policy triggered a massive influx of women and children, who could then not be appropriately cared for. Many drugs ran out in a number of places; consumables completely ran out in most places; patients waited too long in difficult conditions. Months after the launch, water and electricity; equipment; ambulances; and the lack of blood banks are still major problems nationwide. Target beneficiaries continue to be charged in many places for services and drugs. Moreover, many factors that drive maternal mortality and morbidity remain unaddressed, such as unsafe abortions, female genital mutilation, early marriage, and the lack of sexual and reproductive education.
>
> (Amnesty International, 2011, p. 5)

Notice the limited scope of these services, which in effect redefine women as a narrow category (a vessel for childbearing), clawing back the progress made at 1994 International Conference on Population and Development and the 1995 Fourth World Women's Conference held in Beijing (Helen Olsen, personal communication, 11 December 2013). In a peculiar twist for a country with high levels of poverty and unemployment, the free care initiative eliminates the services of traditional birth attendants, criminalising their activities and stripping them of the ability to practise their craft and earn a living (McGough, 2015).

In Congo and Sierra Leone, so much of the state and private sector infrastructure was destroyed in the civil wars that rebuilding health and education services and the economy that sustained them is a massive task. Although there is much talk about public health as a public good and the need to invest in basic health services (Smith *et al.*, 2003; World Bank, 2007), foreign aid is still directed to the private sector and to privatising what is left of public infrastructure. In Sierra Leone's attempts to address widespread malnutrition, Denney *et al.* (2014, p. 12) found that capacity development focuses overwhelmingly on the individual and organisational levels as opposed to the system level; notably, procurement and delivery chains are focused in this narrow way, contributing little to rebuilding the government's capacity. Targeting increased resources, skills and knowledge is 'generally cheaper and less time-consuming' than 'addressing incentives or politics and power' for the 14 agencies involved (ten from the private sector and four from the United Nations) (Denney *et al.*, 2014, p. 12).

Like other countries struggling with the need for outside help in a complex global health landscape, Congo confronts a multiplicity of actors and partners (Zinnen, 2012). Despite a desire to better the health scene, Véronique Zinnen (2012) noted a lack of national leadership, recurrent problems of governance, and resistance from some partners to adopt the principles of primary health care, which acted as a continual brake on progress. Donors themselves controlled a majority of projects dependent on foreign aid. Ties between the Ministry of Public Health and donors are weak, and donor-financed projects seem to proceed as parallel or satellite structures. Such projects are responsible for the disorganisation of public health services.

Conclusions: women under siege

Personal aspects of reproduction are seemingly hidden behind compound walls and closed bedroom doors, yet religious authorities and government lawmakers expose them in order to regulate behaviour in the interests of wide political and economic objectives. Population numbers and population health are critical to the composition of national armed forces and the labour force; motherhood is central to both, and consequently subject to moral, cultural, social, political and economic controls. Intimacy is shuttlecocked between public and private arenas (for example, in laws on contraception and abortion), and lives are caught in the net on either side of the supposedly inviolate threshold. Private details of gender relations are publicised in episodes of rape and domestic violence reported to the police, adjudicated in courtrooms and captured by media. Mass rape in wartime, previously neglected as too insignificant to report (Brownmiller, 1975), became headline news during the 1990s Yugoslav conflict.[18] Violence against women continues to be analysed within the narrow frame of interpersonal violence, even as some feminists distinguish public, state-inflicted rape from private, individual acts of rape, and others protest that the state has a responsibility in all cases. The violence of social reproduction, in the broad definition used in this chapter, is mostly missing from this record.

Ambiguous facets of social reproduction are occluded in the ideologies of separate male/female spheres; these dogmas cannot account for the changing sexual division of labour in wartime, the shifting scope of public and private realms over time and across cultures, or the unclear assignment of exchange value and use value to reproductive activities. The lower value that the corporate sector places on social reproduction surfaces in budgetary politics (for example, military outlays for national security versus welfare expenditures for human security) as well as in the labour market. Radical feminists and queer theorists have dissected the fiction of separate spheres, and social activists have challenged the idea that reproductive activities make no material contributions to production. But the myth persists and influences pertinent fields of inquiry, which continue to overlook the issues. Scholars of international political economy, with few exceptions, continue to analyse the world as if men's experience encompassed women's lives, making gender an irrelevant analytical category. Of the five books[19] reviewed by Georgina Waylen (2010), only the work by Isabella Bakker and Rachel Silvey uses the concept of social reproduction to understand how the global political economy is being transformed; they engage with both the scholarship and the concepts necessary for a gendered international political economy.

This chapter has named the violence in biological and social reproduction through the manipulation of the terms' definitions and the uses/abuses of women's reproductive capacities. Retracing the historical context of the division of labour, it has identified the political ecology of violent social reproduction. Case studies of social reproduction and resource extraction in war-torn Congo and Sierra Leone showcase the consequences for women, and the evidence of their struggles to survive is marked by the impact of neoliberalism. As to the role of the state in social reproduction, the most important new development is the plan for a social protection floor to address poverty. This is an initiative of several UN agencies, which advocate making social protection coverage universal in the form of a basic set of essential social rights and transfers, in cash and in kind, to provide a minimum income and livelihood security for all. The plan also calls for the supply of an essential level of goods and social services, such as health, water and sanitation, education, food, housing, life and asset-saving information, which is accessible for all (Turshen, 2014).

Notes

1 See Cordell *et al.* (1987).
2 For a discussion of rural women's experiences of production and reproduction in socialist development see Croll (1981). For a review of the theoretical literature on women's domestic labour, see the introduction to Bakker and Silvey (2008).
3 Humphries (1991, p. 285) finds another motive for the sexual division of labour: by having men and women perform different tasks, thereby precluding heterosexual contact, capitalists could exert control over sexuality and marriage.
4 Humphries (1991) suggests that labour needs shaped moral philosophy and determined social controls that regulated marriage and pregnancy; in nineteenth-century Britain, parish officers enforced the Poor Laws keeping one eye on the public purse and the other on illegitimacy.
5 According to the laws of Victorian England a woman effectually surrendered her legal existence on marriage. Girls' education suffered because the British medical

profession argued that the physical demands of menstruation and the intellectual demands of study were incompatible (www.st-andrews.ac.uk/~bp10/pvm/en3040/women.shtml, accessed 13 December 2014).

6 For details of converted girls' preparation for Christian marriage and motherhood in Nigeria, see Bastian (2000).

7 Women who laboured as missionaries for CMS ceased to receive wages on marriage, though their missionary work often continued.

8 See Chapter 2 above for details.

9 The justices of the US Supreme Court argued over the meaning of the 1978 Pregnancy Discrimination Act, debating whether the law allows companies to suspend pregnant workers, while allowing other workers with temporary disabilities to remain on the job (www.npr.org/2014/12/03/368282883/supreme-court-case-puts-focus-on-pregnancy-discrimination-act, accessed 13 January 2015).

10 In El Salvador, between 2000 and 2011, the state tried 129 women who had miscarried and found 49 of them guilty of homicide; they were condemned to jail terms as long as 30 years (http://agrupacionciudadana.org/, accessed 27 January 2015).

11 For the details of sexual coercion of enslaved women, see Scully and Paton (2005).

12 According to the ILO (2014, p. 102), 17 per cent of the population in sub-Saharan Africa is afforded total health coverage.

13 Anaemia, which is low levels of haemoglobin in the blood, is especially serious in pregnancy as it can lead to premature delivery and low birth weight.

14 The reference here is to Naomi Klein's theories of economic and political shocks that have operated on a global scale to create what she terms 'disaster capitalism'.

15 Ndaywel è Nziem (2002, pp. 156–157) writes that the treachery of those around them complicates the women's attempts to earn a living; they are cheated at every turn and making a profit is impossible. Neither their education and training nor their post as nurses at the capital's foremost university clinic guarantees them a living; they must experiment with raising fowl and selling eggs, baking bread, knitting baby clothes, and if one enterprise fails, they try another. Becoming a concubine seems like a luxury, if one can pull it off. No division exists between production and social reproduction in this instance; the functions merge nearly seamlessly.

16 Information based on the Report of the Secretary-General to the Security Council (A/68/878–S/2014/339) issued on 15 May 2014 (https://childrenandarmedconflict.un.org/countries/democratic-republic-of-the-congo/, accessed 20 May 2015).

17 For some of the colonial history of medical services in Sierra Leone, see Patton (1996).

18 For an account of the legal history and UN action on sexual violence in wartime, see Horvitz and Catherwood (2006).

19 The five books are Bakker and Silvey (2008); Blyth (2009); Hobson and Seabrooke (2007); Klein (2007); and Pogge (2008).

References

ActionAid (2012) *Women's land rights project in Guatemala, India and Sierra Leone.* Johannesburg: www.actionaid.org.

African Development Bank (2013) Championing inclusive growth across Africa: recognizing Africa's informal sector, www.afdb.org/en/blogs/afdb-championing-inclusive-growth-across-africa/post/recognizing-africas-informal-sector-11645/, accessed 20 July 2014.

Amnesty International (2011) *Sierra Leone: continuing human rights violations in the post conflict period. Amnesty International submission to the UN universal periodic review, May 2011.* London: Amnesty International.

Baaz, Maria Eriksson and Maria Stern (2013) *Sexual violence as a weapon of war? Perceptions, prescriptions, problems in the Congo and beyond*. London and New York: Zed Books; Uppsala, Sweden: Nordic Africa Institute.

Bakker, Isabella (2003) Neo-liberal governance to the reprivatization of social reproduction, social provisioning and shifting gender orders. In *Power, production and social reproduction: human in/security in the global political economy*, edited by Isabella Bakker and Stephen Gill, pp. 66–82. London: Palgrave.

Bakker, Isabella (2004) Neo-liberal governance and the reprivatization of social reproduction. Conference papers, International Studies Association, 2004 annual meeting, Montreal, Canada.

Bakker, Isabella and Stephen Gill (2003) Global political economy and social reproduction. In *Power, production and social reproduction: human in/security in the global political economy*, edited by Isabella Bakker and Stephen Gill, pp. 3–16. London: Palgrave.

Bakker, Isabella and Rachel Silvey, eds (2008) *Beyond states and markets: the challenges of social reproduction*. London: Routledge.

Bastian, Misty L. (2000) Young converts: Christian missions, gender and youth in Onitsha, Nigeria 1880–1929, *Anthropological quarterly* 7(3): 143–158.

Belloula, Nacéra (2000) *Algérie, le massacre des innocents*. Paris: Fayard.

Bennholdt-Thomson, Veronika (1988) The future of women's work and violence against women. In *Women: the last colony* by Maria Mies, Veronika Bennholdt-Thomson, and Claudia von Werlhof, pp. 113–129. London: Zed Books.

Bitar, D. (1998) *Reproductive health in refugee situations: review of existing reproductive health indicators*. Geneva: United Nations High Commissioner for Refugees.

Blanc, Ann K. (2004) The role of conflict in the rapid fertility decline in Eritrea and prospects for the future, *Studies in family planning* 35(4): 236–245.

Blyth, Mark, ed. (2009) *Routledge handbook of international political economy (IPE): IPE as a global conversation*. London: Routledge.

Bouju, Jacky and Mirjam de Bruijn, eds (2014) *Ordinary violence and social change in Africa*. Leiden/Boston: Brill.

Braeckman, Colette (2004) The looting of the Congo, *New internationalist* 367, May: 13–16.

Braudel, Fernand (1977) *Afterthoughts on material civilization and capitalism*. Baltimore, MD: the Johns Hopkins University Press.

Briffaerts, Jan (2014) *When Congo wants to go to school. Educational realities in a colonial context*. Amsterdam: Rozenberg Publishers, http://rozenbergquarterly.com/when-congo-wants-to-go-to-school-the-educational-climate/?print=print, accessed 30 December 2014.

Brownmiller, Susan (1975) *Against our will*. New York: Simon and Schuster.

Bryceson, Deborah Fahy, Jesper Bosse Jønsson and Hannelore Verbrugge (2013) Prostitution or partnership? Wifestyles in Tanzanian artisanal gold-mining settlements, *Journal of modern African studies* 51(1): 33–56.

Bryceson, Deborah Fahy, Jesper Bosse Jønsson and Hannelore Verbrugge (2014) For richer, for poorer: marriage and casualized sex in East African artisanal mining settlements, *Development and Change* 45(1): 79–104.

Bush, Ray (2007) *Poverty and neoliberalism: persistence and reproduction in the global south*. London: Pluto Press.

Caffentzis, George (2002) On the notion of a crisis of social reproduction: a theoretical review, *Commoner* 5, autumn: 1–22.

Caldwell, John C. (2004) Social upheaval and fertility decline, *Journal of family history* 29(4): 382–406.

Campbell, Catherine (1997) Migrancy, masculine identities and AIDS: the psychosocial context of HIV transmission on the South African gold mines, *Social science and medicine* 45(2): 273–281.

Chanock, Martin (1985) *Law, custom and social order: the colonial experience in Malawi and Zambia*. Cambridge: Cambridge University Press.

Commonwealth Foundation (2013) *National report: Sierra Leone, a civil society review of progress towards the Millennium Development Goals in Commonwealth countries*. Harrisburg, PA: Commonwealth Foundation.

Cordell, Dennis D. (2013) Interdependence and convergence: migration, men, women, and work in sub-Saharan Africa, 1800–1975. In *Proletarian and gendered mass migrations: a global perspective on continuities and discontinuities from the 19th to the 21st centuries*, edited by Dirk Hoerdera and Amarjit Kaur, pp. 173–215. Leiden: Brill.

Cordell, Dennis D., Joel W. Gregory, and Victor Piché (1987) African historical demography: the search for a theoretical framework. In *African population and capitalism: historical perspectives*, edited by Dennis D. Cordell and Joel W. Gregory, pp. 14–32. Boulder, CO: Westview Press.

Coulter, Chris (2009) *Bush wives and girl soldiers: women's lives through war and peace in Sierra Leone*. Ithaca, NY: Cornell University Press.

Croll, Elisabeth Joan (1981) Women in rural production and reproduction in the Soviet Union, China, Cuba, and Tanzania: socialist development experiences, *Signs: journal of women in culture and society* 7(2): 361–375.

Denney, L., M. Jalloh, R. Mallett, S. Pratt and M. Tucker (2014) *Developing capacity to prevent malnutrition in Sierra Leone: an analysis of development partner support*. London: ODI, www.securelivelihoods.org/resources_download.aspx?resourceid=290&document id=302, accessed 20 January 2015.

Dunn, Richard (2014) *A tale of two plantations: slave life and labor in Jamaica and Virginia*. Cambridge, MA: Harvard University Press.

Ensler, Eve (2011) Vday-project website: http://drc.vday.org/conflict-minerals, accessed 13 September 2011.

Foucault, Michel (1981) *The history of sexuality*, vol. 1. Harmondsworth: Penguin.

Galtung, Johan (1969) Violence, peace and peace research, *Journal of peace research* 6(3): 167–191.

Goldberg, Philipp M. (2012) *Trade unions in sub-Sahara Africa*. Johannesburg: Friedrich Ebert Foundation South Africa Office, www.fes-southafrica.org/media/pdf/Database% 20on%20Trade%20Unions%20in%20Sub.pdf.

Harnes, Helga (2014) Pioneer workers, invaluable helpmeets, good mothers: a study of the role of the missionary wife in the Church Missionary Society, *Social sciences and missions* 27: 163–191.

Harries, Patrick (1990) Symbols and sexuality: culture and identity on the early Witwatersrand gold mines, *Gender and history* 1(3): 318–336.

Hennessy, Rosemary (2006) Returning to reproduction queerly: sex, labor, need, *Rethinking Marxism* 18(3): 387–395.

Heuveline, Patrick and Bunnak Poch (2007) The phoenix population: demographic crisis and rebound in Cambodia, *Demography* 44(2): 405–426.

Hill, Kenneth (2004) *War, humanitarian crises, population displacement, and fertility: a review of evidence*. Washington, DC: National Academies Press.

Hobson, John M. and Leonard Seabrooke, eds (2007) *Everyday politics of the world economy*. Cambridge: Cambridge University Press.

Hole, Charles (1896) The early history of the Church Missionary Society for Africa and the East. London: Church Missionary Society, https://archive.org/stream/earlyhistory-ofch00hole/earlyhistoryofch00hole_djvu.txt.

Horvitz, Leslie Alan and Christopher Catherwood (2006) *Encyclopedia of war crimes and genocide.* New York: Facts on File.

Humphries, Jane (1990) Enclosures, common rights, and women: the proletarianization of families in the late eighteenth and early nineteenth centuries, *Journal of economic history* 50(1): 17–42.

Humphries, Jane (1991) The sexual division of labor and social control: an interpretation, *Review of radical political economics* 23(3&4): 269–296.

Hunt, Nancy Rose (2008) An acoustic register, tenacious images, and Congolese scenes of rape and repetition, *Cultural anthropology* 23(2): 220–253.

ILO (2014) *World social protection report 2014/15.* Geneva: International Labour Organisation.

Jackson, Regine O. (2014) The failure of categories: Haitians in the United Nations Organization in the Congo, 1960–64, *Journal of Haitian studies* 20(1): 34–64.

Jackson, Stephen (2005) Protecting livelihoods in violent economies. In *Profiting from peace: managing the resource dimensions of civil war,* edited by K. Ballentine and H. Nitzchke, pp. 153–182. Boulder, CO: Lynne Rienner.

Jaspers, Suzanne and Sorcha O'Callaghan (2010) Challenging choices: protection and livelihoods in conflict. London: ODI Humanitarian Policy Group policy brief 40.

Jayaraman, Anuja, Tesfayi Gebreselassie and S. Chandrasekhar (2009) Effect of conflict on age at marriage and age at first birth in Rwanda, *Population research and policy review* 28(5): 551–567.

Jok, Jok Madut (1998) *Militarization, gender, and reproductive health in South Sudan.* Lewiston, NY: Edwin Mellen Press.

Kalusopa, Trywell, Rudi Dicks and Clara Osei-Boateng, eds (2012) Social protection schemes in Africa. Lomé, Togo: International Trade Union Confederation-Africa, www.ituc-africa.org/IMG/pdf/SOCIAL_SECURITY_BK_FINAL_COPY_5_March_2012_V11_1_.pdf, accessed 18 January 2015.

Kalusopa, Trywell, Kwabena Nyarko Otoo and Hilma Shindondola-Mote, eds (c.2011) *Trade union services and benefits in Africa.* Johannesburg: African Labour Research Network, www.ituc-africa.org/IMG/pdf/BENEFITS_REPORT_FINAL_DRAFT.pdf, accessed 20 May 2014.

Kirby, Paul (2012) Rethinking war/rape: feminism, critical explanation and the study of wartime sexual violence, with special reference to the eastern Democratic Republic of Congo. Unpublished thesis. London: London School of Economics and Political Science (University of London).

Kisangani, Emizet François and F. Scott Bobb (2010) *Historical dictionary of the Democratic Republic of the Congo,* 3rd edn. Lanham, Md.: Scarecrow Press.

Klein, Naomi (2007) *The shock doctrine: the rise of disaster capitalism.* New York: Metropolitan.

Laliberté, Danielle, Benoît Laplante and Victor Piché (2003) The impact of forced migration on marital life in Chad, *European journal of population* 19(4): 413–435.

Land, Isaac and Andrew M. Schocket (2008) New approaches to the founding of the Sierra Leone Colony, 1786–1808, *Journal of colonialism and colonial history* 9(3): 1–15.

Laudati, Ann (2013) Beyond minerals: broadening 'economies of violence' in eastern Democratic Republic of Congo, *Review of African political economy* 40(135): 32–50.

Lewis, Barbara (1982) Fertility and employment: an assessment of role incompatibility among African urban women. In *Women and work in Africa*, edited by Edna G. Bay, pp. 249–276. Boulder, CO: Westview.

Lindisfarne, Nancy and Jonathan Neale (2013) What gender does, *International Socialism* 139, http://isj.org.uk/issue-139/, accessed 23 December 2014.

Lindstrom, David P. and Betemariam Berhanu (1999) The impact of war, famine, and economic decline on marital fertility in Ethiopia, *Demography* 36(2): 247–261.

Lovgren, Stefan (2007) Congo gorilla killings fueled by illegal charcoal trade, *National Geographic News*, 16 August, http://news.nationalgeographic.com/news/2007/08/070816-gorillas-congo.html, accessed 20 May 2014.

McGough, Fredanna M. (2015) Locating the informal in the formal?, *African and Asian studies* 14(1/2): 40–60.

Meillassoux, Claude (1983) Female slavery. In *Women and slavery in Africa* edited by Claire C. Robertson and Martin A. Klein, pp. 49–66. Madison: University of Wisconsin Press.

Ministère du Plan et Macro International (2008) Enquête démographique et de santé, République Démocratique du Congo 2007. Calverton: Ministère du Plan et Macro International.

Ndaywel è Nziem, I. (2002) Le territoire médicale à l'épreuve de l'informel. In *Manières de vivre: économie de la 'débrouille' dans les villes du Congo/Zaïre*, edited by Gauthier de Villers, Bogumil Jewsiewicki and Laurent Monnier, pp. 141–169. Paris: L'Harmattan.

Oakland Institute (2012) *Understanding land investment deals in Africa: SOCFIN land investment in Sierra Leone*. Oakland, CA: Oakland Institute.

Omilola, Babatunde and Sheshangai Kaniki (2014) *Social protection in Africa: a review of potential contribution and impact on poverty reduction*. New York: United Nations Development Programme.

Patton, Adell (1996) *Physicians, colonial racism and diaspora in West Africa*. Gainesville, FL: University Press of Florida.

Peterman, Amber, Tia Palermo and Caryn Bredenkamp (2011) Estimates and determinants of sexual violence against women in the Democratic Republic of Congo, *American journal of public health* 101(6): 1060–1067.

Pogge, Thomas (2008) *World poverty and human rights: cosmopolitan responsibilities and reforms*, 2nd edn. Cambridge: Polity.

Powell, V. (1987) Relationships between gender and fertility: insights from the case of the baby boom. PhD thesis. Ann Arbor, MI: University Microfilms International.

Robertson, Claire C. and Martin A. Klein, eds (1983) *Women and slavery in Africa*. Madison: University of Wisconsin Press.

Rockmore, Marc (2012) Living within conflicts: risk of violence and livelihood portfolios. Brighton: IDS Sussex, HiCN working paper 121.

Rothenberg, Daniel (2014) *'Everything is there in the tunnels.' Selected oral histories from the artisanal mining industry in North Kivu and South Kivu*. Chicago: Heartland Alliance for Human Needs and Human Rights and Arizona State University.

Scully, Pamela and Diana Paton, eds (2005) *Gender and slave emancipation in the Atlantic world*. Durham, NC: Duke University Press.

Shepler, Susan (2011) The real and symbolic importance of food in war: hunger pains and big men's bellies in Sierra Leone, *Africa today* 58(2): 43–56.

Smith, R., R. Beaglehole, D. Woodward and N. Drager, eds (2003) *Global public goods for health: health economics and public health perspectives*. Oxford: Oxford University Press.

Statistics Sierra Leone (2013) *Sierra Leone demographic and health survey*. Freetown, Sierra Leone.

Stein, Zena, Mervyn Susser, Gerhart Saenger and Francis Marolla (1975) *Famine and human development: the Dutch hunger winter of 1944–1945*. New York: Oxford University Press.

Sturgess, Patricia and Christopher Flower (2013) Land and conflict in Sierra Leone: a rapid desk-based study. Redhill: Evidence on Demand, http://dx.doi.org/10.12774/eod_hd.dec2013.sturgess_flower, accessed 15 February 2015.

Tarawallie, Mariama (2013) Women in Sierra Leone: resisting dispossession, *Open democracy*, 16 December, www.opendemocracy.net/5050/mariama-tarawallie/women-in-sierra-leone-resisting-dispossession, accessed 23 October 2014.

Tolson, Michelle (2014) Working Cambodian women 'too poor' to have children, www.ipsnews.net/2014/05/working-cambodian-women-too-poor-to-have-children/, accessed 13 January 2015.

Turner, Terisa and Leigh Brownhill (2001) Women never surrendered: the Mau Mau and globalization from below in Kenya 1980–2000. In *There is an alternative: subsistence and worldwide resistance to corporate globalisation*, edited by Veronika Bennholdt-Thomsen and Claudia von Werlhof, pp. 106–132. London: Zed Books.

Turshen, Meredeth (2010) Reproducing labor: colonial government regulation of African women's reproductive lives. In *The demographics of empire: the colonial order and the creation of knowledge*, edited by Karl Ittmann, Dennis Cordell and Greg Maddox, pp. 217–144. Athens: Ohio University Press.

Turshen, Meredeth (2014) A global partnership for development and other unfulfilled promises of the millennium project, *Third world quarterly* 35(3): 345–357.

Turshen, Meredeth, Hélène Bretin and Annie Thébaud-Mony (1993) Prescription de contraception aux femmes immigrées en France. In *Population, reproduction, sociétés: perspectives et enjeux de démographie sociale*, edited by Dennis D. Cordell, Danielle Gauvreau, Raymond R. Gervais and Céline Le Bourdais, pp. 217–234. Montreal: Presses de l'Université de Montréal.

UN (2008) Letter dated 10 December 2008 from the Chairman of the Security Council Committee established pursuant to resolution 1533 (2004) concerning the Democratic Republic of the Congo addressed to the President of the Security Council. New York: United Nations document S/2008/773.

UNDAP (2014) *Tanzania delivering as one. Annual report 2013–2014*. Dar es Salaam: United Nations Development Assistance Plan,http://tz.one.un.org/index.php/core-commitments/millennium-development-goals, accessed 10 April 2015.

UN MDGs (2015) Millennium Development Goals Indicators. New York: United Nations, http://mdgs.un.org/unsd/mdg/SeriesDetail.aspx? srid=553&crid, accessed 10 April 2015.

Urdal, Henrik and Chi Primus Che (2013) War and gender inequalities in health: the impact of armed conflict on fertility and maternal mortality, *International interactions: empirical and theoretical research in international relations* 39(4): 489–510.

Verhaegen, Benoit (1990) *Femmes zaïroises de Kisangani: combats pour la survie*. Paris: L'Harmattan.

Vlassenroot, Koen and Chris Huggins (2004) Land, migration and conflict in Eastern D.R. Congo, *African Centre for Technology Studies Eco-conflicts* 3(4), October: 1–4.

Vlassenroot, Koen and Timothy Raeymaekers (2008) Crisis and food security profile: the Democratic Republic of the Congo. In *Beyond relief: food security in protracted crises*, edited by Luca Alinovi, Günter Hemrich and Luca Russo, pp. 157–168. Rugby, Warwickshire; Practical Action Publishing.

Vlassenroot, Koen, Salomé Ntububa and Timothy Raeymaekers (2006) Food security responses to the protracted crisis context of the Democratic Republic of the Congo, ftp://ftp.fao.org/docrep/fao/009/ag307e/ag307e00.pdf, accessed 20 January 2013.

Waylen, Georgina (2010) Book reviews, *Signs* 36(1): 237–244.

Weijs, Bart, Dorothea Hilhorst and Adriaan Ferf (2012) Livelihoods, basic services and social protection in Democratic Republic of the Congo. Working paper 2. London: ODI Secure Livelihoods Research Consortium.

Woldemicael, Gebremariam (2008) Recent fertility decline in Eritrea: is it a conflict-led transition?, *Demographic research* 18(2): 27–58.

Women for Women (2014) 'Women inherit wrappers, men inherit fields': the problem of women's access to land in South Kivu, Democratic Republic of Congo. London, UK: Women for Women International.

World Bank (2007) Global public goods: a framework for the role of the World Bank, http://siteresources.worldbank.org/DEVCOMMINT/Documentation/21510685/DC2007-0020(E)GlobalPublicGoods.pdf.

World Bank (2014) Poverty data, http://povertydata.worldbank.org/poverty/region/SSA, accessed 20 July 2014.

WHO (2008) *Closing the gap in a generation: health equity through action on the social determinants of health*. Geneva: World Health Organisation.

World Vision (2009) Children's rights in the Democratic Republic of Congo; Stakeholder report on DRC. Submission by World Vision for universal periodic review, sixth cycle, November.

Wright, Melissa W. (2006) *Disposable women and other myths of global capitalism*. London: Routledge.

Zinnen, Véronique (2012) Documentation des résultats de la mise en œuvre des principes de l'efficacité de l'aide dans le secteur de la santé: étude de cas de la République Démocratique du Congo. Groupe de recherche en appui à la politique pour la mise en oeuvre de l'agenda pour l'efficacité de l'aide, www.grap-pa.be/attachments/article/69/201202_capitalisationdp_rdc3.pdf, accessed 20 January 2015.

5   The construction of lives in armed conflict

Fighters, male and female, had their own 'families' within the compound, which consisted of children they had captured and who were under their protection and care. Girl fighters could and did serve as heads of these 'families'. Food and loot were distributed on the basis of these 'families' ... older children and adolescents who were not attached to a 'family' were not given food and had to survive as scavengers.

(Mazurana and Carlson, 2004, p. 14)

In considering how lives are lived in war zones and how armed conflict changes relations of production and reproduction, two salient findings emerge from the preceding chapters: these two spheres cannot be considered separately as they are inextricably related to one another; and consigning men to the productive sphere and women to the reproductive sphere is specious as it expands biological reproduction to encompass the whole of social reproduction. The acceptance of such false binaries only abets capitalists' attempts to hide the use they make of sexist ideologies in their search for cheap labour and high profits. The apparent split between production and social reproduction is an artefact of the industrial revolution in Europe, an ideology man-made for economic purposes, and a depiction that is spurious in its inaccurate portrayal of human lives. The division of labour for the functions of Fordist factory production was confounded with the sexual division of labour, which became a class-bound aspiration that did not reflect the realities of either working-class lives in Europe or subaltern existence in Africa. These chapters show that the sexual division of labour is no less fluid than gender roles, that it is subject to economic and political exigencies, and that it varies in time and place. In wartime new gender roles are manifest in the changed sex-specificity of labour. When villages in Congo or Sierra Leone are invaded, some people are forced to flee and others are forcibly recruited into participation in violent conflicts; in the process gender assignments are reconfigured, underscoring the lability of gender identity.

Yet the assertion persists that woman's place is in the home because of her childbearing potential; it is a recurrent theme of post-war promises to return to a mythical norm, of normative gender relations as reassuring solace, and an explanation of the baby boom in the United States after the Second World

War. (Or perhaps it is evidence of an anti-feminist backlash.) One way to overcome this fiction is to demonstrate the articulation of production and social reproduction throughout history and modern economies, which continue to transform their integration. This chapter exposes the hypocritical ideology of separate public (male) and private (female) spheres by showing that neoliberal capitalist regimes deliberately structure production and social reproduction in ways that mask the reality of the continuing interdependence of these domains. A theory of the permanent articulation of production and social reproduction enhances feminist arguments for gendered labour markets by taking account of modified market requirements. Conventional gender ideologies regarding appropriate occupations for women and men are continuously adapted in response to varying political economies. The divide between economics and politics mirrors the artificial dissociation of the public (masculine) from the private (feminine) sphere.

Neoliberal macro-economic policies assume or promote the commoditisation of human life through the privatisation of health and education services and the end of subsidised food and housing, leading to more inequitable distribution of these necessities and the dismantling of communal welfare. While social institutions are being marketised, more and more people are being exploited rather than benefiting from development (Bakker, 2003). In the process of macro-economic policy formulation, decision-makers appear to neglect the reproductive economy – the production and social reproduction of human beings – and turn away from the negative effects of their policies on women (Elson, 1999). This singular focus on for-profit macro-economic policies is deliberate, and it is not new. Unequal gender effects are not accidental; they are integral to economic restructuring as part of a conflict over the supposed boundary between public and private spheres. Whether gender bias is accidental or deliberate matters: accidental bias can be corrected with better theory and better facts; deliberately biased policy-makers will resist gender-sensitive theory (Brodie, 2003, p. 55).

The ostensible split between production and reproduction in the industrial revolution parallels developments in colonial Africa. In Europe the divorce occurs when productive labour is transferred to the factory and reproductive labour is confined to the home; in Africa, productive labour is shifted to enclaves of mines and plantations and reproductive labour is confined to the farm/homestead. In both cases, reproductive labour in the home subsidises productive labour; in both cases, reproductive labour is thereby commoditised. In both cases, new cohorts of labourers – the draft of women and children – are assimilated to the labour market; and reproductive costs, instead of a charge on the wage bill, are a form of new wealth collected by capitalists. It is the power of the capitalist mode of production to first make use of and then destroy all other modes of production; it mobilises and uses workers by manipulating their precapitalist modes of production (Verhaegen, 1990, p. xiv).

After independence in many African countries the contribution of reproductive labour was characterised as rural support of urban growth, while investment favoured the cities and neglected the countryside. Increased industrialisation, which came with the outsourcing of low-wage work to young female hands, was subsidised by the reproductive labour of children and older women. With international migration, the subsidy to households takes a new name – remittances. International remittances (which governments skim for foreign exchange) keep the reproductive economy functioning, just as reproductive work keeps the wage earner functioning and produces the next generation of workers. Historical and transnational perspectives make clear that externalising the cost of the social wage was always a strategy of capitalist production. There is little new in this respect in neoliberalism's retraction of the welfare state.

Economic globalisation has reorganised the welfare state and parallel arrangements of paid, unpaid and voluntary civic work (Lenz, 2005, p. 217). Neoliberal capitalist regimes use budgetary discipline as a justification for many of the cuts in state services that are critical to social reproduction. Ray Bush (2007, p. 49) shows that the current capitalist strategy is to ensure that non-capitalist societies pay the costs of the reproduction of labour; when workers are paid wages lower than the cost of subsistence, the (false) assumption has always been that the worker's family provides its own subsistence. By increasing inequality, by widening the gap between rich and poor and intensifying poverty, these regimes force more women into the workforce on unfavourable terms. The irony lies in overturning earlier idealised versions of women as mothers raising their children at home. Today working-class and subaltern women must do waged work in addition to housework, care work and the labour of pregnancy and delivery as they are integrated into the global market and as social reproduction is transnationalised. Neoliberal regimes readily reshape gender roles whenever required to fit the needs of the globalising economy, not hesitating to expound a new rhetoric of gender equality (Prügl and True, 2014).

Production/reproduction in slavery and under colonial rule

The study of slavery is a field in which production and reproduction are routinely articulated. Since the 1980s historians have researched the traffic of women into domestic slavery in Africa and through the transatlantic slave trade to plantation life in the Americas (Campbell *et al.*, 2007; Robertson and Klein, 1983). These studies vivify the employment of enslaved women and men in the regeneration of material life, depicting the detailed strategies of master and slave in essential matters of production and reproduction. Violence in every form from humiliation and whiplashes to murder was always an imminent matter of life or death in the discontinuous and insecure lives of slaves, and the use of violence was always part of the masters' strategy to raise productivity and profitability.

Robert Harms (1983, p. 95) writes of the advantages to Congolese masters of owning female slaves:

> to ensure the long-term continuity of their firms, rich traders wanted offspring who were totally under the control of the firm and who had no

obligations to maternal uncles or other outsiders. To this end, slave owners blatantly manipulated the marital arrangements of their female slaves. The women responded by maintaining an extremely low birthrate.[1]

Slavery was a way of recruiting women to work in the fields, and slave women were little distinguished from free women in production: both produced food and enjoyed autonomy. Some slave women carved out successful careers in the production and trade of foodstuffs, and they even purchased slaves. Future labour needs could be met even after the end of the transatlantic trade: 'the political and social processes that produced slaves – warfare, judicial condemnation, debt foreclosure, and kidnapping – could not easily be halted' (Harms, 1983, p. 96). These details of domestic slavery reveal the intimate calculus of production and reproduction. Both master and slave from their different viewpoints reckoned the costs and benefits of bearing and raising children, unable to separate the spheres of production and reproduction.

The transition from slavery to colonialism was not the break in European exactions that Africans hoped for as forced labour replaced slave labour, depriving Africans of the ability to choose solutions to colonists' demands for taxes that might have been paid from sources other than wages. In response to the lack of freedom to choose, Africans organised new forms of resistance, refusing cooperation or compliance with authorities. Interestingly, resistance centred not only on conditions within the workplace but also on intersecting relations of production and reproduction.

Colonists used labour recruitment policy to remake women into homebound mothers and men into wage labourers in ways that clarify the uninterrupted connection of production to reproduction. In Congo the colonial model of the family centred on three aspects of marriage – monogamy, domesticity and male authority (Rubbers, 2015). The Church and commercial companies like the UMHK (Union Minière du Haut-Katanga) preached this model. The Church's purpose was to indoctrinate youth, and companies aimed to gain a stable workforce. To prevent the wives of its workers from having extramarital affairs, the UMHK encouraged women to cultivate plots, look after their houses and take children to school, at the risk of losing their food ration.[2]

There is another side to this story of working for the UMHK, which reveals the workers' strategies in regard to links between production and reproduction. Given the failure of the mining company to provide amenities for the maintenance and reproduction of the workforce, Africans organised friendly societies and lodges, not only the male workers but also women who figured prominently in the

> smuggling networks that brought reminders from home – indigenously prepared beer and spirits, regional food and spices, and marijuana – onto the worksites. Women were much in the limelight because such activities were very lucrative and gave the lodges a source of funds for bribing African policemen and lower-level European officials....

By the end of the 1920s African women had created their own closed voluntary associations. Perhaps the most important series of them were the infamous *kufunga* bars. These institutions were a crucial facet of urban African life until independence. They served as a means by which women could make money and initiate younger women from the hinterland into the mysteries of town life. They were an important way station in the attempt to construct a stable form of conjugal life and to give male migrants some idea of the assets women of different ages and from different locations might bring with them in the making of urban households. The frequent arrests of African women in both the town and the rural areas for the illegal sale of beer and *lutuku*, a spirit made from either corn or cassava, suggests that there was more organization among the female population of the industrial towns of Katanga than met the eye of the average colonial administrator.

(Higginson, 1989, pp. 83, 250, n. 100)

Colonists' desire to shape gender relations for the purposes of production seems to have been a common preoccupation in the early twentieth century. In Senegal the French government cultivated a class of workers whose lifestyle and children's education corresponded to European standards; once designated as *evolués*, these workers deserved benefits like the family allowance. To be classed as *evolué* one had to have not only a salaried job, but also one's wife's maternal health had to be monitored by colonial medical services (Rodet, 2014). For this minority of workers the separation of male and female spheres was clearly defined. The same was not the case for common labourers or single men, who had to cook, wash up and wash their own clothes. Notions of femininity and masculinity tied to work assignments clearly were full of contradictions.

This European portrait of the *evolué* confined African masculinity to men's productive labour and gave colonists the workforce control they sought, but Africans associated masculinity with marriage and family, which were the foundations of social status and adult autonomy in African society. The colonial state's definition of manhood effectively denied African labourers a normal family life and frustrated their social aspirations in their local communities. This clash of ideas led men to resist forced labour recruitment in colonial French West Africa (Rodet, 2014), and in the Belgian Congo to desert worksites frequently (Marchal, 1999). Paradoxically, working for Europeans in the modern sector gave young men the ability to circumvent the age-dominated patriarchal social order; with the money they earned they could pay bride price, marry and found their own families outside the conventional route to matrimony that led through the elders. In Mali, these new arrangements challenged the power of elders to control young workers and to accumulate resources, provoking an inter-generational conflict over notions of masculinity (Rodet, 2014, p. 117).

Both the French and Belgian colonial administrations relied heavily on local authorities to ensure successful recruitment, and chiefs routinely selected young single men, protecting established families. Young people resisted, not just colonial domination, but also local authorities and the elders who were often complicit with the colonial agents (Rodet, 2014). Migration to centres of commercial agricultural exploitation was one way that young men could succeed in securing their independence, marrying and starting a family without having to adopt either colonial or traditional models of masculinity.

Children and child labour

Because so much of the ideology of separate male and female spheres turns on the birthing and raising of children, it seems pertinent to review changing attitudes to childhood in the contexts of slavery, colonialism and current economic and political crises including children's participation in civil war. That the birth of children is closely tied to production in every society is easily illustrated. In nineteenth-century England, the fate of the increased number of children born out of wedlock was linked to the sexual division of labour: children were illegitimate because there was no economic space for them (not vice versa), families could ill afford to protect daughters given the declining value of home-based work, and new mothers could not both work and breastfeed, so the child's survival was imperilled (Humphries, 1991, p. 287). In Africa in times of famine, patriarchal communities tried to reduce problems of feeding the people they were responsible for by selling off girls and women who bore children in numbers they could not support – a defensive strategy (Campbell *et al.*, 2009, p. 3). And today the severe effects of the recession are linked in Uganda to the disappearance of children whose parents send them to orphanages set up by Pentecostalist pastors in search of converts or NGO funding (Caplan, 2010).

Given the elaborate strategies described above of masters, male slaves, Churches and employers in the pre-colonial and colonial periods to ensure human reproduction, it is clear that children were desired and welcomed into households and that women were valued if not venerated for their fecundity. It is also evident that ideas of children's worth were vested in their productive capacities, which were exploited from a very early age. Childhood, in the contemporary western conception of this period of life, barely extended to the age of five in societies that were not mechanised and had too few adult workers. In urbanised cash economies, even young children could earn money to contribute to the household economy. Formal education was neither universally available nor affordable for the majority. In African terms, however, children are social actors, and today they seem to occupy the frontier of the reconfiguration of integration and exclusion (De Boeck, 2000) or, in the words I keep coming back to, the terms and conditions under which production and reproduction are being integrated within the global economy.

Several events conspired to change the position of children in society; a few may be cited. First, the post-Second World War population growth, interpreted by Paul Ehrlich (1971) as an explosion that endangered life on earth, inaugurated decades of population control programmes all over the world, overcoming theological opposition and even Marxist dissent. Neo-Malthusianism would inform some of the worst social planning on record, as the global North made clear that children were unwanted. Second, the end in Africa of protective colonial rule, which paradoxically had held at bay the most unregulated forms of competitive capitalism, meant that the former colonies were now open to exploitation by all. Third, the Cold War launched prolonged proxy wars in Africa that impoverished the countryside. Lastly, structural adjustment and austerity budgets ensured, not only that there would be no expansive era of indigenous African production, but also that Africans would not have the minimum services needed to maintain social reproduction.

By the end of the twentieth century, street children had become a common sight in all big cities. The reasons are manifold. Unemployment undercut households' ability to function as viable economic units, divorce rates soared, and AIDS deprived many children of their parents; children were shunted into the care of their extended families, which were themselves increasingly strained and unable to bear this burden (Waddington, 2006). As the basic security of the family unit was threatened, women and men sought to establish new relationships that might offer access to employment or income-generating schemes. In these situations women tried to support their children alone, whereas many men shirked this responsibility. Children who live on the streets generally occupy marginal places in their families.

Witchcraft accusations against children

The charge of sorcery is the single most frequently cited reason families give for pushing children out of their homes and into the streets. Accusations of witchcraft are a response to tensions in social relations within the family and to the struggle for survival. On one level, these conflicts may concern material issues such as the wish to deprive orphaned children of their inheritance (Aguilar Molina, 2005, p. 22). On another level, they reflect a deep crisis in the process of social reproduction that liberalisation and globalisation have produced (Federici, 2008). Many consider the accusations as cover for an alarming form of child abuse; children accused of sorcery are tortured by their community, sometimes by their own parents (Gouby, 2011).

A growing number of witchcraft accusations against children are recorded in Freetown and several cities in Congo (Human Rights Watch, 2006; Koroma, 2012). Many families bring the accused children to pastors, who force them to undergo 'deliverance' ceremonies in an attempt to rid them of 'possession'. There are 2,600 primary schools in Kinshasa (RDC, 2010, p. 8), and it is said that more evangelical Churches practise exorcism than there are schools in the city. Although Churches may also serve families that have no access to or confidence in basic social services, exorcism is a highly lucrative business. According to Human Rights Watch (2006, p. 4), children who undergo deliverance rituals in Congo are sequestered inside churches for anything from a few hours to several days or weeks. They may be denied food and water to encourage them to confess to practising witchcraft. In the worst cases, children are beaten, whipped or given purgatives to coerce a confession. After the ceremonies, whether or not they confess, children are often sent away from their homes.

Filip De Boeck (2000, p. 32) believes that Congolese children have come to occupy an unprecedented central position in the public sphere, not as passive consumers but as major social actors with access to the new global economy. They exist between a local economy of accelerating violence and the eruption of violence in the world economy. Judith Lavoie, head of child protection for the UN's peacekeeping mission in the DRC says of witchcraft accusations, 'It's not about the children themselves – it's about a society turning to its children to solve its problems' (UN, n.d., p. 6). And when calamities like illness, accidents and deaths occur, society blames the children.

Silvia Federici (2008) has written thoughtfully about the phenomenon of witch hunting, reflecting on its meaning: she finds that it mirrors women's devalued social position in the intense conflicts between young and old, women and men, over the use of crucial economic resources. It is startling to find that so many confessions end with the children naming their grandmother as the instigator, an accusation that provides the family with a reason for acquiring her assets and expelling her as well. Witchcraft accusations against children, it seems to me, are the most egregious signs of the violence of reproduction and of the failures of the productive system to which social reproduction is attached. Witchcraft exorcisms reveal the violence of production, of systems that do not generate enough jobs or provide income, and ultimately the violence of reproduction.

The articulation of production and reproduction

Wilma Dunaway (2014, p. 69) outlines five ways in which reproductive labours are now routine elements of international production. First, the socialisation of workers in the attributes of a productive labourer takes place in the reproductive sphere, reducing significantly the time and money employers spend on training new workers. Second, capitalism co-opts the larger share of the material and social bases of household production, whether fiscal resources for public goods or ecological resources from the commons, both of which are critical to social reproduction. Co-option includes pollution (of air, soil and water) and destruction (for example, of forests), as well as simply squandering the wealth of environments that indigenous peoples had husbanded for centuries. Third, capitalist production assimilates many household activities such as artisanal crafts, medicinal and herbal plant collection, and harvesting of snails and fingerling fish; this formerly non-waged work that was closely tied to the reproductive sphere is now part of the informal economy that enables the poor to subsist. Similarly, women's reproductive labours are extended to capitalist enterprise when wives provide cleaning, food preparation and family networking functions for husbands' export textile shops or commercial fishing businesses. And when women work as subcontractors in the home, the demarcation between reproduction and commodity production is blurred by their use of reproductive resources and their children's labour. This ties in with the fourth way in which reproductive labours are routine elements of international production, namely the continuing socialisation of reproductive functions with the monetisation of subsistence resources: the need to purchase water, fuel and food, the push to sell caregiving labour, and the demand for body parts (for example, oocytes and organs) and bodily functions (surrogate pregnancies).

Dunaway's (2014, p. 71) final point questions the confusion of workplace and home when it comes to women's sexuality and asks whether such management policies are profitable. Why are capitalists not more assiduous in policing what she calls 'the murky space' between productive and reproductive labour? Knowing that waged labour does not mitigate women's responsibility for unpaid household work and childcare, employers might be expected to ensure that the efficiency and profitability of their productive systems are not threatened by the additional time their female workers spend on unpaid tasks (for example, by providing childcare). And, if the gendered separation between production and reproduction is so ingrained in society, why is it not maintained in the workplace where men frequently demand 'reproductive services' from female production workers, whether in the benign form of expecting to be served coffee or in malignant acts of sexual harassment and physical assault? The answers may be found in the control these policies enable employers to exercise over male and female workers (McCann, 2005).

Maria Mies (1986) might answer that the sexual division of labour was not and is not an evolutionary and peaceful process, based on the ever-progressing development of productive forces and specialisation; rather, it is a violent conflict in which, first, certain categories of men and, later, certain groups of people, by virtue of arms and warfare, establish an exploitative relationship between themselves and women, as well as other peoples and classes. An updated version that takes account of globalisation and civil war might read: these struggles are over the terms and conditions under which production and reproduction are being integrated within the global economy.

Reflecting on the articulation of production and reproduction, Deborah Bryceson and Ulla Vuorela (1984, p. 140) consider the question in terms of modes of production and modes of human reproduction, which they see as separate theoretical entities, each embodying a development dynamic unique to itself (labour productivity in the former and population dynamics in the latter), but never existing in isolation from one another. They argue that modes of human reproduction and modes of production are of equal importance; neither one is subordinate or dominant. Further, modes of human reproduction are constituted by relations and forces of reproduction. Forces of reproduction signify the degree of control men and women exert over nature in relation to birth and death, which in turn is influenced by knowledge of public health and birth control. Relations of human reproduction refer to male/female social relationships regarding access to and control of sexual union, procreation and children. Although human reproduction and material production are the universal constants of human existence through time and space, their social forms and contents are historically determined.

Socially, the unifying linkage between modes of production and human reproduction is effected through the social rationalisation of labour time, which generates particular configurations of the division of labour (Bryceson and Vuorela, 1984, p. 144). A balanced social division of labour successfully ensures viable reproduction and aims for the expansion of the social formation, but labour differentiation spells sexual asymmetry, and sexual asymmetry is ubiquitous. Women's alienation, which Bryceson and Vuorela say is caused by sexual asymmetry, entails restricted access and control of the means of reproduction as well as the means of production. The social act of childbearing provides the material basis for the origin of women's alienation and its perpetuation in specific forms under different modes of production. For Bryceson and Vuorela (1984), the sexual division of labour is the link between mode of production and mode of human reproduction; the two modes are integrated in the sense that the site of production and human reproduction are one and the same – the extended family household.

The marriage transaction in many African societies is a social arrangement concerning the reproduction of labour – directly through the transfer of a woman's labour power to her husband, and indirectly through her capacity to have children and hence reproduce labour from one generation to another for her husband's family. In patrilineal societies, children are 'legally' part of their fathers' families, though they retain social ties with their mothers' relatives (Cordell, 2013). Clearly marriage plays a critical role in providing agricultural labour and is an institution that is partly political and partly economic. These gendered roles and their contribution to family labour units are co-opted to sustain corporate capitalism today.

In later work, Bryceson revisited these arguments in the context of Tanzania's transition from stable, low population density, decentralised, non-capitalist, agrarian societies to urbanised concentrations, not only in major cities, but also in new artisanal mining communities. Although still primarily rural (73.6 per cent of the population), Tanzania is feeling the deepening impact of the global economy in new forms of trade, investment and work relations, which are spreading capitalist interpersonal relations that permeate sexual and family relations (Bryceson *et al.*, 2013, p. 37). As the spread of capitalist modernity weakens the association of sex with human reproduction, the young in mining communities not only escape ritualised and symbolically controlled kinship systems that previously determined marriage arrangements, but also actively experiment with independent, ad hoc coupling in an evolving spectrum of de facto conjugal relations. The significance of this analysis for the argument that production and reproduction are permanently articulated is that Tanzanians at mining sites, both men and women, regard reproductive activities as integral to the choices and decisions of their productive lives.

Looking at Kisangani in Zaire during the Mobutu years, Benoit Verhaegen (1990, p. xx) sees marginality as a permanent status fundamentally linked to the capitalist mode of production. He found four types of women in the city: the best off are the bourgeois traders who travel from Kisangani to Kinshasa and

Europe; next are women specialising in long-distance trading who transport goods by river, rail or road (they regard sexual favours as part of the job and part of their calculation of profit); third are the market women who as a last resort may also pay taxes with sexual favours; and fourth are the petty traders who sell individual items at tiny profit margins. This description of informality and mobility resembles that of women displaced by war. These characteristics are now features of the global economy, since a majority of economically active women in developing countries work in informal conditions, as do migrant workers (Phillips, 2013, p. 184). For capitalists, informality, actively harnessed and entrenched, has become critical to accumulation as a means of increasing competitiveness, reducing the costs of social reproduction and ensuring labour flexibility.

The reorganisation of the reproductive economy

Much has been written about how neoliberal globalisation has reorganised the productive economy but little about how it has reorganised the reproductive economy, and even less about how the two go hand in hand. Violence is manifest in the reorganisation of the reproductive economy no less than in the productive economy, and it has significant effects on women's and men's lives, gender relations and inter-generational interactions. Violence affects outcomes, too, as interpersonal aggression increases with the pressures of neoliberal policies on families. This section of Chapter 5 attempts to sketch the dimensions of a reorganised reproductive economy and to describe the contribution of armed conflict to the redesign of social reproduction.

The privatisation of social reproduction is a strategy of neoliberal policy that individualises the provision of human security (Bakker, 2003, p. 82). The strategy is implemented by the state, which plays a critical role in negotiating the public/private boundaries of production and reproduction. One way it does this is by tying human security to citizenship: immigrants, undocumented and trafficked workers who provide care for others, are not themselves eligible to receive state benefits; in these situations national identity becomes a salient issue, easily translated into conflict. Another way to police boundaries of production and reproduction is by using fiscal policy to shift the risks of structural adjustment and austerity downwards from public to private responsibility. Decentralisation transfers obligation down to the subnational and local levels of government, often without increasing their resources or capacity to carry out these new functions. Unprepared local authorities shift the burden down to communities and households, particularly economically and socially defenceless women. This last move amounts to the most comprehensive way in which the provision of human security is individualised: the diffusion of responsibility effectually removes services from the public sector. When neoliberal policies mandate cutbacks in funding for public institutions, the simultaneous loss of community spaces diminishes social life.

The term public, as in public services like public utilities and public libraries, has many meanings, some of them contradictory: public space is open to everyone, public life is contrasted with private life, a public corporation is a private sector company, and public services are government-provided, not normally restrictive or exclusive, and usually free of charge at point of service. When public services are privatised, these meanings are subverted. Several steps may be taken: barriers to access are created such as means tests for eligibility and user fees; the government may sell its facilities to private companies or enter into public–private partnerships, in effect commercialising the service; some public services may be commoditised and outsourced to private firms (anything from hospital laundry and food services to routine lab work and drug supplies); and individuals may be shunted into private facilities, whether prisons or nursing homes. In the chaos that ensues from the rapid implementation of these policies, corruption and criminal activity are common.

Privatisation appears to be a decision taken at the national level; the global context in which the policy is implemented is not obvious to the users of services, whether they are consumers, clients, patients or prisoners. First, the policy itself is part of the international programme of structural adjustment required of all countries seeking loans from the World Bank or the commercial banking market. Second, the General Agreement on Trade in Services (GATS) of the World Trade Organisation (WTO), discussed in Chapter 4 above, regulates trade in services, for example in health care by providing specialised and general health personnel, nursing, hospital and ambulance services, as well as physiotherapeutic and paramedical services. In principle, WTO members agree to open all public service sectors to trade and foreign competition, though only 50 have done so to date (www.who.int/trade/glossary/story033/en/). To reach its goal of liberalising trade in services, GATS covers four modes of provision: cross-border supply, consumption abroad, movement of individuals (rather than companies) to work abroad temporarily, and foreign commercial presence. This last raises the third way that the mechanisms of privatisation may elude detection.

When countries decide to allow foreign private suppliers to provide services, they may become part of global supply chains, which embed hidden surplus extraction at every node. As discussed in Chapter 1 above, firms set up production and maintain trade by exploiting unpaid household and informal sector labour (Clelland, 2014). Retailers like supermarkets and department stores use their power in supply chains systematically to push business costs and risks onto producers, who in turn pass them on to working women. This is the Wal-Mart business model, which focuses on maximising returns for shareholders, demands increasing flexibility through 'just-in-time' delivery, and exercises tighter control over inputs and standards, and ever-lower prices (Oxfam International, 2004). Hired short term or without contracts, women work at high speed for low wages in unhealthy conditions without benefits. The consequences of their precarious employment extend beyond the workplace since most women are also raising children and caring for sick and elderly relatives. They are doubly burdened, with little support from their governments or employers; the stress can destroy their own health, break up their families and undermine their children's chances of a better future. The capitalist sector, having received a labour subsidy from women's unpaid work, still takes no responsibility for the labourer or her family during periods of unemployment – another aspect of sub-contracting (Wilson, 2012).

For women living in conflict zones, two problems recur. First is the absence of the state, or more specifically the absence of any social welfare provision by the state, sending households back into subsistence mode unless they can access charities; often the only functioning authority is the traditional leader whose power and legitimacy vary from place to place (some manage community disputes; others profit personally from their position). Second, in the aftermath of conflict, instead of international assistance enabling the state to resupply the social services necessary to reproduction, we see capitalists taking advantage of the situation to institute neoliberal policies of so-called self-sufficiency. Survivors can at best hope for underpaid work from firms moving in to capitalise on the devastation and desperation in their hunt for low-wage labour. After 25 years of civil war in Sri Lanka, despite criticism of the government's wartime conduct, firms moved into the war-torn north-east offering jobs to the vanquished: Brandix Lanka, the country's largest apparel exporter and a supplier to Gap, Victoria's Secret, Marks & Spencer and other large retailers added five factories, including one in the battle-scarred north-east, hiring workers straight out of camps for the internally displaced (Montlake, 2011).

For this study of gender and conflict in Africa, the most pertinent example of labour exploitation by global supply chains comes from a study of minerals extracted by Congolese women and men in militarised conflict zones under near slave-like conditions (see Chapter 1 above for additional details). Artisanal mines are nominally under the control of a single authority, but multiple actors – criminal elements in well-organised groups or small-scale thieves – exerting highly asymmetrical relations of power, threaten workers and use violence to achieve their ends. Of the coltan mined in the DRC in 2000, 58 per cent was consumed in Germany, the US, China, the UK and Japan (Moran *et al.*, 2015, p. 361). A typical coltan supply chain runs from the DRC to Rwanda and thence for processing to the US, where the mineral is used in the manufacture of electronic capacitors, resistors, coils, transformers and the like. These products are then sold to the South Korean radio, television and communications equipment sector, and Koreans most likely purchase them as game consoles and mobile phones. Collusion and corruption of national and local authorities enable these global supply chains to operate with impunity, committing human rights violations that evade detection. The operations also require international buyers to turn a blind eye.

The worst labour abuses occur at the beginning of the supply chain in the forcible recruitment of workers and the terms under which they work. For women, sexual harassment is the norm. Whether the workers are women or men, issues of social reproduction are always part of the story of mineral extraction. A recent project documents miners' lives and experiences of human rights violations in artisanal mining in eastern Congo (Rothenberg and Radley, 2014). Between one and two million people are dependent on artisanal mining for their livelihood in the Kivu provinces, and the number is even greater if one factors in secondary economies and supply chains. In the following excerpt 'XX' is used to respect the miner's preference for anonymity.

> XX wanted to join some other women in the area, who had begun work sifting through the abandoned rock produced by miners to try and find some cassiterite [tin] and earn a little money. To be able to access the abandoned rock, the pit boss told XX she would have to sleep with him. When XX started working, the pit boss then imposed a tax on the small quantities of cassiterite that she managed to find. The local authorities also impose a special tax on all women working in the mining site, simply because they are women. Women who refuse to pay this tax are summoned in front of the traditional authorities and sometimes even the military. XX is then only allowed to sell the little cassiterite that remains after she's paid these taxes to one specific buyer, unlike the men. This buyer – or 'shashuleur' – doesn't use scales to weigh the minerals, but instead simply estimates and buys at the price he wants; often well under what the women report to be the true weight and value of the cassiterite.
>
> (Rothenberg and Radley, 2014, p. 42)

Global supply chains, reliant on low wages imposed by beatings and torture, underpayment, non-payment of wages or wage theft, also depend on high levels of collusion among various authorities and powers in suppressing and controlling the miners. Mining bosses collude with government agencies, mining police, national police, the national army or multiple non-state armed groups. In interviews miners described abuses like forced labour, threatened or overt violence, illegal taxation and theft of minerals at mine sites and along nearby and distant transit routes (Rothenberg and Radley, 2014).

Globalised production has reorganised reproduction in complicated ways, some of which trace back to this use of unlicensed artisanal mining that ignores basic rules of health and safety in a highly dangerous industry. We know almost nothing about miners' lung diseases in this unregulated sector of the industry and therefore nothing about the consequences in the reproductive sector for care of the sick. Poor hygiene in remote Congolese mines, where access to health care is limited, leads to illness and disease. No one assumes responsibility for fatal accidents on mine sites, nor is compensation paid to the miner's family. Workers who survive with serious disability have no way to offset lost wages; many mine bosses punish them for their absence and refuse to allow them to return to work (Rothenberg and Radley, 2014). These are issues of social reproduction implanted in the production process.

Miners know that the dangers they face threaten their own lives and the future of their families. A 36-year-old mother of five children was forced to start working as a porter after her husband was seriously injured.

I work in the mines carrying rocks only because my husband was injured in December 2012 in Mugerero in a landslide that killed two people that were in a tunnel. The mine boss gave us nothing for the care or support of our family, even as my husband is now disabled. Now, I carry sand and stones from the quarry to the river which is about three kilometers. I have to climb hills with a heavy burden of over 20 kilograms. If I were to fall and break my back, that would be the end of my whole family.

(Rothenberg and Radley, 2014, p. 60)

The militarised exploitation that miners interviewed in Congo describe is not a case of history repeating itself; unfree labour today is not the same as slavery 200 years ago. Nor is it a case of history coming full circle – independent Africans are better off than when their countries were choked by colonial rule. The informalisation of economies today, including the casualisation of labour, is fundamentally different partly because of the many links between informal production and global supply chains. But one does observe an economic regression in Congo. Transport in Kisangani has reverted from motorised vehicles back to head porterage (Omasombo Tshonda, 2002). Churches in Kinshasa are performing brutal exorcisms on children accused of witchcraft that hark back to the sixteenth and seventeenth centuries when the Catholic Church in Europe inspired witch hunts and conducted witch trials (De Boeck, 2000; Federici, 2004, 2008). Public mass education has shrunk back to private tuition for those who can afford to pay (although this distinction is illusory when parents pay the salaries of public school teachers), and illiteracy is rising among girls in rural areas (Mujanji, 2002). This regression has profoundly affected gender and generational relations.

The violent reorganisation of the reproductive economy in wartime

To consider the reorganisation of reproduction in wartime, let's begin with what should be an easy question to answer: how is biological reproduction affected by armed conflict? Unfortunately this issue is baffling because there are almost no demographic data on birth rates in wartime (see discussion in Chapter 4 above). Congo is one of ten nations with the world's lowest registration of births (28 per cent) and the numbers fell during the conflict. Yet the evidence for a different demographic regime in civil war is so strong that women successfully pressed the 1993 World Conference on Human Rights to adopt in the Vienna Declaration and Programme of Action article 38, which names violations of the human rights of women in situations of armed conflict, including murder, systematic rape, sexual slavery and forced pregnancy, as violations of the fundamental principles of international human rights and humanitarian law (www.ohchr.org).

The Vienna Declaration was prompted in part by accounts of brutal violations of women's reproductive rights that had just emerged from the Yugoslav wars. Serbian soldiers had expressed their intent to impregnate Muslim women, detention centres were created for this purpose in Bosnia, gynaecologists were present in the rape camps to examine women, and pregnant women were intentionally held until it was too late legally or safely to procure an abortion (Salzman, 1998, p. 359). The deliberate impregnation of some women on the one hand, and the termination of pregnancies on the other, were such prominent features of those wars that this category of gender harm could not be ignored. David Mitchell (2005) argues that the prohibition of sexual violence in humanitarian law has emerged as one of the most fundamental standards of the international community, as a norm of *jus cogens*, a fundamental principle of international law that is accepted by the international community of states as a norm from which no derogation is permitted. Although the courts have not formally designated prohibition of rape as a *jus cogens* rule, its peremptory status, like that of torture, is likely to become an important normative standard within the international legal system.[3]

Widening the circle of concern beyond sexual assault, consider these impacts of war on reproduction: mutilation, enforced widowhood, loss of fertility, nakedness, deprivation of sanitary provisions for menstruation, and HIV transmission (Aolain, 2008, p. 220). None of these gendered harms is defined as a war crime. Violent conflict has lasting effects that are rarely the same for men and women. A narrow focus on sexual and gender-based violence screens from policy-makers a far wider set of gender issues that the new wars have lodged in social relations of production and reproduction (Buvinic *et al.*, 2012).

War-impoverished societies turn men (and some women) into predators and women (and some men) into prey, affecting gender relations in production and social reproduction. Men, writes Falangani Mvondo (2002) of the situation in Congo, concerned about keeping up appearances and not working at jobs beneath their former status, steal from their wives; and women (perhaps because so few ever had high-status jobs) will try anything to bring money into the household. This change in morality occurs in the context of high rates of unemployment, high rates of men's dismissal from jobs in the private sector, and women losing public sector jobs in teaching and health care (or finding salaries not paid or salaries so far below the cost of living that they cannot continue in these jobs, or cannot continue to have only this one job). The recourse to self-employment in the informal sector, the necessity of selling any available asset to accumulate enough capital for an entrepreneur's stake, the attempt to set up one's children in self-employing informal businesses, mostly fall to women. Children are not always responsible, squandering the capital they have been given, and young daughters are targets for leeches. Not only is there no private sector investment to create employment, but also the state fails to make or maintain the rudimentary infrastructure necessary for women to work in the informal sector. The roads are so poor, for example, public transport so lacking, that it is nearly impossible to profit from intercity commerce. Worse, on any road traders will encounter improvised roadblocks, usually created and manned by soldiers to fleece them – either by devising new 'taxes' or by simply helping themselves to the goods in transport.

This picture of people turning on each other, preying on the weak, resorting to illegal and criminal acts in order to survive is not new, and is not particular to the global South, or urban or industrial centres; in war zones the behaviour is economically and politically driven. In Congo, Mvondo (2002) found that the first sacrifice people make is education of daughters and then sons, because even when enrolment is free, books, supplies, uniforms and transport are not. Next to go is morality – the values of a society, which include customary gender and inter-generational relations; for example, male heads of household complain about loss of respect from children for whom they can no longer provide. Children's attitudes change when they are out of school with nothing to do and no support. Boys are prey to pederasty and girls to precocious pregnancy. Next to go is the regime of three meals a day: most families live from day to day and cannot always assemble enough money to purchase the evening meal – they may go two or thee days without eating. When they do eat, the meals are not nutritionally balanced, consisting mainly of cornmeal and some kind of generic spinach. After food, the next concern is health, which means resorting to home remedies for all but the most serious cases requiring medical care. To pay for hospital visits, families will borrow money; if the maternity hospital does not receive payment, it will hold hostage any woman who has just given birth. Some financially strapped families resort to dispensaries that are dirty, exposing mothers and new-borns to infection. Funerals also present a problem; the state no longer provides hearses, and families must also find the money for the private purchase of a coffin as well as a burial plot. Some simply abandon the dead.

In considering how the privatisation of social reproduction has reorganised the reproductive economy, the multiple levels – from the immediate and personal to the ultimate and public – on which neoliberal policies operate become salient. The ways in which economic (production) plans determine, entangle and twist social (reproduction) policies are evident in agreements like GATS and networks like global supply chains. Ethnographic studies of labouring communities reveal the daily realities of 'divisions of labor, notions of worth, rituals of collectivity, claims to identity, and relations of power' (Smith, 2015, p. 578); but these spaces of dense social ties are dogged by violence in conflict zones. Wars may clear away impediments – both moral and material – to regeneration, but without the kind of economic development that also removes extreme poverty, how are these communities to revitalise and reimagine their future?

Conclusions: regression

Conflict seems to exaggerate and intensify women's and men's experiences in production and reproduction. Work is harder – harder to find, harder to secure, more difficult to execute, more stressful and dangerous, more exploitative and precarious – and payment is less reliable, less able to provide basic needs. Social reproduction – pregnancy and childbirth, the maintenance of family life, the preservation of the social and political relations of community, and the promotion of education and creativity – unravels. Death prevails, families disperse, communities split, schools close. Child labour is necessary from a very early age. In military life, men do the work normally accomplished by women – they may create 'families' in bush camps and serve as mothers to child soldiers, as described in the epigraph at the head of this chapter – even as masculinity is aggrandised (Mazurana and Carlson, 2004, p. 14). In war zones, women undertake men's tasks, not only productive work but also political activities. The homestead, if it survives intact, becomes once more a centre of social reproduction and subsistence production, as travel is curtailed, markets close and communications are interrupted. On the run, fleeing from attack, people discard the distinctions of the old social order, including the sexual division of labour and the eminence of the elderly. The dead cannot be buried and ancestors cannot be reverenced. Youth are now in ascendance (De Boeck, 2000).

Violence is met with everywhere, in every kind of economic and social transaction. Weapons of war enforce production. Corruption and criminality, bribery and dishonesty distort social relations of production and reproduction. Labour practices honoured in peacetime – the right to unionise, to strike for better working and living conditions – are suspended. The conduct of hostilities normalises violence and eliminates regular economic activity. Refugee camps become, not havens for the displaced, but recruitment centres for armed groups and labour pools for traffickers. As the shadow economy becomes central to survival in these long conflicts, the dismantling of criminal networks becomes more complicated and disruptive to the lives of ordinary people caught up in collusion and collaboration.

In the aftermath of armed conflict, while people are still disoriented, neoliberals set up shop, an advance party of charities and emergency relief organisations having paved the way. Once again separating economics (post-war recovery) from politics (the work of reconciliation and accountability), advocates of free market economics mobilise international financial institutions and private companies to take over the resources of these countries. The new market-oriented moral order privileges the private over the public and the individual over the collective; it reasserts the family as a gender-neutral self-sufficient unit of care-giving and reciprocal obligations (Bakker, 2003, p. 80). One might ask whether there was ever a functioning public sector to privatise in Sierra Leone or a free labour market to unfetter in Congo.

Neoliberals believe in the perfection of market economies based on models that assume perfect information, perfect competition, perfect risk markets. These beliefs 'were never based on solid empirical and theoretical foundations, and even as many of these policies were being pushed, academic economists were explaining the limitations of markets – for instance, whenever information is imperfect, which is to say always' (Stiglitz, 2007, p. 1). No matter that 70 per cent of the population of post-war Sierra Leone (79 per cent in rural areas) lived below the poverty line of Le 2,111 (less than US$1) per day and that 26 per cent lived in extreme poverty, meaning that their income was insufficient to buy the adult equivalent of 2,700 calories per day (Poate *et al.*, 2008, p. 6). Never mind that after Africa's first world war – which involved nine nations as near as Rwanda and as far as Namibia – 70 per cent of Congolese lived below the poverty line or that poor health and education limited their ability to earn a living (Weijs, Hilhorst and Ferf, 2012, p. 7). Disregarding abundant evidence of the unity of production and reproduction – a unity that is universal and indivisible of spheres that are interdependent and interrelated – neoliberals are certain that government is an impediment to economic recovery and that social reproduction is a sphere unto itself: if families cannot provide for themselves, let charities step in.

The next chapter returns to the consequences to women of separating economics (post-war recovery) from politics (the work of reconciliation and accountability) and to what Saskia Sassen (2010) calls a savage sorting of winners and losers.

Notes

1 Traditional techniques to prevent pregnancy included douching with a chemical mixture after intercourse and muscular movements after intercourse to make the sperm flow out of the vagina. Abortion techniques were also well known: douche with a liquid from the bark of the *mondengu* tree or root of the *ingongo* vine in the first three months (Harms, 1983, p. 106). Low birth rates may also be attributable to high rates of sexually transmitted infections (Hunt, 1999).
2 Compare this company's control of working-class life with what unions were able to accomplish in the West Virginia coal mines (Smith, 2015, p. 571).
3 For a review of all relevant law, see Hunter (2014).

References

Aguilar Molina, Javier (2005) The invention of child witches in the Democratic Republic of Congo: social cleansing, religious commerce and the difficulties of being a parent in an urban culture. London: Save the Children.

Aolain, Fionnuala Ni (2008) Expanding the boundaries of transitional justice, *Ethics & international affairs* 22(2): 213–222.

Bakker, Isabella (2003) Neo-liberal governance to the reprivatization of social reproduction, social provisioning and shifting gender orders. In *Power, production and social reproduction: human in/security in the global political economy*, edited by Isabella Bakker and Stephen Gill, pp. 66–82. Basingstoke: Palgrave Macmillan.

Bakker, Isabella and Stephen Gill, eds (2003) *Power, production, and social reproduction: human in/security in the global political economy*. Basingstoke: Palgrave Macmillan.

Brodie, Janine (2003) Globalization, in/security, and the paradoxes of the social. In *Power, production, and social reproduction: human in/security in the global political economy* edited by Isabella Bakker and Stephen Gill, pp. 47–65. Basingstoke: Palgrave Macmillan.

Bryceson, Deborah Fahy and Ulla Vuorela (1984) Outside the domestic labor debate: towards a theory of modes of human reproduction, *Review of radical political economics* 16(2/3): 137–166.

Bryceson, Deborah Fahy, Jesper Bosse Jønsson and Hannelore Verbrugge (2013) Prostitution or partnership? Wifestyles in Tanzanian artisanal gold-mining settlements, *Journal of modern African studies* 51(1): 33–56.

Bush, Ray (2007) *Poverty and neoliberalism: persistence and reproduction in the global south.* London: Pluto Press.

Buvinic, Mayra, Monica Das Gupta, Ursula Casabonne and Philip Verwimp (2012) Violent conflict and gender inequality: an overview. Brighton: Institute of Development Studies, University of Sussex, HiCN working paper 129, www.hicn.org/wordpress/wp-content/uploads/2012/06/HiCN-WP-1291.pdf, accessed 20 July 2014.

Campbell, Gwyn, Suzanne Miers and Joseph C. Miller, eds (2007) *Women and slavery.* Athens: Ohio University Press.

Campbell, Gwyn, Suzanne Miers and Joseph C. Miller, eds (2009) *Children in slavery through the ages.* Athens: Ohio University Press.

Caplan, Pat (2010) Child sacrifice in Uganda? The BBC, 'witchdoctors' and anthropologists, *Anthropology today* 26(2): 4–7.

Clelland, Donald A. (2014) Unpaid labor as dark value in global commodity chains. In *Gendered commodity chains: seeing women's work and households in global production,* edited by Wilma A. Dunaway, pp. 72–87. Stanford, CA: Stanford University Press.

Cordell, Dennis D. (2013) Interdependence and convergence: migration, men, women, and work in sub-Saharan Africa, 1800–1975. In *Proletarian and gendered mass migrations: a global perspective on continuities and discontinuities from the 19th to the 21st centuries,* edited by Dirk Hoerder and Amarjit Kaur, pp. 173–215. Leiden: Brill.

De Boeck, Filip (2000) Le 'deuxième monde' et les 'enfants-sorciers' en République Démocratique du Congo, *Politique africaine* 80: 32–57.

Dunaway, Wilma A. (2014) Bringing commodity chain analysis back to its world-systems roots: rediscovering women's work and households, *Journal of world-systems research* 20(1): 64–81.

Ehrlich, Paul R. (1971) *The population bomb.* London: Ballantine and Friends of the Earth.

Elson, Diane (1999) Labor markets as gendered institutions: equality, efficiency and empowerment issues, *World development* 27(3): 611–627.

Federici, Silvia (2004) *Caliban and the witch: women, the body and primitive accumulation.* New York: Autonomedia.

Federici, Silvia (2008) Witch-hunting, globalization, and feminist solidarity in Africa today, *Journal of international women's studies* 10(1): 21–35.

Gouby, Mélanie (2011) Kivu children accused of sorcery, Institute for War & Peace Reporting, http://iwpr.net/report-news/kivu-children-accused-sorcery, accessed 20 June 2014.

Harms, Robert (1983) Sustaining the system: trading towns along the middle Zaire. In *Women and slavery in Africa,* edited by Claire C. Robertson and Martin A. Klein, pp. 95–110. Madison: University of Wisconsin Press.

Higginson, John (1989) *A working class in the making: Belgian colonial labour policy, private enterprise, and the African mineworker, 1907–1951.* Madison: University of Wisconsin Press.

Human Rights Watch (2006) What future? Street children in the Democratic Republic of Congo. New York: Human Rights Watch.

Humphries, Jane (1991) The sexual division of labor and social control: an interpretation, *Review of radical political economics* 23(3&4): 269–296.

Hunt, Nancy Rose (1999) *A colonial lexicon of birth ritual, medicalization, and mobility in the Congo.* Durham, NC: Duke University Press.

Hunter, Jane (2014) Rape in conflict: what does the law say? Stratford, UK: Action on Armed Violence, https://aoav.org.uk/2014/rape-in-conflict-legal-status, accessed 20 June 2015.

Koroma, Dauda (2012) In Sierra Leone, young boys confess to witchcraft, 17 September, http://news.sl/drwebsite/exec/view.cgi?archive=8&num=21118&printer=1, accessed 20 January 2014.

Lenz, Ilse (2005) Recovering translation – translating recoverings? Towards integrative perspectives on the labor and other social movements, *Labor history* 46(2): 214–219.

McCann, Deirdre (2005) Sexual harassment at work: national and international responses. Geneva: ILO Conditions of work and employment series no 2.

Marchal, Jules (1999) *Travail forcé pour le cuivre et pour l'or: l'histoire du Congo, 1910–1945*. Borgloon: Paula Bellings.

Mazurana, Dyan and Khristopher Carlson (2004) From combat to community: women and girls of Sierra Leone, www.womenwagingpeace.net, accessed 31 July 2013.

Mies, Maria (1986) *Patriarchy and capital accumulation on a world scale: women in the international division of labour*. London: Zed Books.

Mitchell, David S. (2005) The prohibition of rape in international humanitarian law as a norm of *jus cogens*: clarifying the doctrine, *Duke journal of comparative & international law* 15: 219–257.

Montlake, Simon (2011) Brandix adapts to Sri Lanka's post-civil war world, www.forbes.com/global/2011/1205/companies-people-ashroff-omar-brandix-apparel-sri-lankan-montlake.html, accessed 20 January 2014.

Moran, Daniel, Darian McBain, Keiichiro Kanemoto, Manfred Lenzen and Arne Geschke (2015) Global supply chains of coltan: a hybrid cycle assessment study using a social indicator, *Journal of industrial ecology* 19(3): 357–365.

Mujanji, Tshiamala (2002) Quelques visages de l'informel: le cas de la ville de Mbuji-mayi. In *Manières de vivre: économie de la 'débrouille' dans les villes du Congo/Zaïre*, edited by Gauthier de Villers, Bogumil Jewsiewicki and Laurent Monnier, pp. 65–90. Paris: L'Harmattan.

Mvondo, Falangani (2002) Paupérisation de familles petites-bourgeoises et transformation des valeurs en période de crise. In *Manières de vivre: économie de la 'débrouille' dans les villes du Congo/Zaïre*, edited by Gauthier de Villers, Bogumil Jewsiewicki and Laurent Monnier, pp. 113–140. Paris: L'Harmattan.

Omasombo Tshonda, Jean (2002) Vivre à Kisangani: le cas de l'économie du transport. In *Manières de vivre: économie de la 'débrouille' dans les villes du Congo/Zaïre*, edited by Gauthier de Villers, Bogumil Jewsiewicki and Laurent Monnier, pp. 91–111. Paris: L'Harmattan.

Oxfam International (2004) *Trading away our rights: women working in global supply chains*. Oxford, www.maketradefair.com, accessed 30 June 2014.

Phillips, Nicola (2013) Unfree labour and adverse incorporation in the global economy: comparative perspectives on Brazil and India, *Economy and society* 42(2): 171–196.

Poate, Derek, Paul Balogun, Ines Rothmann, Mark Knight and Fatmata Sesay (2008) *Country programme evaluation: Sierra Leone*. London: Department for International Development.

Prügl, Elisabeth and Jacqui True (2014) Equality means business? Governing gender through transnational public–private partnerships, *Review of international political economy* 21(6): 1137–1170.

RDC (2010) Annuaire statistique de l'enseignement primaire, secondaire et professionnel année scolaire 2008–2009. Kinshasa, www.eduquepsp.cd/annuaire-statistique.html, accessed 20 June 2015.

Robertson, Claire C. and Martin A. Klein, eds (1983) *Women and slavery in Africa*. Madison: University of Wisconsin Press.

Rodet, Marie (2014) Forced labor, resistance, and masculinities in Kayes, French Sudan, 1919–1946, *International labor and working-class history* 86: 107–123.

Rothenberg, Daniel and Ben Radley (2014) 'We miners take our lives in our hands, save nothing, and believe only in luck.' The lived experience of human rights and labor violations in select artisanal mining sites in North and South Kivu. Chicago: Heartland Alliance for Human Needs and Human Rights and Center for Law and Global Affairs and the School of Politics and Global Studies at Arizona State University.

Rubbers, Benjamin (2015) When women support the patriarchal family: the dynamics of marriage in a Gécamines mining camp (Katanga province, DR Congo), *Journal of historical sociology* 28(6): 213–234.

Salzman, Todd A. (1998) Rape camps as a means of ethnic cleansing: religious, cultural, and ethical responses to rape victims in the former Yugoslavia, *Human rights quarterly* 20(2): 348–378.

Sassen, Saskia (2010) A savage sorting of winners and losers: contemporary versions of primitive accumulation, *Globalizations* 7(1–2): 23–50.

Smith, Barbara Ellen (2015) Another place is possible? Labor geography, spatial dispossession, and gendered resistance in central Appalachia, *Annals of the association of American geographers* 105(3): 567–582.

Stiglitz, Joseph E. (2007) Bleakonomics, *New York Times Sunday Book Review*, 30 September, www.nytimes.com/2007/09/30/books/review/Stiglitz-t.html?_r=0, accessed 3 January 2013.

UN (n.d.) DR Congo's 'child witches'. New York: United Nations 21st century show #54, www.un.org/webcast/pdfs/21century54.pdf, accessed 20 June 2015.

Verhaegen, Benoit (1990) *Femmes zaïroises de Kisangani: combats pour la survie*. Paris: L'Harmattan.

Waddington, Mark (2006) *'Child witches', child soldiers, child poverty and violence: street children in crisis in the Democratic Republic of Congo*. Report by the All Party Parliamentary Group on Street Children on its mission to the Democratic Republic of Congo and recommendations for addressing the escalating street child crisis. London: Consortium for Street Children.

Weijs, Bart, Dorothea Hilhorst and Adriaan Ferf (2012) Livelihoods, social protection and basic services in DRC. London: Overseas Development Institute Secure Livelihoods Research Consortium working paper 2.

Wilson, Tamar Diana (2012) Primitive accumulation and the labor subsidies to capitalism, *Review of radical political economics* 44(2): 201–212.

Part III

Social movements and social justice

6   Social movements and the struggle for social justice

Ô mes amis, il n'y a nul ami...[1]

(Abadie, 2010)

Social movements – those thrilling and heart-breaking expressions of popular discontent, desperation and despair, steeled threats and single-minded demands, familiar aspirations and hope-inflated desires – have been critical in determining the course of African history. By definition, social movements comprise networks of informal interactions that tie together informal groups and individuals, and at times formal organisations, in struggles for social change on the basis of shared affinity (Eschle and Stammers, 2000). They emerge in response to situations of inequality, oppression, racism and unmet social, political, economic or cultural demands. Women's movements may not conform to the standard profile since they often lack common objectives, continuity and unity; some focus on gender identity, others on social transformation, even as all are political and reject patriarchal privilege (Antrobus, 2004).

The social movements explored in this chapter challenge continuing conflict and persistent violence in the public and private spheres in Africa in both historical and modern times. They are the collective campaigns and crusades people undertake to resist war and oppose violence. They are also the organised efforts to pursue social and racial justice in the productive and reproductive arenas of lives altered by war's brutality. My purpose is to read these struggles through a gendered lens and from the perspective of gender justice, all the while recognising that 'racism and neocolonialism are more key to black women's oppression and lack of resources than gender hierarchy' (Day, 2008, p. 495). The most prominent kinds of protest against visible violence are anti-war movements, for example those of Women Against War; food riots, frequently led women, are protests against the less visible violence of hunger. Social movements assume solidarity and some form of union among adherents, but civil wars break down social cohesion, making social solidarity more problematic. Civil conflict removes the basis for collective resistance by breaking up communities along ethnic, racial and religious lines and turning one neighbour against another; in the process, identities may be reshaped and new alliances forged, sometimes based on the desire for revenge rather than justice. Resistance and a counter-mobilisation of new political forces may come to constitute a new global politics, as the neoliberal model intensifies the globalisation of power.

The negotiations of social movements, their antagonism to capital (both public and private), encompass much of the overt social struggle of the last 20 years: whether campaigns for women's welfare, or gay rights or indigenous peoples, lobbies to save the environment or rallies to end the use of nuclear power and nuclear weapons, these struggles have become class movements (Caffentzis, 2002, pp. 14–15). They follow unpredictable trajectories: how movements identify themselves and what they actually do may diverge. In practice, social movements run the gamut reflecting their origins, funding sources, links to particular governments, ideological roots and divergent social forces. At one end of the spectrum are large non-membership nongovernmental organisations (NGOs, more properly private voluntary organisations) that depend on state or commercial funding; at the other end are grassroots, local or membership-based groups with little or no outside funding. Placing particular movements along such a range is less than straightforward in practice: movements dominated by middle-class educated activists may powerfully articulate an apparently radical agenda for change on behalf of the poor with whom they have no effective links, while grassroots movements may articulate their aspirations and grievances through religious or ethnic discourses that are rarely emancipating (Larmer, 2010, p. 254).

From the early nineteenth to the twentieth centuries, African social movements brought about the end of some of the worst forms of violence on the continent: they achieved the abolition of the slave trade, the legal termination of slavery and, with the election of Nelson Mandela in 1994, the conclusion of the century of formal colonial rule, albeit with the aid of important international allies. These changes in the status of women and men, peasants and workers, for worse and for better, did not come without struggle; the capture of slaves entailed bloody warfare, as did the colonial conquest, and some Africans won liberation from colonial control only after violent combat. More than one million Algerians lost their lives over the course of the eight-year war for independence from France that began in 1954. Women participated in all of these movements, alongside male comrades. At the same time, one could say that nonviolence originated as a movement in Africa when, in 1906, Mohandas Gandhi launched Satyagraha, the nonviolent resistance campaign on behalf of Indian voting rights in South Africa. If African social movements did not coalesce to bring about the changes that the labour movement was able to secure in Europe, if instead, since independence, Africans have seen new forms of violence in their daily lives, it is not for lack of vibrant social movements seeking to bring about progressive political and social change.

Social movements are not exempt from the contradictions and hierarchies of the societies in which they operate; exploitation and social conflict are characteristic, and inequalities of resources, influence and education are typical of these societies, as well as differences of class, gender and ethnicity (Larmer,

2010, p. 252). Their very diversity complicates the problem of conceptualising solidarity among protesters and between social movements (Lenz, 2005, p. 214). For most women, progressive social change starts in the reproductive sphere, not in parliament or on the factory floor, lending different forms of action and mobilisation to women's social movements and the adoption of contentious concepts of citizenship and democracy.

Social movements encompass an astonishing breadth of concerns, and they also change dramatically over time. Analysts distinguish several post-Second World War periods of social struggle in Africa: anti-colonial, nationalist and liberation struggles in the 1950s and early 1960s; a period in the mid-1960s and 1970s when liberation movements held state power and in some countries were more repressive than many local and international supporters had hoped; economic crisis and structural adjustment from the mid-1970s to the end of the 1980s; and in the early 1990s, pro-democracy movements, political transformation and hopes for democratic civil societies, which were sooner or later co-opted by international agencies and donors such as the World Bank (Brandes and Engels, 2011; Larmer, 2010, p. 257). The history of struggles against incorporation, repression and co-optation – the history of anti-slavery, anti-colonialism, labour movements and women's movements – is the heart of the pursuit of social justice in Africa.

Civil society

Social movements are not coterminous with civil society, which has become a popular concept in the analysis of the social bases of recent political change in Africa and in external policy support for processes of liberal democratic political reform. A set of (largely urban) formal organisations and especially NGOs with external links is frequently portrayed as the driving force behind civil society and as the guarantee of democratisation and the containment of the state (Allen, 1997, p. 329). Conceptually, however, civil society is diffuse, hard to define, empirically imprecise and ideologically laden. Analytically it is shallow, and concepts such as class prejudice, racism or gender bias contribute far more to our understanding of recent political change than can civil society. Its popularity and continued use rest on its ideological claim that civil society is necessarily distinct from the state, inevitably in opposition to the state, and the source of (liberal) democratic values and pressures. Although based on flimsy evidence at best, civil society is a concept useful to proponents not only of liberal democratic reform, but also of neoliberal economic change; most of these advocates are not in Africa (Allen, 1997, p. 329).

African analysts, for example those associated with CODESRIA, prefer the term social movements, together with class, gender, ethnicity and the state, to civil society (Allen, 1997, p. 334). Nonetheless, it is important to note that women often predominate in civil society, whereas men are more active in formal political institutions, raising questions as to what is politics, and what is democratic participation (Bell *et al.*, 2004). Long-time feminist scholars of

African social movements like Aili Mari Tripp (1994) regret that the analyses of civil society ignore the gender implications of small informal women's groups (in countries like Tanzania). Because civil society is supposed to stand between the public and private spheres and separate them, these discussions unloose the basic ties between the public activities of the state and the private lives of households – an issue that has been a theme throughout this book. The implications for political economy of preferential use of civil society are clear: for neoliberal regimes to be legitimate, they require a flourishing civil society, which in turn needs a state that is limited, does not intervene in the economy and furthers the freedoms of individual citizens, notably their market freedoms (Allen, 1997, p. 335). In the neoliberal package, civil society is associated with notions of good governance and the arguments of international financial institutions about the links between economic and political reform. Since political reform is essential to economic reform, civil society, which connects the two by influencing policy and holding regimes accountable, is critical. It follows that these arguments justify the conditionalities attached to loans and the redirection of aid flows from bad government (ignoring existing official state arrangements and seeking to rid people of overbearing, autocratic, inefficient and corrupt government) to good NGOs that elevate private and public non-state actors (Allen, 1997, p. 335).

The support of civil society in contradistinction to social movements has both political and economic consequences for women. Associations like the International Federation of Business and Professional Women and Women's Learning Partnership are readily integrated into civil society; women's anti-war movements like Women in Black and the Women's Peace Camp at Greenham Common in Berkshire, England, are less easily assimilated. Service organisations like the Red Cross and Red Crescent Societies further the aims of the neoliberal agenda, while protest groups like Pussy Riot and their followers are disruptive. With changes in development funding and practice over the past ten to 15 years many different actors are competing for a role in saving the world – and saving women and girls in particular. They focus on short-term gains, success in reaching targets and changing lives within clearly defined goals (Wallace and Porter, 2013). UN organisations and local and international nongovernmental organisations seem to be carrying out a concerted campaign for women's social mobilisation that is actually in the interest of globalising capitalist production (Archarya, 2008, p. 55).

Women activists meet with resistance to the recognition of gender equality within social movements: gendered attitudes, behaviour and stereotypes are ingrained in many movements, and ideas around gender, culture, tradition and the private sphere also pose obstacles to women's participation (Horn, 2013). The reasons for the marginalisation of progressive women's movements are rooted in their demands for social transformation, which challenge the social and economic fallout from neoliberal globalisation. In view of persistent gender violence, some African women's movements are demanding nothing less than a new social contract, one that rejects their pre-existing social, economic and legal status, as well as patriarchal gender constructions (AAWORD, www.afard. org).[2] These are the conditions that led to armed conflict in the first place and they must be dismantled (Lemaitre and Sandvik, 2014). Lynda Day (2008, p. 491) writes of the resistance faced by such women in Sierra Leone:

> male pushback results from a neo-liberal women's movement that frames women's economic marginality and lack of access to political power as the result of patriarchy and male privilege, rather than using an African feminist framework which recognizes women's lack of resources as primarily the result of the appropriation of the country's wealth by multinational corporations, lending agencies and members of the elite. If viewed from this perspective, the women's movement would be framed as a socially transformative struggle for all sectors of society, and not as a contest between men and women for power.

NGOs and civil society organisations have some of the same elements of social movement praxis as self-defined social movements, strikes and riots, but they are far more diverse and their missions vary widely from service delivery to advocacy. A tension arises between globalised organisations like international NGOs and locally initiated social movements of resistance, even when the latter link up with like-minded groups in other countries; the tension stems from the situation of NGOs in the neoliberal orbit. 'The myriad day-to-day struggles for change are Africa's true story of struggle; messy, ideologically confused, inherently contradictory, such struggles and movements may contain genuinely organic seeds of indigenous change' (Larmer, 2010, p. 260).

Labour movements

One particular social movement deserves special mention: labour movements have mobilised for decent work, higher wages and social welfare to counter unequal distribution of wealth and the insecurity of the labour market (Lenz, 2005, p. 215). Labour is a crucial part of contemporary global justice and solidarity movements, and in Africa it was critical to the movement for independence. As the most important African mass organisations of that time, unions played a singular role in the anti-colonial movements; they very early on realised the extent of their power to interfere with colonial plans by disrupting production and transport. Immediately following the Second World War, unionists in manufacturing, transport, extractive industries and the professions (lawyers, teachers and the like) were leaders in ousting colonial regimes. All of this played out in the competitive militarised environment of the Cold War; by its end, the international financial institutions (IFIs) had mobilised to foist anti-union reforms on African workers and their governments. Structural adjustment programmes, which devastated the formal sector and led to massive job losses, took their toll on membership, breaking the unions (Schillinger, 2005). In an era of deindustrialisation and disinvestment, the Washington Consensus identified labour market deregulation as one of the tenets of structural adjustment, and IFI country-level policy advice frequently included recommendations to weaken labour market regulations. Today the World Bank sedulously promotes labour market flexibility – on a continent where 80 per cent work in the informal sector.

Trade unions have been one of the social movements most resistant to women, ignoring their concerns and creating barriers to their participation and leadership. Beyond South Africa, which is relatively industrialised and has a larger formal sector, few women are prominent in labour relations or have a history of organising. Women tend to succeed when they organise sectors in which they hold a majority, like food marketing. Examples of market women's early unionisation in Sierra Leone were given in Chapter 3 above. Organising women in the informal sector is especially challenging: self-employed or independent operators, such as street vendors, shebeen owners, hairdressers and artisans, who are doing business directly with local consumers, dominate the sector. Without a shared work space in which to meet and build trust, without a common adversary to whom demands can be addressed, organising campaigns are costly and meet with little success.

Scattered reports tell of women workers striking to organise unions. For example, in 2003 in Uganda, Apparels Tri-Star, a Sri Lankan textile factory that sells clothes to Target, Children's Place and Dollar General in the US under the African Growth and Opportunity Act (AGOA), saw 400 young women workers (known as the 'Agoa girls') go out on a two-week strike accusing the management of gross abuse of rights, including sexual exploitation, work under inhumane and unsafe conditions, and restrictions on workers' freedom of association; when hundreds were fired, hundreds more protested the dismissals outside parliament, and they too were fired (PANA, 2003). In some instances, women are caught up in men's strikes, as in the deadly disruptions in Sierra Leone at African Minerals Limited (AML) in 2012: police fired live ammunition at unarmed community members, killing one woman, Musu Conteh, who worked for an AML contractor, while she was singing and dancing alongside several dozen women demonstrators (HRW, 2014). AML, an iron ore mining firm headquartered in London, was formerly the Sierra Leone Diamond Company.

With renewed investment and development coming at the end of civil war in Congo, women began to join trade unions and eventually to assume leadership positions. Marie Josée Lokongo Bosiko is the vice-president of the National Union of Congolese Workers (UNTC), which has 64 trade unions across Congo (www.ituc-csi.org/spotlight-on-marie-josee-lokongo?lang=en). The UNTC is one of the three organisations in Congo affiliated with the International Trade Union Confederation (ITUC). The UNTC has created women's committees in every company where the union is represented to channel problems specific to women workers into discussions with employers. The UNTC is also trying to organise informal sector workers by, for example, setting up women's committees in Kinshasa markets to teach women how they can avoid many of the problems they face with various authorities if they join a union. The UNTC operates a mutual health fund that offers beneficiaries cut-price treatment and a clinic for union members and their families. Maternity is one of the biggest issues: employers don't want to hire women who take time off during pregnancy, for medical check-ups, the baby's vaccinations, and so on. The union is fighting to protect workers' maternity rights while also advising on family planning. Sexual harassment is a serious problem, and women are urged to report it and receive counselling.

ITUC (2010) took a major stand on the distinct role of women trade union-ists in conflict prevention and resolution, especially with regard to violence per-petrated against women during conflicts. The union maintains that conflicts are the result of fundamental problems such as the unequal distribution of wealth, corruption, impunity, bad governance, and the neoliberal policies imposed by international financial institutions and the WTO. The trade union struggle against violence in the workplace cannot be dissociated from the fight against violence within society, they maintain. Unionists are experienced actors in the field of conflict management: witness the millions of collective agreements around the world negotiated by workers' organisations to improve living and working conditions. ITUC insists that effective action requires unions that are independent, democratic and representative, and such unions will be strength-ened by a greater involvement of women.

Resistance

Resistance, that refusal to accept or comply – whether individual unwillingness, deliberate slow-downs or unresponsiveness, whether group nonviolent action, concerted boycott or underground insurgent organisation, whether expressed through political satire, body language or cartoons and graffiti – is the motor of many social movements. Even when resistance is the act of an individual, it requires collusion among participants as well as the development of some degree of mutual support to prevent denunciations. The civil resistance discussed here is transgressive and non-institutional; it is purposive, coordinated and sustained in nature (Chenoweth and Cunningham, 2013). The examples are drawn from the histories of Sierra Leone and Congo. The purpose is to reveal African women's continuous presence in these social movements and make visible their contribution to social justice.

Resisting the violence of slavery

The international struggles to abolish the slave trade and slavery were the world's first broadly based peaceful reform movements to achieve their goals (Northrup, 1997). The late eighteenth century was the age of revolutions, and no account of insurrection in Africa can be divorced from the wave of rebellions sweeping the Caribbean, the Americas and France (Hochschild, 2005). Indi-vidual Africans opposed the Atlantic slave trade[3] – for example, Naimbana (c.1710–1793) of Koya (Temne Kingdom) and Gumbu Smart (1750–1820) (Ijagbemi, 1978). African calls for the end of slavery emerged in Britain at this time, voiced by freed African slaves like Ottobah Cugoano (John Stuart, c.1757–1791), Ignatius Sancho (c.1729–1780) and Olaudah Equiano (Gustavus Vassa, c.1745–1797); they gave impetus to the British movement for abolition and eventually to the founding of Sierra Leone (Fyfe, 1993, p. 13). The story of Edmund Morel's exposé of slavery in Congo, which led to the end of de jure slavery there and the demise of Congo Free State, is well known (Marchal, 1996; Morel, 1903).

The slave revolts of the 1870s and 1880s took place in the context of the British anti-slavery campaign and supportive missionary activity. Rebellions against enslavement in Africa were met with forceful suppression and were not peaceful. Recorded by European observers as early as the eighteenth century, slave revolts, which grew into a social movement, occurred in every setting, at every step in the process of enslavement, and used violent and nonviolent means. In Sierra Leone an uprising, which broke out in 1785 among several thousand slaves held by Mandingos, lasted more than ten years until it was finally suppressed in 1796; women were certainly among the rebels, if not initially then later at the settlements the insurgents founded (Nowak, 1986).

In addition to outright uprisings, revolts in Africa took many other forms: opposition during the process of enslavement or capture; escape during the long march to the coast; redemption of family and friends; and rebellion in the pens where slaves were warehoused awaiting buyers prior to shipment (Diouf, 2003; Mouser, 2007). Strategies ranged from the defensive and protective to the offensive; they included resettlement in remote areas, construction of fortresses and establishment of free villages for escaped slaves, as well as more militarised styles of leadership; immediate responses featured the defence of communities by secret societies, women's organisations and young men's militias, children acting as sentinels, the use of venomous plants and insects, and wearing amulets created by spiritual leaders (Diouf, 2003).

The organisation of slaves in Zanzibar was a much later phenomenon than the West African slave market. The first recorded revolt on Zanzibar island did not occur until 1840 (Akinola, 1972). Hadrami Arabs from Makulla and Sheher organised their slaves into urban labour gangs from the 1860s and initially used them to transport merchandise to and from the docks of Zanzibar (Akinola, 1972). Urban slaves lived wretchedly in hovels, worked seven days a week and could be hired out for all kinds of work, with payment going to their masters; escape was the most common way they resisted their condition. The other categories of slavery are familiar: domestic slaves, who were mainly women, often concubines, and plantations slaves. This last group was prone to violent uprisings and revolts from the 1870s, provoked by the intolerable conditions in which they lived and worked. They were often brutalised by the callous administration of cruel punishment: free application of whips, fetters, stocks, manacles, chains and iron collars (Akinola, 1972, p. 222).

*Resisting the violence of colonial control in production and
reproduction*

Resistance began before the colonial powers were able fully to impose their rule,
often taking the form of armed struggle, and it continued well into the twentieth century; many European powers did not achieve control of their African
colonies until after the First World War. Much has been written about political
resistance to colonialism (see, for example, Maddox, 1993); little analysis of
women's resistance is available from a feminist viewpoint beyond the now
classic descriptions of women's participation in liberation wars (for example,
Guinea Bissau, Mozambique, South Africa and Zimbabwe). Debates on decolonisation that took place in the UN General Assembly from 1946 to 1960 were
masculinised on both sides: colonialists relied on a paternalist masculinity to
legitimate their rule ('our dependencies require our rule the way a child requires
a father'); anti-colonialists replied with a resistance masculinity ('colonialism is
emasculating, decolonisation is necessary for a return of masculine dignity')
(Patil, 2009). Case studies give a glimpse of women's resistance in production
and social reproduction.

In Sierra Leone rebellions against colonial rule were immediate in the wake
of colonial acquisition: for example, in 1898 most of the districts rose up in
opposition to taxation (Fyle, 2006; Grace, 1975). Resistance continued throughout the colonial period with women participating predominantly in Freetown.
In 1940 the women's auxiliary of the West African Youth League created two
trade unions, the Sierra Leone Market Women's Union, led by Mary M. Martyn
and Christiana England, and the Sierra Leone Washer-women's Union led by
Violet Johnson (Denzer, 1987, p. 445; Luke, 1985). In 1947 the Sierra Leone
Market Women's Union called for the lowering of market stall fees, improve-
ments in market hygiene, an end to unpopular wartime controls still in effect,
and a halt to permits that allowed hawkers and petty traders to compete for customers in and around markets (Denzer, 1987, p. 445). The Sierra Leone
Women's Movement, established in 1951, was directly involved in the mobilisation of demonstrators and petitioners protesting against the rising cost of
living: they organised cooperatives and bulk purchasing (Abdullah, 1997;
Denzer, 1987, p. 447). Some of these groups are still active today – the Sierra
Leone Market Women's Union, the Sierra Leone Women's Movement – and
were central advocates for women after the civil war (King, 2006, p. 258).

The British wanted to incorporate the Sierra Leonean working class into a
system of industrial relations that would contain post-depression militant
working-class agitation that enveloped the country in the years leading up to
Second World War. Sierra Leone's recently discovered mines promised new
economic wealth and, together with the strategic importance assigned to Freetown, should have translated into higher wages and a decrease in unemployment; instead, most people experienced an inflationary rise in the cost of living
(Spitzer and Denzer, 1973). In the post-Second World War context of decolonisation, however, workers and their unions recognised the administration's

tactics as attempts to keep wages down, and they began a series of strikes in the early 1950s, culminating in the general strike of 1955 (Abdullah, 1997). We know that women were present because one was killed in the rioting that followed the strike (UK House of Commons, 1955).

In rural areas of Congo, where the Belgians imposed compulsory cultivation, peasant resistance took many forms in the struggles against forced production, levies of cash, labour for public projects and conscription. Colonial economic demands undermined the social reproduction of communities, and everyday forms of resistance were the efforts of women and men to define the terms under which they wanted to produce and reproduce within the colonial economy. Mbole peasants (in today's Orientale Province) employed flight to the forest and marshes, sabotage of agricultural calendars and migration – 'weapons of the weak' – to resist demands to produce palm oil, rubber, rice and other compulsory crops for the colonial economy (Likaka, 1994, p. 590).

In the industrial areas of Congo, resistance was almost continual. Skirmishes over tax collection were frequent and resistance was common, especially among labourers. The most important catalyst for worker unrest at the Union Minière du Haut-Katanga between 1918 and 1930 was the increasing divergence between the basis of authority in the industry and the changing requirements of production (Higginson, 1988). Workers preferred non-confrontational sabotage to conflict; in early 1929 they chose the vulnerable new hydroelectric power lines as their easiest target, bringing work almost to a standstill (Higginson, 1988, p. 18). Compulsory overtime, new machinery that set a faster pace of work and overzealous supervisors were the most common reasons for acts of sabotage.

African women living at the urbanised mine sites created their own closed voluntary associations; the most important among them were the *kufunga* bars, which were a crucial facet of urban African life before independence. The bars enabled women to make money and initiate young women from rural areas into the mysteries of town life. They were an important way station in the attempt to construct a stable form of conjugal life and to give migrant men some idea of the assets women of different ages and from different locations might bring with them in the making of urban households. The frequent arrests of African women in both towns and rural areas for the illegal sale of beer and *lutuku*, a spirit distilled from either corn or cassava, suggests that there was more organisation among women in the industrial towns of Katanga than average colonial administrators were aware of (Higginson, 1989, p. 250, n. 100).

Overthrowing colonialism

Sierra Leone and Congo achieved independence at roughly the same time, in 1960/61 at the height of the Cold War, along with most other African countries, but their paths to independence were different. In part this was because the colonial powers, with empires of vastly uneven scope, chose disparate trajectories for decolonisation. The British created the Commonwealth in 1949, providing a route for newly independent former colonies to maintain economic and security ties with the metropole. The transition to independence in Sierra Leone was relatively peaceful, although the legacies of colonialism – particularly the dissimilarities between the colony and the protectorate – left difficulties that have yet to be overcome. Belgium, with its single colony (as opposed to more than 20 British colonies in Africa alone) and limited imperial experience, relinquished control of Congo (which it administered together with Rwanda and Burundi) in a matter of months.

Not all nationalist leaders appreciated women's importance as a base of mass support, relegating them to women's leagues or auxiliaries. Women's organisations, especially market women, merchants and traders, were active anti-colonialists in Guinea, Nigeria, Sierra Leone and Tanzania. Kwame Nkrumah (Ghana) and Ahmed Sékou Touré (Guinea) were two leaders who supported the mobilisation of women; Nkrumah's party reserved 10 per cent of parliamentary seats for women, and Touré had an indirect impact on Congo.

Mobilisation of women came late in the independence movement in Congo. Pauline Opango, wife of Patrice Lumumba, was an early member of the Mouvement National Congolais. In 1960 Antoine Gizenga asked Andrée Blouin (originally from the Central African Republic, her father was French, her mother African), who had been working with Sékou Touré in Guinea, to come and work with women in Congo; she quickly created the Feminine Movement for African Solidarity and enrolled tens of thousands of women (Bouwer, 2010, pp. 90–91). Their platform called for literacy, health education, women's rights and progress, a campaign against alcoholism and a service to protect abandoned women and children.

Women's participation in the armed rebellions against Mobutu's rule following Lumumba's assassination was significant. In the resistance, which cost perhaps one million lives, Pierre Mulele, assisted by his wife Léonie Abo, led a struggle in the Kwilu region from 1963 to 1968; teams of female nurses, instructors, peasants and high school students joined him. The women, who accounted for between 20 and 35 per cent of the teams, were fighters, officials, trainers and recruiters, as well as informers, spies and servants (Bouwer, 2010, p. 104). Women were part of the assault teams at Idiofa and Dibaya, a woman served as a judge on the popular tribunal of Yene, and women were physical education instructors for young people (Verhaegen, quoted in Bouwer, 2010, p. 105). In Orientale and the eastern provinces, women also participated in the rebellions where they performed tasks like surveillance and meal preparation.

Movements after independence

Perhaps it is the invisibility of women's participation in the anti-colonial struggles that contributed to the ease with which men newly installed in political power seemed to abandon their late comrades and erstwhile sisters. One would like to think that the nature of the new African governments had some influence, but the dismissal of women's claims was as senseless in revolutionary

Algeria as it was in the authoritarian regimes that assumed power in Congo and Sierra Leone. William Reno (2005, p. 127) believes that 'in violent conflicts in places like Congo, Liberia and Sierra Leone, economic interests have crowded out ideologically articulate mass-based social movements for reform or revolutionary change to a degree that was not apparent during earlier anti-colonial struggles'.

Although they were marginalised, women did enter the political arena in Sierra Leone: Constance Cummings-John, active in the struggle for independence, stood for a seat in parliament and became mayor of Freetown in the 1960s. Other women who stood for or were appointed to political offices in the post-independence era include June Holst-Roness, Florence Dillsworth and Nancy Steele, a woman known for her militancy (Abdullah *et al.*, p. 3). From 1996 to 2002, the number of women running for parliament rose from 65 to 156 and the number elected from five to 18; at the local government level, 54 women won councillorship elections, 5.3 per cent were elected as mayors/chairpersons and 10.5 per cent as deputies (Abdullah, 2014). Freetown was the site of both organised and disorderly protests against austerity from 1978 when economic stabilisation measures were imposed and the national currency was delinked from the British pound, precipitating steep economic decline (Walton and Seddon, 1994, p. 142). The public excesses on display at the 1980 OAU annual conference fuelled popular discontent at rising prices and shortages of basic commodities (the three-day conference cost $200 million), prompting the slogan 'OAU for you, IOU for we'. Escalating prices of staples like rice and palm oil, wage freezes and import curbs led to strikes in 1981, bringing public transport to a halt, cuts to power supplies and school closures. School children, students and unemployed youth barricaded roads and looted shops, offices and cars; paramilitary police suppressed their disorderly conduct. Unrest continued: in 1986 the IMF forced another devaluation of the currency and removal of price subsidies; inflation rose 300 per cent, prompting another round of student demonstrations (Walton and Seddon, 1994, p. 143).

The same pattern of corrupt mismanagement and an austerity regime wracked the populations of Congo, prompting outbreaks of unrest, strikes and riots. Food riots, also associated with IMF-imposed structural adjustment measures, broke out in Congo in 1990 as inflationary prices of staples touched even those on ministerial salaries: disturbances occurred in Bukavu (South Kivu), Kinshasa, Lubumbashi and Mbuji Mayi. Six months later, in July 1991, the military broke out of their barracks and looted Kinshasa 'comprehensively' (Walton and Seddon, 1994, p. 163). Inflation was now at 10,000 per cent, and the government put down demonstrations and riots with violence. The corruption and venality of the Zairiean regime are well documented, as is the support it received from western powers that bent their own IMF rules to bolster Mobutu's regime (Wrong, 2002).

Congolese civil society developed during the Mobutu era as the main voice of political opposition expressing complaints about violations of human rights (Davis, 2013, p. 295). We know of at least one tax revolt led by women:

hundreds of women demonstrated in 1982 against taxes being levied on the cassava and groundnuts they transport to sell at markets (Newbury, 1984). The revolt against Mobutu in the early 1990s failed, leading to civil war and the overthrow of the dictator by a largely external political and military force in 1997; some believe that this transition by military means frustrated the impetus towards truly democratic governance (Dwyer and Zeilig, 2012, p. 167). Can a case be made for civil war as social movement?

Civil wars as resistance?

Mark Duffield (2002) suggests an alternative view of the new wars as a form of resistant and reflexive modernity – a modernity that attempts social transformation which globalisation has made possible by creating opportunities for an organisational form of network war. The encounter between this reflexive modernity and the international will to govern has caused the radicalisation of development and its reinvention as a strategic tool of conflict resolution and social reconstruction. The use of aid as a tool of global liberal governance is equivocal, he contends, and the nature of its influence is contested. Policy failure, however, tends to result in a fresh round of reinvention and reform rather than reconsideration. One effect is the increasing normalisation of violence.

Reno (2005) argues that the political strategies of key actors have created structural obstacles to mass-based protest movements, and that these strategies make mass violence distinctive in states where formal institutions of government have collapsed or are very weak.

> In most failed states politicians have built systems of personal rule behind the façade of formal statehood. Their power is not founded on controlling effective state agencies or standard concepts of legitimacy. Instead they control markets and use their ability to regulate access to these resources through naked force and selective enforcement of the law to enhance their power. Armed groups that develop in this type of regime reflect a political economy in which power is tied to exclusive control of even clandestine economies. This competition empowers individuals whose social capital enables them to grab resources quickly and to manipulate the failed state's commercial networks of political control at the expense of ideologues and popular organizers.
>
> (Reno, 2005, p. 128)

One outcome of these political strategies is a confusion of categories: in Sierra Leone's 1991–2002 war distinctions between regime and rebel became so blurred that people used the term *sobel* to designate someone who acted as soldier or rebel, depending upon the immediate circumstances. Rebellion on these terms does not represent independent collective action, as fighters try to maximise their gains from the existing political society as much as possible, even when members hold personal convictions and critiques that reject such accommodations (Reno, 2005, p. 128).

Another consequence of these strategies is the proliferation of NGOs as international aid agencies flood in looking for local partners through which services can be delivered. For example, between 1994 and 1997 World Bank funding through NGOs in Africa grew to 40 to 50 per cent from 6 per cent of the total 1989 budget (Gutiérrez, 2010, p. 33). In response, local groups or, sometimes, single individuals, formed private voluntary organisations, often lured by the money or by special import licences granted to local NGOs. For governments rendered dysfunctional by civil war, NGOs are a cloud cover, delivering services the state cannot supply. In the developing world a substantial part of liberal reform was not oriented towards the organisational strengthening of the state but towards the creation of a *cordon sanitaire* around it – that is, the creation of a ring of NGOs directly linked with transnational actors that bypass national political institutions and bureaucracies whenever possible. Coordination is a nearly impossible task: the competing and overlapping interests of hundreds of NGOs overwhelm even the best governments. Equally important but largely overlooked are other long-term effects of humanitarian aid on the state's capacities of control. For one, humanitarian corridors sometimes turn into entry points for alliances that hinder the re-establishment of regular political authority. For another, the interests of NGOs and those of war actors become intertwined very quickly, and this collaboration can grow into power alliances that make the political centre more dependent on local power holders than ever before (Schlichte, 2002, p. 34).

International NGO policy influences the actions of local civil society organisations. In the Congo peace negotiations of 2002, for example, various peace organisations had gained sufficient strength to participate in the Inter-Congolese dialogues held in Sun City, South Africa.[4] The prospect of jobs and power in the future administration preoccupied the delegates, and instead of forming coalitions they competed as individuals, setting up an antagonistic dynamic that was to embitter social movements for a decade (Davis, 2013, p. 295). Women's associations concerned with insecurity and sexual violence participated in the meetings and, although many had on-going direct contact with armed groups near their villages, they were not invited to (nor did they demand to attend) discussions related to military reform, the security sector or the UN DDR programme for disarmament, demobilisation and reintegration (Davis, 2013, p. 296). Laura Davis (2013, p. 296) wonders whether national and international facilitators pressed the women to unite, and if disparate voices could not find a common line other than on sexual violence. Similar questions might be asked about the Congolese report to the meeting of the International Conference of the Great Lakes Region on sexual and gender-based violence in December 2011 (RCD, 2011). One of 11 national reports, it alone considered only the issues of rape and sexual violence; the other reports were remarkable for their frank exposés of women's issues specific to their countries and at variance with the international feminist agenda.

Indigenous groups that arise spontaneously in response to years of civil war may pursue local goals with few ties to international partners. Women from all classes and ethnic groups in Sierra Leone mobilised extensively to facilitate an end to the civil war and to build peace at home and across borders. Among the best-known examples are the Mano River Women's Peace Network (MAR-WOPNET), the Women's Movement for Peace, the Sierra Leone Women's Forum (a network of 50 women's groups that worked together for an end to the war and progress towards democracy), the Network of Women Ministers and Parliamentarians, and the Sierra Leone Women's Movement for Peace (Abdullah *et al.*, 2006). They lobbied behind-the-scenes with warlords and political leaders; they organised public rallies and demonstrations; and they provided services related to peacemaking such as civilian electoral education and training. As early as 1996, a delegation of women's groups led by Women Organized for a Morally Enlightened Nation pressured the military government to hold democratic elections. However, when the elections that brought President Kabbah to power were held, only five women were on the victorious party's list of 68 candidates. In 1999, women played a leading role in the negotiations that led to the signing of the 1999 Lomé peace accord. They insisted that RUF be included in a power-sharing arrangement, even though that meant a blanket amnesty for their atrocities. It was to be another three years before the war finally ended. Several articles in the accord that called for attention to victimised women in the plans for rehabilitation and reconstruction reflected women's involvement in the Lomé process (Mama and Okazawa-Rey, 2012).

Can civil wars be considered as resistance? Can we measure the success of resistance by the transformations that follow in the aftermath? In social science it is difficult to attribute causality when an open-ended society exposed to myriad internal and external forces undergoes change. Women in Sierra Leone celebrate the adoption of the Local Government Act of 2004 that ensures a minimum of 50 per cent representation of women in ward committees; the passage in 2007 of the Domestic Violence Act, the Registration of Customary Marriage and Divorce Act, and the Devolution of Estate Act; and a national action plan to integrate UN Security Council Resolution 1325 domestically (M'Cormack-Hale and Beoku-Betts, 2015). But women were unable to secure a bill establishing a 30 per cent threshold for women's representation in parliament, which has fallen steadily since the first post-war elections in 2002. Law and legal processes would seem to play a pivotal role in times of post-war transition, reforming the law and using legal forms to bring about institutional transformation. One wonders about the law's ability to transform the lives of unlettered women. Can the law administer gendered social justice?

Violence and social justice

Social movements – whether struggles for the right to unionise, for emancipation or for recognition of women's dignity, whether bread riots or anti-globalisation protests – are often responses to violence, and they are frequently met with more and repeated violence in return. Mass violence is not just about the casualties counted on battlefields or the militarisation of commerce. Violence is a lived experience of everyday life in and out of war zones, encompassing dense clusters of meaning that require trans-disciplinary exploration, as has been maintained throughout this book. If we take seriously the concept of structural violence, then the judicial responses cannot be framed solely in terms of violations of individual human rights, or reparations for loss of personal property, or compensation for torture and sexual assault. Such symptomatic responses do not answer the underlying causes of violence or alter the aggravating mechanisms of violence. Structural violence contains notions of social harm and social injury; it implicates structural arguments that acknowledge groups and encompass economies of violence that are material and symbolic. If violence is structural, then harms to persons are social as well as individual; if injury is social, then we must address the social dimensions of trauma in our analyses and in our replies.

A gendered reading of structural violence engages new concepts of gender harms that reflect patterns of social injury. Gender harms are not only about sexual violence as a harm that affects women and girls. If we are to realise gender justice for such injuries, we must acknowledge the full range of perpetrators and victims, recognising that women as well as men, girls as well as boys, not only are subjected to violence but also commit violent acts. Women are part of a gender group, but legal responses to gender-based sexual violence don't look at relations within gender groups, they don't consider how hegemonic norms of masculinity and femininity are enacted on bodies in violence in a relational way (Kirsten Campbell, personal communication, 4 July 2014). A gendered reading of structural violence does not rest at the individual level. Crimes of mass violence – both the visible crimes of state repression and massacres and the hidden crimes of infant deaths, slow starvation, disease, despair and humiliation (Scheper-Hughes and Bourgois, 2003, p. 2) – are committed against communities. They interfere with public and private relationships as well as with social relations of production and reproduction, the very bases of society. It is the historical context of social relations and the contemporary economic, political and social settings that give acts of mass violence their resounding impact.

In the quest for a transformative gender justice, in wondering how international justice can reassemble social relations in more just forms after conflict, some feminists have turned to relational justice, which is a concept of justice in relation to other persons. Relational justice is defined as justice produced through cooperative behaviour, agreement, negotiation or dialogue among actors in post-conflict situations. A relational approach to justice reveals the extent to which our choices are made possible by and realised with the help of others and how our decisions affect others. This is a dispute resolution framework that focuses on violations of civil and political rights. The concept of relational justice contrasts with the emphasis in many political institutions and social systems in the global North on an independent, self-sufficient individual who seeks protection and security in rights that hold others at bay; who seeks safety in a justice system that lays blame and punishes the individual at fault; who finds success through his or her own efforts; and who sees freedom as being able to act without the involvement or interference of others (Llewellyn, 2012).

Relational justice seems to controvert the analytical strength, spirit and meaning of structural violence. The concept takes the first step back from the solipsistic individual to couples and groups, but in the formulation given above it does not appear to touch on the systemic forces that undergird violence. It deals with personal distress in a relational context but it does not take an intersectional approach to large-scale social forces such as poverty, inequality, sexism and racism that structure the risks of violation and violence. Nor does it rise to the institutional level of the global economy. Relational justice by itself cannot address the fundamental question of how to create a more just society after conflict, a question of critical importance to women who do not want to return to the status quo ante bellum. Reassembling social relationships after prolonged struggle is a project of great magnitude. Relational justice, transitional justice and international criminal law each take a different approach. Transitional justice seeks to reassemble a society divided by conflict through processes that invoke justice discourses, while international criminal law seeks to invest social ties through legal precepts (Campbell, 2013, p. 53).

Transitional justice pursues accountability for past abuses of civil and political rights for the purposes of restoring societies pulled apart by conflict and preventing the recurrence of abuses. The goal is to end conflict and move to a stable and peaceful society; it is not always about social transformation and may not address the roots of violence or alter post-conflict societies. A focus on security, says Rosalind Shaw (2010), may defeat local efforts to right the structural and systemic injustices that caused the conflict. In Sierra Leone the concurrent operation of a truth commission and international criminal prosecution coincided with the final two years of national DDR and local reintegration practices. Transitional justice takes a victim-centred approach, DDR a security-centred approach. The result in Sierra Leone was unequal treatment of ex-combatants (those who committed human rights abuses received DDR resources) and non-combatants (victims did not receive reparations or received inadequate compensation after delays). Narrow definitions of justice failed to engage what justice and reintegration meant to all war-affected groups in the context of Sierra Leone's socio-economic abjection and enduring structural violence. Given decades of political corruption, economic free fall, massive unemployment, successions of institutional failure, extractive rural institutions and social exclusion of youth, Shaw insists it is not enough to address only the violations committed during armed conflict itself.

Lisa Laplante (2008, p. 331) points out that increasing numbers of violent street protests and riots caused by socio-economic grievances occur in countries in which truth and reconciliation commissions have studied similar past episodes of violence and repression. Can the expansion of truth commissions' mandates to include a legal framework that examines the causes of violence rooted in violations of economic, social and cultural rights remedy these shortcomings of transitional justice? This is a fast-moving field. An earlier preoccupation with criminal trials and truth commissions seems to have yielded to feminist questions about the extent to which the law can ever effectively deter violence against women. Many societies accept the compromise of 'some truth and some justice' as a concession that allows for an end to atrocities and provides a route to reconciliation with adversaries who are guilty of collaboration, if not of demonstrable war crimes. However, given the ways in which the law and criminal justice systems often act to reinforce deeply sexist assumptions about sexual and social identities, the extent to which the law or truth-telling can ever effectively deter violence against women seems limited.

Accountability

If mechanisms of transitional justice like truth and reconciliation commissions do not bring transformative justice to women, can international criminal law at least deliver accountability for the crimes of war? The international system is set up to achieve justice through legal proceedings: the International Criminal Court (ICC), ad hoc criminal tribunals and national criminal prosecutions. Its framework is built on criminal law and, increasingly, on human rights law (UN Secretary-General, 2004). The questions are whether these legal approaches can reach the women, children and men whose lives were fractured by the violent new wars and whether the 1948 UN Universal Declaration of Human Rights, which declares that victims should have an effective remedy for violations of fundamental rights, can be honoured in a meaningful way. Will the prosecution of those responsible enable their victims to voice their needs to mend the spiritual and material damages they incurred? In some of these legal venues, judges have listened to individual women, and the UN Children's Fund (UNICEF) and some NGOs have attempted to capture the voices of children, especially those who served as soldiers. A theme that runs through their testimony is loss of community. Current plans for restitution, reparations and the reconstruction of communities are not designed to help victims accommodate personal losses to gender and inter-generational relations that have shifted in the midst of a ruined economy. Amnesty arrangements force displaced women returning home to confront their persecutors living in the same village. Low-level crimes are not pursued because the ICC can prosecute only a very small number of cases; the court focuses on those individuals who bear the greatest responsibility, which has been interpreted to mean leaders at the national rather than local or international level. In the case of Congo, no military or political establishment figure has been indicted; only a few non-state actors have been called to account.[5] All of this raises questions about accountability – to whom and for what?

The northern powers' response to the new wars was to institute additional interventions in the domestic affairs of the South, exceeding what structural adjustment programmes had allowed. Inventing novel terminology to justify this seizure of control – failed states, fragile regimes, fractured states, conflict-affected countries – the international community proceeded with its programme to extend the neoliberal model of market democracy (Chomsky, 1997). One framework for conflict resolution frequently imposed is power sharing, a strategy that depends upon the joint exercise of power by warring parties (Lemarchand, 2007). Did power sharing enable the government of Sierra Leone to end the civil war in 1999 and marginalise RUF (Binningsbø and Dupuy, 2009)? Or were attempts at implementation so beset by profound levels of mistrust among the various parties involved that ultimately there was no more political will to make Lomé work (Bright, 2000)? Do power-sharing structures result in impunity for international crimes and lead to continued domestic abuses? Or are power-sharing agreements – supposedly intended to end deadly conflict, secure peace and build democracy in divided societies – one more western conflict resolution experiment being tested in Africa (Levitt, 2014)? Given the post-conflict history of Sierra Leone, especially the resumption of war just months after the Lomé peace accord was signed in 1999, power sharing appears to reproduce insurgent violence (Tull and Mehler, 2005). Power sharing and transitional justice are clashing paradigms because power sharing, in the name of national reconciliation, in practice means amnesty for war crimes. Thus in Congo, most of the armed perpetrators were integrated into the national army and never brought to account for their past violations of human rights law (Davis, 2013). Amnesty showed fighters that impunity would prevail and provided an incentive to renewed fighting. Reparations were never part of the conversation.

In an interesting discussion based on a case study of the DRC, Alex Veit (2011, p. 17) analyses the continuous increase and expansion of international treaty regimes, intrusions by international organisations into previously domestic policies, and the takeover of governmental functions by commercial actors and nongovernmental organisations. He calls this direct internationalised rule, based on relationships of authority between international actors and individuals. Under this regime international agencies exert influence on state policies, or they take over governmental functions, severely restricting national sovereignty. 'Humanitarian military interventions, development cooperation, refugee regimes, and the takeover of governmental functions by private corporations are widespread forms of internationalized rule in the global South, where they become increasingly involved in the regulation of societies' (Veit, 2011, p. 37).

If the nations of the global North at the receiving end of global supply chains, which are also the national homes of corporations that profit from the new wars, are running the institutions through which victims hope a reckoning will take place, how can justice be done? International justice and international courts such as the ICC are increasingly important in internationalised rule and, in the case of refugees, an international juridical regime structures these processes (Veit, 2011, p. 21). Contesting international intervention policies is particularly difficult, taking into account the very asymmetrical balance of power and 'a legal framework for demanding accountability and making claims [that] does not exist, or only in skeletal form' (Veit, 2011, p. 21). Given the element of violent coercion, humanitarian military intervention is a particularly clear demonstration of how direct internationalised rule affects political spaces and what challenges arise for societal contestation of such rule. The take-over of governmental functions by the private corporate sector, especially in countries of the global South, sometimes in ways reminiscent of concessions granted to colonists, is another instance of direct internationalised rule.

The UN's scope for accountability is narrow, and for Congo the International Criminal Court has so far achieved only two convictions with one case pending. Thomas Lubanga, founder and president of Union des Patriotes Congolais (UPC), and founder and former commander-in-chief of Forces Patriotiques pour la Libération du Congo (FPLC), was accused in 2006 of war crimes; his conviction in 2012 was based on the limited charge of recruiting and using child soldiers for which he was sentenced to 14 years in prison. Germain Katanga, commander of Force de Résistance Patriotique en Ituri (FRPI), was found guilty of one count of crimes against humanity (murder) and four counts of war crimes (murder, attacking a civilian population, destruction of property and pillaging) committed on 24 February 2003 during the attack on the village of Bogoro, Ituri district; he was sentenced in 2014 to 12 years' imprisonment. Bosco Ntaganda, former deputy chief of staff and commander of operations of the FPLC, went on trial in the Hague in July 2015 for 13 counts of war crimes including murder, attacks on civilians, rape, sexual slavery, pillaging, displacement, and enlistment and conscription of child soldiers, and five counts of crimes against humanity (murder, rape, sexual slavery, persecution and forcible transfer of population) allegedly committed in 2002–2003 in Ituri Province. This case is of special interest to women for its indictments on charges of rape and sexual slavery.

The power-sharing framework suggests that civil wars are internal affairs between governments and non-state actors, but are they? The international community assumes that East–West proxy warfare ended with the conclusion of the Cold War; these new wars are dubbed internal affairs, even though Congo's conflict was widely called Africa's first world war (Prunier, 2009) and Sierra Leone's struggles were intimately linked with those of Liberia and Guinea (Sawyer, 2004). An accounting of the full array of nations and criminal organisations involved in these wars – the transnational geography of crime and corruption that sustains violent economies – requires indictments of those who supplied the weapons and military training to the previous corrupt regimes as well as the rebels who challenged them, and all the criminal intermediaries in the supply chain.[6] As to who bears responsibility for policies like structural adjustment, which created many of the conditions that led to war, apologists point to the need in the early 1980s to respond rapidly and rationally to the debt crisis. Critics of the international financial institutions find an association between the adoption of IMF programmes and the onset of civil war (Hartzell *et al.*, 2010). International criminal law focuses on who committed the act rather than what criminal actions are punishable (McGregor, 2010). Global supply chains that originate with unfree labourers in shadow economies and end in legitimate transactions by transnational corporations (the trail reaches far into the realm of ordinary commercial activity) are not called to account.

Accountability for economic crimes

The 1966 East–West split of the UN Universal Declaration of Human Rights into two treaties – the International Convention on Economic, Social and Cultural Rights (ICESCR, supported by the eastern bloc) and the International Convention on Civil and Political Rights (ICCPR, supported by western allies) – still dominates international approaches to social justice.[7] The West (now the global North) benefits from the separation of politics from economics, which keeps accountability for neoliberal economic crimes out of the spotlight of international criminal prosecutions for war crimes. Historically, domestic, hybrid and international tribunals prosecute violations of civil and political rights that constitute international crimes. A new generation of jurists and feminists counters that position and insists that economic, social and cultural rights are entitlements, not aspirational expectations to be fulfilled by market-driven economic or political processes (Arbour, 2006; Balakrishnan and Elson, 2011). The realisation of economic, social and cultural rights requires the state to act, and regimes operating on neoliberal market principles would rather see the state refrain from acting.

Pillage of public and private property is a well-established war crime (Lundberg, 2008), but this violation does not rise to the level of the economic crimes such as the theft and illegal trade of minerals that kept the fighters armed and profiting from conflicts in Congo and Sierra Leone. The ICC can charge individuals with pillaging[8] in international conflicts under Articles 8(2)(b)(xvi) and in internal conflicts under Article 8(2)(e)(v); the remit is limited to 'natural persons' (as opposed to 'legal persons'), and the Rome statute does not recognise corporations as natural persons (McGregor, 2010). Corporations can thus avoid criminal responsibility for aiding and abetting pillaging. This evasion is possible despite significant, detailed information about corporate crimes: numerous UN expert panels have collected meticulous accounts of economic violations in both Congo and Sierra Leone, naming parent and subsidiary companies (see, for example, UN, 2010; UNSC, 2000). The ICC's jurisdiction is limited to addressing the crimes of genocide, war crimes and crimes against humanity, which are violations of core civil and political rights; it is not retrospective and applies only to crimes of this nature committed after the Rome Statute, the treaty that established the court, came into force in 2002 (Davis, 2013, 297). That means it does not apply to most of the atrocities in Congo and Sierra Leone, which were committed before that date.

Economic crimes are violations of economic, social and cultural rights not recognised by the United States, which has not ratified the ICESCR or the Rome Statute. The US government claims that it 'strongly supports transitional justice initiatives and has long supported efforts to hold responsible the perpetrators of atrocities, such as genocide, war crimes, crimes against humanity, and other serious human rights abuses' (US, 2009); but the focus of this statement is violations of civil and political rights. Some states do not want to prosecute economic crimes against corporations because they don't want to inhibit foreign investment or economic development. States that fail to prosecute civil rights violations may lack incentives to account for economic crimes (Vandeginste and Sriram, 2011, p. 496). For example, the power-sharing Lomé peace accord for Sierra Leone provided RUF with control over significant economic resources, as the position allocated to Foday Sankoh gave him effective control over the country's diamond mines.[9] Given RUF's brutal treatment of civilians, many victims saw this provision as an unfair reward (Vandeginste and Sriram, 2011, p. 497).

William Schabas, eminent jurist and former member of the Sierra Leone Truth and Reconciliation Commission, says of the impunity of corporations:

> private sector actors such as transnational corporations have been highly invisible in armed conflict fuelling war and atrocity yet operating deep within the shadows and often from remote and privileged environments. At best they are conceptualised as secondary participants in international crimes, in a world where impunity, amnesty and immunity ensure that even the central architects of systematic human rights violations are still about as likely to be held accountable as they are to be struck by lightning.
>
> (Schabas, 2008, p. 512)

The international community has failed to use its influence to force Rwanda to account for the economic consequences of its 1996 invasion and occupation of eastern Congo, in particular the Rwandan army's occupation of mine sites and its forced labour practices, which not only continued the practices of unfree labour markets, but also left Congolese workers impoverished and exhausted (Renton *et al.*, 2007, p. 192).

The Rome Statute criminalises intentional environmental damage as a war crime in international armed conflict. No mention was made of this issue in the proceedings of the International Criminal Tribunal for Rwanda, however, or in any of the mandates it authorised despite evidence of extensive damage; for example, refugees trampled and stripped two national parks, and systematic resettlement exhausted the agricultural capacity of lands in eastern Congo (Drumbl, 2009, p. 10). It would be difficult to prosecute and punish these crimes under the ICC's limited jurisdiction, as no corporate, institutional or state culpability is possible. One should note that, nonetheless, the United Nations Security Council created the Compensation Commission (UNCC) in 1991 with the sole function to compensate governments, international organisations, companies and individuals for losses and damage suffered as a direct result of Iraq's unlawful invasion and occupation of Kuwait in 1990–1991 (www.uncc.ch).

In addition to the need to hold legitimate corporations accountable for pillage (Lundberg, 2008; McGregor, 2010), there is the problem of indicting international criminal organisations. Transnational organised crime is commonly defined as any offence committed in more than one state, including offences that are planned, controlled and may have a substantial effect in another state (Paulose, 2012, p. 94). Specific crimes are illegal narcotic drug trafficking and arms trafficking and sales. Perhaps the ICC, under Article 7 (crimes against humanity), could also indict organised crime syndicates for trafficking and smuggling people (Aston and Paranjape, 2012); these violations of human rights are emblematic of the new wars. Facilitated by neoliberal deregulation, by the destabilisation of governments by insurgents and by regional insecurity, organised criminal groups have grown in economic size and strategic military power, becoming a significant global threat.

Accountability for forced displacement

Displacement is the UN euphemism for forced eviction, ethnic cleansing, expulsion, forced removal, forced migration, population transfer, relocation and resettlement, house demolition and land expropriation. Transitional justice is largely disconnected from forced displacement. The field of refugee protection has moved from its political roots to a depoliticised humanitarian project, dividing the displaced from the wider political context and violence that led to their exile (Hovil, 2012). The displaced are often marginalised in peace processes, political transitions and other mechanisms designed to enable return and reintegration. None of the transitional justice mechanisms effectively and explicitly deals with identifying individual criminal responsibility for forced displacement and its consequences. This is not a trivial issue; the numbers are staggering. In Sierra Leone 2.6 million of an estimated pre-war (1990) population of four million were displaced during the conflict. In Congo, 'the waves of violence have been so chronic over the years that they have created a culture of displacement that has touched nearly every inhabitant living in the eastern provinces' (White, 2014, p. 4). The number of internally displaced persons (IDPs) in eastern Congo has hovered around two million for over a decade, with an estimated 2.6 million displaced in 2014; most do not live in settlements but are dispersed among the local population. Another 500,000 took refuge in neighbouring countries in 2014.

The causes and consequences of displacement are often strongly gendered. Three gender-specific dynamics of conflict-related displacement stand out: sexual and gender-based violence against women and men of all ages and at all stages of displacement (prior to, during and after displacement), causing additional physical and psychological trauma; gender-specific economic consequences of displacement, including the difficulties of reintegration and reclaiming assets upon repatriation; and the threats to young men and women who participated in armed groups and are questioned by family and community when they return home (Hovil, 2012). When young mothers, formerly associated with armed groups in Sierra Leone, return to their communities, they are typically socially isolated, stigmatised and marginalised (McKay et al., 2011). Research in Congo's Kivu provinces found high levels of post-traumatic stress disorder and depression in the population (Pham et al., 2010). Many women and men who have been subjected to extreme brutality and sexual violence fear to return to their villages (Hovil, 2012).

Displacement to camps in which freedom of movement and access to liveli-hoods are restricted can affect gender relations. Humanitarian agencies typically perform many of men's traditional tasks, which may leave some men feeling angry, helpless and prone to lash out at women and children. The social and cultural norms and networks that men and women would ordinarily rely on to help them address problems such as domestic violence seldom exist in a camp environment. Humanitarian assistance strongly emphasises the vulnerability of women and children, letting men and boys cope on their own with the viola-tions that led to their displacement and to injustices experienced during exile. How men deal with their compromised masculinity has a direct effect on women's chances of recovery; in Sierra Leone men whose wives were victims of sexual crimes needed psychological support (King, 2006). Men who leave camp to seek work may lose their legal status as refugees; the ambiguity of their situ-ation opens them to charges of association with rebel, criminal or political activity, and they may suffer additional abuses like arbitrary arrest and rape (Hovil, 2012).

Refugee and IDP camps and settlements are not isolated islands; they do not have an independent existence outside national jurisdiction. What takes place inside the camp is relevant to wider national and international processes. The 1954 UN Convention on Refugees prohibits the expulsion or forcible return of refugees, but it did not protect Rwandans who fled to Zaire after the genocide. In 1994, 1.1 million refugees crossed the border; among them were 40,000 ex-FAR (Forces Armées Rwandaises) of the defeated regime and tens of thou-sands of militia, primarily *interahamwe*, who soon controlled and militarised the camps. The Zairian army forcibly repatriated 15,000, and 640,000 returned after a rebel force supported by Zaire, Rwanda and Uganda broke up the camps (Adelman, 1999). Forced eviction requires the same type of immediate action and redress as the prohibition of torture (Arbour, 2006, p. 11).

Regular criminal justice systems that rely exclusively on legal remedies to rectify grievances fail to account for the limits of law, particularly in cases of mass crimes such as genocide, ethnic cleansing and crimes against humanity. In trying to come to terms with crimes like these, 'not only does our moral discourse appear to reach its limit, but it also emphasizes the inadequacy of ordinary measures that usually apply in the field of criminal justice' (Boraine, 2004).

Gendered reparations

Unlike the treaties ending inter-state wars, the ceasefires of civil conflict rarely separate opposing sides across international boundaries. Nor does every civil conflict end with a clear victor. Some wars are resolved with power-sharing arrangements, which bestow amnesty for all sorts of violations of human rights. Projects to repair the injuries inflicted during political violence are especially challenging in power-sharing situations. In 2002 the ICC explicitly recognised individual criminal accountability for war crimes and rejected immunity for heads of state; in 2006 the UN General Assembly adopted basic principles and guidelines on the right to a remedy and reparation for victims of gross violations of international human rights law and serious violations of international humanitarian law.[10] These legal steps represent progress but are a long way from addressing the structural characteristics of the new wars and the gendered nature of sexual violence.

Social harm and social injury are central to the concept of structural violence, which creates material and moral economies of violence that affect production and social relations of production and reproduction. Current law does not encompass reparations that would address the roots of structural violence or speak to its impact on society. As discussed in the section on accountability for economic crimes, the law does not recognise economic crimes as violations of economic, social and cultural rights, and therefore no case law has established remedies for these wrongs. If profiteers, traffickers and corrupt officials are allowed to continue to operate in the wake of war, how can social injury be repaired?

One reason for returning to structural violence and social harms, discussed in the introduction to violence and social justice above, is to resolve the tension between individual and collective approaches to reparations. Reparations involve the direct distribution to victims of a set of goods including economic transfers, but, according to Pablo de Grieff (2009, p. 2), there are

> countervailing considerations to broadening the mandate of transitional justice measures to include violations of social and economic rights, or at least economic crimes, including questions about the capacity and effectiveness of measures that have a hard enough time satisfying their more traditional, narrower, mandates.

This equation of collective reparations with development programmes is problematic for at least three reasons: first, because most development programmes are designed by the nations implicated in economic crimes in Africa. Second, development programmes cannot answer to the very diverse conflicts in Africa – from the struggle against apartheid in South Africa, to the continuing civil wars in Sudan and the Horn of Africa, to the decade-long conflicts in West Africa and Algeria, and the interrelated wars in the Great Lakes Region. Conflicts in Asian and Latin American societies are undoubtedly different if equally varied, and perhaps individual reparations programmes are justified. Third, individual and collective reparations have dissimilar consequences for women and men because of their unequal positions in patriarchal societies.

Collective reparations are tied, not to development, but to economic, social and cultural rights; and there are precedents for collective responses (Arbour, 2006, p. 19). Confronting the consequences of political violence and serious human rights violations committed during *les années de plomb* after Morocco's independence in 1956, the government was aware that an approach focused solely on individual victims of such crimes would offer inadequate support for communities affected by repression. The Moroccan Justice and Reconciliation

Commission therefore determined to treat the issue of reparations in symbolic and material form involving individuals, communities and regions.[11] The commission recommended communal reparations to strengthen specific marginalised and excluded regions that were particularly affected by political violence.

Structural violence demands collective solutions; this is the correct framework in which to consider the gendered nature of sexual violence, its continued social, psychological and economic impacts on society, and the reparations due to its victims. Singling out individual women or men, putting them through an administrative ordeal to select those worthy of compensation, and subjecting them to public humiliation in the process, only compounds the injustice of the sexual violence they have endured. War is a collective experience: witnessing the destruction of a social world embodying collective history, identity and values produces distress that is normal (Summerfield, 2000). To label this reaction as psychological disturbance, to single out some women and men as more damaged or less able to 'cope', denies social meaning to what the community has suffered collectively. This denial is especially detrimental to social activists whose political protests against inhuman living and working conditions met with violence.

Reparations programmes that benefit an entire society devastated by war and ensure community-based compensation require acceptance of a new social contract that binds all members together in interdependence. To devise such programmes, governments and affected communities need to study and reflect on the legacies of conflict. There may be a new constitution to write, new legislation to draft, land reform to adopt and electoral quota systems to devise. These institutional issues are arguably the most important consequences of war. Tangible effects are obvious: landmines, destroyed roads, schools and health facilities, and a new cohort of disabled people. Less apparent, less known and less understood are the social outcomes of civil war: the changed perceptions of womanhood/femininity and of manhood/masculinity; the changed relations of women to men and to kin and ethnic identity; the changed configuration of families; the changed place of children, childhood and adolescents/adolescence; and changed inter-generational relations. Collective reparations need to be seated in these realities and in a better comprehension of war-wearied societies, their visions of a reformed future and the quality of peace they seek.

Without this level of serious thought and consideration, the gendered harms of war cannot be addressed successfully. Women in Bosnia-Herzegovina complain of a conservative backlash as gender identities are being reconstructed, reconfigured and redefined through interactions between the liberal peace-building discourse and nationalism, culture and religion (Björkdahl and Selimovic, 2014). Women in Sierra Leone speak of the complexities involved in translating women's wartime activism into positive post-war changes in women's lives, of the obstacles to overcoming marginalisation, and of new threats to their established locations of power and patronage (M'Cormack-Hale and Beoku-Betts, 2015). Women from Congo say, yes, we have a new constitution adopted in 2006 that upholds the principle of equality between men and women; however, many provisions of the Congolese family, labour and penal codes still discriminate against women, particularly in the areas of civil liberties and ownership rights (GI-ESCR, 2013). If the principal goals of reparations are recognition of injuries, the establishment of civic trust among the communities split by civil war, and social solidarity between men and women, then the pro-grammes must look forward and backward, seeking to clarify, expose and come to terms with repressive, violent and abusive pasts, as well as aim to promote peace and democracy in the future (Laplante, 2008).

Conclusions: the persistence of violence

Social injustice is another name for violence (Galtung, 1969, p. 171). And we live in a violent world, a world of overt aggression and silent killers. In 2015, 35 wars and armed conflicts were being fought (Goldstein, 2015).[12] The UN High Commission for Refugees reported a record high of nearly 60 million people dis-placed by war, conflict or persecution in 2014. The greatest silent killer is hunger, the number one risk to health worldwide, greater than AIDS, malaria and tuberculosis combined. In a world of 7.3 billion, one in nine people is undernourished and does not eat enough to be healthy. Our world is defined by economic inequality: 24 countries have a Gini coefficient above 50, 14 of them in Africa.[13] More countries have even greater internal inequalities: India has seen a sharp increase in regional inequality (Punjab, the richest state, is 4.7 times wealthier than Bihar, the poorest) since liberalisation of the economy (Pal and Ghosh, 2007). Bryan Stevenson (n.d.), founder and executive director of the Equal Justice Initiative, Montgomery, Alabama, says, 'The opposite of poverty is not wealth, the opposite of poverty is justice.'

Social justice is a condition of the egalitarian distribution of power and resources and the absence of structural violence (Galtung, 1969, p. 183). Expressions of social justice are found in declarations of human rights, but those norms about equality are stated in personal rather than structural terms. 'They refer to what individuals can do or can have, not to who or what decides what they can do or have; they refer to distribution of resources, not to power over the distribution of resources' (Galtung, 1969, p. 188, n. 18). Such human rights are compatible with paternalism, with elite men holding onto the ultimate power, which is the distribution of resources without any change in the power structure. Concessions are not enough, not even equality is enough to satisfy the dispossessed; the fight is about the way in which decisions over resource distri-bution are arrived at and implemented.

Much has been written about inequality as a source of conflict (Cederman *et al.*, 2013), less about the rise in inequality following civil war. A study of poverty and inequality in post-war Rwanda, which had a Gini coefficient of 50.8 in 2011, up from 28 in 1983, found stark differences in vulnerability to poverty by region, gender and widow status of the head of household, as well as signi-ficant changes in the ability of Rwandan households to generate income; important determinants of inter-household shares of income are distribution of land and financial assets like savings or cattle (Finnoff, 2015). The percentage of households headed by women in Rwanda has risen to 33.3 (2010) from 20.8 (1992).

Women suffer disproportionately in the aftermath of civil war. The proliferation of armed conflicts and the high levels of military and civilian casualties have resulted in large numbers of widows in many countries. Widowhood changes the social and economic parts played by women in the household and community, alters the structure of the family, and can affect the physical safety, identity and mobility of women and children. Widowhood can also act on access to basic goods and services necessary for survival, rights to inheritance, land and property, and status within the community. Ostracism and other punishments may follow the death of a husband associated with an opposition group of the armed conflict, leaving the widow exposed to intimidation, violence, abuse or even repudiation (ICRC, 1999). In Rwanda, the loss of male family protection led to painful and humiliating situations for women who survived the genocidal conflict (Twagiramariya and Turshen, 1998).

In long civil wars, political elites shift their attention and activity into violent clandestine rackets to control economic opportunity, exercise power and control people (Reno, 2005, p. 128). Women and girls, men and boys are caught up in these rackets and enter what Saskia Sassen (2000, p. 540) calls 'alternative circuits for survival, profit-making and hard-currency earnings'. Most profits are made off the bodies of disadvantaged women and girls who are illegally trafficked for the sex industry and other labour markets. The collapse of distinctions between productive labour and reproductive work in the sex industry is evident to the ILO, which called for official economic recognition of the sex sector in 1998, citing the expanding reach of the industry and its unrecognised contribution to countries' gross domestic product (Lim, 1998). Although the ILO promised that recognition would extend labour rights and benefits to sex workers and improve their working conditions, the real motive would seem to be the collection of taxes, which would bring additional revenue to heavily indebted governments. Critics of the ILO position say the organisation severely underestimates violence against prostituted women and girls (Raymond, 2003).

The links between rackets, neoliberal policies and the sex sector are easily perceived: on one hand, barriers to the migration of capital are eased through decreased tariffs on foreign investment, and on the other, barriers to cross-border migration increase. This double standard affects the sex industry by limiting access to travel for cross-border migrants while simultaneously improving the market for trafficking in persons by making cross-border migration legally more difficult (Shah, 2012/2013). The institutional supports of the neoliberal global economic system, aided by new communications technologies and certain conditions within underdeveloped and war-torn countries, make possible the transnational and trans-local networks that are the conduits for the new slavery. And the post-war climate of impunity ensures that corrupt officials and criminal organisations will continue to collude in running these networks. War undermines local systems of production and distribution, causes the closure of small national enterprises, and raises rates of unemployment; in the general chaos of ruined economies that succeeds civil war, these forces propel people to search desperately for work/labour/livelihood/income.

Under pressure from these forces, human and physical capital continues to flood out of Africa, exceeding the flow of aid and investment to the continent. Rather than reforming the existing neoliberal international order, the UN Millennium Development Goals in 2000 was an exercise in consolidation of neoliberal power (Turshen, 2014). The vaunted eighth goal, to develop a global partnership for development, did not address the need to turn Africa's vast oil and mineral wealth to the advantage of Africans; rather, it ensured the continuing trend to export raw materials and import finished goods, leaving the economy undeveloped. Politicians and economists who fail to balance the extraction of non-renewable resources with reinvestment, who factor out society and the environment in the calculus of economic growth, promote the myth of African economic expansion while ignoring the crisis of social reproduction. The real MDG goals, Samir Amin (2006) asserts, amount to an extreme form of privatisation, aimed at opening new fields for the expansion of capital, the generalisation of the private appropriation of agricultural land, commercial expansion within a context of maximum deregulation, and the equally uncontrolled expansion of capital movement.

The new wars have spawned a broad set of gender issues in social relations of production and reproduction. In an era of liberalising and globalising economies, armed conflict has devalued women's social position and generated intense conflicts between women and men and between the young and the old over the use of critical economic resources, beginning with land. New, more violent social relations of production and reproduction are the core of gender and the political economy of conflict in Africa. Why does violence persist? Violence persists because it is profitable to those who employ it in the interests of capital. As the epigraph to this chapter says, 'Ô mes amis, il n'y a nul ami…' (Abadie, 2010).

Notes

1 O my friends, there is no friend … (attributed to Aristotle).
2 AAWORD has challenged the rationale behind these policies, as a contribution to the critique raised against the international financial institutions, especially against World Bank lending policies. Additionally, the association has queried the theoretical underpinnings of IFIs, which promote the status of the dominant classes and result in the continued impoverishment of populations in Africa (www.afard.org/indexang.php).
3 I was unable to locate any women abolitionists born in Africa.
4 In March 2002, 400 delegates assembled in Sun City, South Africa, for the second session of peace talks, which ended in agreement between Joseph Kabila's government and Jean Pierre Bemba, president and commander-in-chief of the MLC, who was made prime minister in the 30-month transitional administration. Two vice-presidents represented the MLC and the RCD, and an interim parliament representing all the signatories to the agreement would draft a new constitution. A new

integrated army would be created from government units and rebel soldiers (Lodge *et al.*, 2002).

5 In 2008 the ICC arrested Jean Pierre Bemba. He was charged with two counts of crimes against humanity (murder and rape) and three counts of war crimes (murder, rape and pillaging) in connection with events in the Central African Republic, not Congo. In 2015 he was put on trial in The Hague (www.icc-cpi.int/iccdocs/PIDS/publications/BembaEng.pdf).

6 Viktor Bout, an arms dealer, was arrested by the United States, tried, convicted and sentenced in 2012 to 25 years in prison, not for his dealings in Africa, which included Congo and Sierra Leone, but for a sting operation involving drugs in Colombia (www.bbc.co.uk/news/world-europe-11036569, accessed 15 January 2014).

7 For an excellent discussion of the split of the UN Universal Declaration on Human Rights into two covenants, one for civil and political rights and one for economic, social and cultural rights, in the context of transitional justice, see Arbour (2006, p. 6, n. 11).

8 The ICC interprets pillaging in the context of an international armed conflict of which the perpetrator was aware as the perpetrator appropriating property, intending to deprive the owner of property, intending to appropriate it for private or personal use, and appropriating property without the consent of the owner (www.icc-cpi.int/NR/rdonlyres/336923D8-A6AD-40EC-AD7B-45BF9DE73D56/0/ElementsOfCrimesEng.pdf, accessed 10 June 2015).

9 Sankoh was offered chairmanship of the Commission for the Management of Strategic Resources, National Reconstruction, and Development (Article V), with the status of vice-president, answerable only to the president.

10 For links to relevant international law, see http://iccforum.com/background/reparations, accessed 15 June 2015.

11 For a full account of the various commissions, see Guillerot (2011).

12 The breakdown as of July 2015 is: ten wars (>1,000 fatalities/year), five serious armed conflicts; plus 15 other armed conflicts (fewer than 200 battle-deaths in year) and five serious armed conflicts; Goldstein (2015) defines war as two or more armed groups engaged in ongoing lethal violence over political objectives (control of territory or government).

13 The Gini coefficient is a number between 0 and 100, where 0 corresponds with perfect equality and 100 corresponds with perfect inequality.

References

Abadie, Delphine (2010) Le Canada en République Démocratique du Congo: 'Ô mes amis, il n'y a nul ami…', *Journal des alternatives*, 2 August, Montreal, www.alternatives.ca/fra/journal-alternatives/publications/dossiers/justice-climatique/article/le-canada-en-republiqueAbadie, accessed 24 November 2011.

Abdullah, Hussainatu (2014) Women organising for gender equality in Sierra Leonean politics, http://democracyinafrica.org/women-organising-gender-equality-sierra-leonean-politics/, accessed 2 January 2015.

Abdullah, Hussainatu J., Aisha F. Ibrahim and Jamesina King (2006) Women's voices, work and bodily integrity in pre-conflict, conflict and post conflict reconstruction processes in Sierra Leone, http://r4d.dfid.gov.uk/PDF/Outputs/WomenEmp/Abdullah_SierraLeoneCountryPaper.pdf, accessed 20 January 2014.

Abdullah, Ibrahim (1997) The colonial state and wage labor in post-war Sierra Leone 1945–1960: attempts at remaking the working class, *International labor and working class history* 52: 87–105.

Adelman, Howard (1999) The use and abuse of refugees in Zaire, April 1996 to March 1997, http://web.stanford.edu/~sstedman/2001.readings/Zaire.htm, accessed 30 June 2014.

Akinola, G. A. (1972) Slavery and slave revolts in the Sultanate of Zanzibar in the nineteenth century, *Journal of the historical society of Nigeria* VI(2): 215–228.

Allen, Chris (1997) Who needs civil society?, *Review of African political economy* 24(73): 329–337.

Amin, Samir (1974) *Accumulation on a world-scale: a critique of the theory of underdevelopment*, vol. 2. New York: Monthly Review Press.

Amin, Samir (2006) The Millennium Development Goals: a critique from the South, *Monthly Review* 57(10): 1–10.

Antrobus, Peggy (2004) *The global women's movement: origins, issues and strategies*. London: Zed Books.

Arbour, Louise (2006) Economic and social justice for societies in transition, *International law and politics* 40: 1–28.

Archarya, Meena (2008) Global integration of subsistence economies and women's empowerment: an experience from Nepal. In *Beyond states and markets: the challenges of social reproduction*, edited by Isabella Bakker and Rachel Silvey, pp. 55–71. London: Routledge.

Aston, Joshua Nathan and Vinay N. Paranjape (2012) Human trafficking and its prosecution: challenges of the ICC, http://papers.ssrn.com/sol3/papers.cfm?abstract_id=2203711, accessed 19 July 2014.

Balakrishnan, Radhika and Diane Elson (2011) *Economic policy and human rights: holding governments to account*. London: Zed Books.

Bell, Christine, Colm Campbell and Fionnuala Ní Aoláin (2004) Justice discourses in transition, *Social and legal studies* 13(3): 305–328.

Binningsbø, Helga Malmin and Kendra Dupuy (2009) Using power-sharing to win a war: the implementation of the Lomé Agreement in Sierra Leone, *Africa spectrum* 44(3): 87–107.

Björkdahl, Annika and Johanna Mannergren Selimovic (2014) Gendered justice gaps in Bosnia-Herzegovina, *Human rights review* 15: 201–218.

Boraine, Alexander L. (2004) Address on transitional justice as an emerging field, 11 March. Transcript available at www.idrc.ca/uploads/user-S/10829975041revised-boraine-ottawa-2004.pdf, accessed 20 July 2014.

Bouwer, Karen (2010) *Gender and decolonization in the Congo: the legacy of Patrice Lumumba*. London: Palgrave Macmillan.

Brandes, Nikolai and Bettina Engels (2011) Social movements in Africa, *Stichproben: Wiener zeitschrift für kritische Afrikastudien* 20(11): 1–15.

Bright, Dennis (2000) Paying the price: the Sierra Leone peace process. www.c-r.org/accord-article/implementing-lomé-peace-agreement, accessed 20 June 2014.

Caffentzis, George (2002) On the notion of a crisis of social reproduction: a theoretical review, *Commoner* 5, autumn: 1–22.

Campbell, Kirsten (2013) Reassembling international justice: the making of 'the social' in international criminal law and transitional justice, *International journal of transitional justice* 8(1): 53–74.

Cederman, Lars-Erik, Kristian Skrede Gleditsch and Halvard Buhaug (2013) *Inequality, grievances, and civil war*. Cambridge: Cambridge University Press.

Chenoweth, Erica and Kathleen Gallagher Cunningham (2013) Understanding nonviolent resistance: an introduction, *Journal of peace research* 50(3): 271–276.

Chomsky, Noam (1997) Market democracy in a neoliberal order: doctrines and reality, *Z magazine*, November, http://zcomm.org/zmagazine/market-democracy-in-a-neoliberal-order-doctrines-and-reality-by-noam-chomsky-1/, accessed 20 March 2014.

Davis, Laura (2013) Power shared and justice shelved: the Democratic Republic of Congo, *International journal of human rights* 17(2): 289–306.

Day, Lynda R. (2008) 'Bottom power': theorizing feminism and the women's movement in Sierra Leone (1981–2007), *African and Asian studies* 7: 491–513.

de Grieff, Pablo (2009) Articulating the links between transitional justice and development: justice and social integration. New York: International Center for Transitional Justice research brief.

Denzer, LaRay (1987) Women in Freetown politics, 1914–61: a preliminary study. In *Sierra Leone, 1787–1987: two centuries of intellectual life*, edited by Murray Last and Paul Richards, pp. 439–456. Manchester: Manchester University Press.

Diouf, Sylviane A., ed. (2003) *Fighting the slave trade: West African strategies*. Athens: Ohio University Press.

Drumbl, Mark A. (2009) Accountability for property crimes and environmental war crimes: prosecution, litigation, and development. New York: International Center for Transitional Justice.

Duffield, Mark (2002) Social reconstruction and the radicalization of development: aid as a relation of global liberal governance, *Development and change* 33(5): 1049–1071.

Dwyer, Peter and Leo Zeilig (2012) *African struggles today: social movements since independence*. Chicago: Haymarket Books.

Eschle, Catherine and Neil Stammers (2004) Taking part: social movements, INGOs, and global change, *Alternatives: global, local, political* 29(3): 333–372.

Evans, Brad (n.d.) Histories of violence project, http://historiesofviolence.com/special-series/disposable-life/the-project/, accessed 20 June 2015.

Finnoff, K. (2015) Decomposing inequality and poverty in post-war Rwanda: the roles of gender, education, wealth and location, *Development southern Africa* 32(2): 209–228.

Fyfe, Christopher (1993) *A history of Sierra Leone*. Aldershot: Gregg Revivals.

Fyle, C. Magbaily (2006) *Historical dictionary of Sierra Leone*. Lanham, MD: Scarecrow Press.

Galtung, Johan (1969) Violence, peace and peace research, *Journal of peace research* 6(3): 167–191.

GI-ESCR (2013) Shadow report to the United Nations Committee on the Elimination of Discrimination against Women: Democratic Republic of the Congo, 55th session, 8–26 July. Duluth: Global Initiative for Economic, Social and Cultural Rights.

Goldstein, Joshua (2015) International relations, www.internationalrelations.com/wars-in-progress/, accessed 17 July 2015.

Grace, John (1975) *Domestic slavery in West Africa with particular reference to the Sierra Leone Protectorate, 1896–1927*. London: Frederick Muller.

Guillerot, Julie (2011) Morocco: Gender and the Transitional Justice Process. New York: International Center for Transitional Justice.

Gutiérrez, Francisco (2010) Mechanisms. In *Economic liberalization and political violence: utopia or dystopia?*, edited by Francisco Gutiérrez and Gerd Schönwälder, pp. 13–48. London: Pluto Press. Available online at: www.idrc.ca/EN/Resources/Publications/openebooks/482-6/index.html#ch01.

Hartzell, Caroline A., Matthew Hoddie and Molly Bauer (2010) Economic liberalization via IMF structural adjustment: sowing the seeds of civil war?, *International organization* 64(02): 339–356.

Higginson, John (1988) Disputing the machines: scientific management and the transformation of the work routine at the Union Minière du Haut-Katanga, 1918–1930, *African economic history* 17: 1–21.

Higginson, John (1989) *A working class in the making: Belgian colonial labour policy, private enterprise, and the African mineworker, 1907–1951*. Madison: University of Wisconsin Press.

Hochschild, Adam (2005) *Bury the chains: the British struggle to abolish slavery*. New York: Houghton Mifflin.

Horn, Jessica (2013) *Gender and social movements: overview report*. Brighton: Institute of Development Studies, www.bridge.ids.ac.uk, accessed 21 July 2014.

Hovil, Lucy (2012) Gender, transitional justice, and displacement: challenges in Africa's Great Lakes Region. New York: International Center for Transitional Justice.

HRW (2014) *Whose development? Human rights abuses in Sierra Leone's mining boom*. New York: Human Rights Watch.

ICRC (1999) Widowhood and armed conflict: challenges faced and strategies forward. Geneva: International Committee of the Red Cross, www.icrc.org/eng/resources/documents/misc/57jqha.htm, accessed 20 July 2014.

Ijagbemi, Adeleye (1978) Gumbu Smart: slave turned abolitionist, *Journal of the historical society of Sierra Leone* 2(2): 45–60.

ITUC (2010) Statement: women trade unionists at the centre of conflict prevention, management and resolution: Bukavu, South Kivu, DR Congo, 14 and 15 October 2010, www.ituc-csi.org/IMG/pdf/DECLARATION_-_BUKAVU_18-10-10_FINALE_en.pdf, accessed 20 January 2015.

King, Jamesina (2006) Gender and reparations in Sierra Leone: the wounds of war remain open. In *What happened to the women? Gender and reparations for human rights violations*, edited by Ruth Rubio-Marín, pp. 246–283. New York: Social Science Research Council.

Laplante, Lisa J. (2008) Transitional justice and peace building: diagnosing and addressing the socioeconomic roots of violence through a human rights framework, *International journal of transitional justice* 2: 331–355.

Larmer, Miles (2010) Social movement struggles in Africa, *Review of African political economy* 37(125): 251–262.

Lemaitre, Julieta and Kristin Sandvik (2014) Beyond sexual violence in transitional justice: political insecurity as a gendered harm, *Feminist legal studies* 22(3): 243–262.

Lemarchand, René (2007) Consociationalism and power sharing in Africa: Rwanda, Burundi, and the Democratic Republic of the Congo, *African affairs* 106(422): 1–20.

Lenz, Ilse (2005) Recovering translation – translating recoverings? Towards integrative perspectives on the labor and other social movements, *Labor history* 46(2): 214–219.

Levitt, Jeremy I. (2014) *Illegal peace in Africa: an inquiry into the legality of power sharing with warlords, rebels, and junta*. Cambridge: Cambridge University Press.

Likaka, Osumaka (1994) Rural protest: the Mbole against Belgian rule, 1897–1959, *International Journal of African Historical Studies* 27(3): 589–617.

Lim, Lin Lean, ed. (1998) *The sex sector: the economic and social bases of prostitution in Southeast Asia*. Geneva: International Labour Office.

Llewellyn, Jennifer (2012) A relational vision of justice, www.restorativejustice.org/RJOB/a-relational-vision-of-justice, accessed 15 January 2015.

Lodge, Tom, Denis Kadima and David Pottie, eds (2002) *Compendium of elections in Southern Africa, Democratic Republic of Congo*, p. 73. Johannesburg: Electoral Institute for Sustainable Democracy in Africa, www.content.eisa.org.za/old-page/drc-sun-city-inter-congolese-dialogue-negotiations, accessed 12 February 2013.

Luke, David F. (1985) The development of modern trade unionism in Sierra Leone, Part I, *International journal of African historical studies* 18(3): 425–454.

Lundberg, Michael A. (2008) Plunder of natural resources during war: a war crime (?), *Georgetown journal of international law* 39: 495–525.

McGregor, Michael A. (2010) Ending corporate impunity: how to really curb the pillaging of natural resources, *Case Western Reserve journal of international law* 42(1/2): 469–497.

McKay, S., A. Veale, M. Worthen and M. Wessells (2011) Building meaningful participation in reintegration among war-affected young mothers in Liberia, Sierra Leone and northern Uganda, *Intervention: international journal of mental health, psychosocial work, and counselling in areas of armed conflict* 9(2): 108–124.

M'Cormack-Hale, Fredline A. O. and Josephine Beoku-Betts (2015) The politics of women's empowerment in post-war Sierra Leone: contradictions, successes, and challenges, *African & Asian Studies* 14(1/2): 8–17.

Maddox, Gregory (1993) *Conquest and resistance to colonialism in Africa*. New York and London: Garland.

Mama, Amina and Margo Okazawa-Rey (2012) Militarism, conflict and women's activism in the global era: challenges and prospects for women in three West African contexts, *Feminist review* 101: 97–123.

Marchal, Jules (1996) *E D Morel contre Léopold II: l'histoire du Congo, 1900–1910*. Paris: L'Harmattan.

Morel, Edmund D. (1903) *The Congo slave state: a protest against the new African slavery; and an appeal to the public of Great Britain, of the United States and of the continent of Europe*. Liverpool: John Richardson & Sons.

Mouser, Bruce (2007) Rebellion, marronage and jihad: strategies of resistance to slavery on the Sierra Leone coast, c. 1783–1796, *Journal of African history* 48: 27–44.

Newbury, M. Catharine (1984) Ebutumwa Bw'Emiogo: the tyranny of cassava. A women's tax revolt in eastern Zaïre, *Canadian journal of African studies* 18(1): 35–54.

Northrup, David (1997) Women against slavery: the British campaigns, 1780–1870 (review), *Journal of world history* 8(2): 335–337.

Nowak, Bronislaw (1986) The slave rebellion in Sierra Leone in 1785–1796, *Hemispheres* (Warsaw) 3: 151–169.

Pal, Parthapratim and Jayati Ghosh (2007) Inequality in India: a survey of recent trends. New York: United Nations Department of Economic and Social Affairs working paper 45, ST/ESA/2007/DWP/45.

PANA (2003) US may review Uganda's AGOA benefits, 3 November, www.panapress.com/US-may-review-Uganda-s-AGOA-benefits-13-494261-17-lang2-index.html, accessed 15 January 2011.

Patil, Vrushali (2009) Contending masculinities: the gendered (re)negotiation of colonial hierarchy in the United Nations debates on decolonization, *Theory and society* 38(2): 195–215.

Paulose, Regina Menachery (2012) Beyond the core: incorporating transnational crimes into the Rome Statute, *Cardozo journal of international & comparative law* 21(1): 77–109.

Pham, Phuong N., Patrick Vinck, Didine Kaba Kinkodi and Harvey M. Weinstein (2010) Sense of coherence and its association with exposure to traumatic events, post-traumatic stress disorder, and depression in eastern Democratic Republic of Congo, *Journal of traumatic stress* 23(3): 313–321.

Prunier, Gérard (2009) *Africa's world war: Congo, the Rwandan genocide, and the making of a continental catastrophe*. Oxford: Oxford University Press.

Raymond, Janice G. (2003) Legitimating prostitution as sex work: UN Labour Organization (ILO) calls for recognition of the sex industry (part one). Available at http://sisyphe.org/spip.php?article689, accessed 27 June 2014.

RCD (2011) République démocratique du Congo Ministère du genre, de la famille et de l'enfant rapport de la consultation nationale sur les VSBG en préparation du sommet de la CIRGL de décembre 2011. Kinshasa.

Reno, William (2005) The politics of violent opposition in collapsing states, *Government and opposition* 40(2): 127–151.

Renton, David, David Seddon and Leo Zeilig (2007) *The Congo: plunder and resistance*. London: Zed Books.

Sassen, Saskia (2000) Women's burden: counter-geographies of globalization and the feminization of survival, *Journal of international affairs* 53(2): 503–524.

Sawyer, Amos (2004) Violent conflicts and governance challenges in West Africa: the case of the Mano River Basin area, *Journal of modern African studies* 42(3): 437–464.

Schabas, William A. (2008) *War crimes and human rights: essays on the death penalty, justice, and accountability*. Folkestone: Cameron May CMP.

Scheper-Hughes, Nancy and Philippe Bourgois, eds (2003) *Violence in war and peace: an anthology*. Hoboken, NJ: Wiley-Blackwell.

Schillinger, Hubert René (2005) Trade unions in Africa: weak but feared. Bonn: Friedrich-Ebert-Stiftung occasional papers.

Schlichte, Klaus (2002) State formation and the economy of intra-state wars. In *Shadow globalization, ethnic conflicts and new wars: a political economy of intra-state war*, edited by Dietrich Jung, pp. 27–44. London: Routledge.

Shah, Svati P. (2012/2013) Thinking through 'neoliberalism' in the twenty-first century, *Scholar & feminist online* 11.1–11.2. Available at http://sfonline.barnard.edu/gender-justice-and-neoliberal-transformations/thinking-through-neoliberalism-in-the-twenty-first-century/#sthash.Q5AvTuTA.dpuf, accessed 19 June 2015.

Shaw, Rosalind (2010) Linking justice with reintegration? Ex-combatants and the Sierra Leone experiment. In *Localising transitional justice: interventions and priorities after mass violence*, edited by Rosalind Shaw and Lars Waldorf, with Pierre Hazan, pp. 111–132. Stanford, CA: Stanford University Press.

Spitzer, Leo and LaRay Denzer (1973) I. T. A. Wallace-Johnson and the West African Youth League. Part II: the Sierra Leone period, 1938–1945, *International journal of African historical studies* 6(4): 565–601.

Stevenson, Bryan (n.d.) Equal Justice Initiative, www.eji.org, accessed 12 June 2015.

Summerfield, Derek (2000) War and mental health: a brief overview, *BMJ* 321: 232–235.

Tripp, Aili Mari (1994) Rethinking civil society: gender implications in contemporary Tanzania. In *Civil society and the state in Africa* edited by John W. Harbeson, Donald Rothchild and Naomi Chazan, pp. 149–168. Boulder, CO: Lynne Rienner.

Tull, Denis M. and Andreas Mehler (2005) The hidden costs of power-sharing: reproducing insurgent violence in Africa, *African affairs* 104(416): 375–398.

Turshen, Meredeth (2014) A global partnership for development and other unfulfilled promises of the millennium project, *Third world quarterly* 35(3): 345–357.

Twagiramariya, Clotilde and Meredeth Turshen (1998) 'Favours' to give and 'consenting' victims: the sexual politics of survival in Rwanda. In *What women do in wartime: gender and conflict in Africa*, edited by Meredeth Turshen and Clotilde Twagiramariya, pp. 101–117. London: Zed Books.

UK House of Commons (1955) Situation, Sierra Leone (Commission of Inquiry) HC Deb 17 February, vol. 537, cds560–564, http://hansard.millbanksystems.com/commons/1955/feb/17/situation-sierra-leone-commission-of, accessed 20 September 2015.

UN (2010) Democratic Republic of the Congo, 1993–2003: Report of the mapping exercise documenting the most serious violations of human rights and international humanitarian law committed within the territory of the Democratic Republic of the Congo between March 1993 and June 2003, available at www.ohchr.org/EN/Countries/AfricaRegion/Pages/RDCProjetMapping.aspx, accessed 10 January 2015.

UNSC (2000) Report of the panel of experts appointed pursuant to Security Council resolution 1306 (2000) paragraph 19, in relation to Sierra Leone. United Nations Security Council document S/2000/1195.

UN Secretary-General (2004) *The rule of law and transitional justice in conflict and post-conflict societies*, UN doc S/2004/616 (23 August).

US (2009) United States of America – resolution: transitional justice. UN Human Rights Council, 12th Session. Geneva, 1 October, www.state.gov/documents/organization/153530.pdf, accessed 20 June 2014.

Vandeginste, Stef and Chandra Lekha Sriram (2011) Power sharing and transitional justice: a clash of paradigms?, *Global governance* 17: 489–505.

Veit, Alex (2011) Social movements, contestation and direct international rule: theoretical approaches, *Stichproben. Wiener zeitschrift für kritische Afrikastudien* 20(11): 17–43.

Wallace, Tina and Fenella Porter with Mark Ralph-Bowman, eds (2013) *Aid, NGOs and the realities of women's lives: a perfect storm*. Bourton on Dunsmore: Practical Action Publishing.

Walton, John and David Seddon (1994) *Free markets and food riots: the politics of global adjustment*. Oxford: Blackwell.

White, Stacey (2014) Now what? The international response to internal displacement in the Democratic Republic of the Congo. Washington, DC: Brookings Institution.

Wrong, Michela (2002) *In the footsteps of Mr. Kurtz: living on the brink of disaster in Mobutu's Congo*. New York: Harper Perennial.

Index

For Product Safety Concerns and Information please contact our
EU representative GPSR@taylorandfrancis.com Taylor & Francis
Verlag GmbH, Kaufingerstraße 24, 80331 München, Germany